SO-BES-862

3 120 00317 9999

National Parks with Kids

Open Road *is* Travel!

PUBLIC LIBRARY
DANVILLE, ILLINOIS

CRITICAL ACCLAIM FOR
OPEN ROAD TRAVEL GUIDES!

Whether you're going abroad or planning a trip in the United States, take Open Road along on your journey. Our books have been praised by *Travel & Leisure, The Los Angeles Times, Newsday, Booklist, US News & World Report, Endless Vacation, American Bookseller, Coast to Coast*, and many other magazines, newspapers, and websites.

Remember – Open Road *is* travel!

About the Author

Paris Permenter and John Bigley, a husband-wife travel writing team, are the authors of Open Road Publishing's *Caribbean with Kids, National Parks with Kids,* and *Las Vegas with Kids*. They have also authored numerous other guidebooks to the Caribbean and US and contributed many articles to leading travel magazines and newspapers. Paris and John are frequent television and radio talk show guests on the subject of travel.

From their home base in Texas, Paris and John edit Lovetripper.com Romantic Travel Magazine (www.lovetripper.com), an award-winning online publication devoted to romantic travel worldwide.

Open Road *is* Travel!

Open Road Publishing has guide books to exciting, fun destinations on four continents. As veteran travelers, our goal is to bring you the best travel guides available anywhere!

No small task, but here's what we offer:

• All Open Road travel guides are written by authors with a distinct, opinionated point of view – not some sterile committee or team of writers. Our authors are experts in the areas covered and are polished writers.

• Our guides are geared to people who want to make their own travel choices. We'll show you how to discover the real destination – not just see some place from a tour bus window.

• We're strong on the basics, but we also provide terrific choices for those looking to get off the beaten path and experience the country or city – not just see it or pass through it.

• We give you the best, but we also tell you about the worst and what to avoid. Nobody should waste their time and money on their hard-earned vacation because of bad or inadequate travel advice.

• Our guides assume nothing. We tell you everything you need to know to have the trip of a lifetime – presented in a fun, literate, no-nonsense style.

• And, above all, we welcome your input, ideas, and suggestions to help us put out the best travel guides possible.

∾

National Parks with Kids

Open Road *is* Travel!

Paris Permenter & John Bigley

Open Road Publishing

Open Road Publishing

We offer travel guides to American and foreign locales. Our books tell it like it is, often with an opinionated edge, and our experienced authors always give you all the information you need to have the trip of a lifetime. Write for your free catalog of all our titles.

Open Road Publishing
P.O. Box 284, Cold Spring Harbor, NY 11724
E-mail: Jopenroad@aol.com

2nd Edition

Text Copyright©2004 by Paris Permenter & John Bigley
Maps Copyright©2004 by Open Road Publishing
- All Rights Reserved -
ISBN 1-59360-021-6
Library of Congress Control No. 2004105643

Maps by Mike Hermann, Purple Lizard Maps, Lemont, Pennsylvania.

The authors have made every effort to be as accurate as possible, but neither they nor the publisher assume responsibility for the services provided by any business listed in this guide; for any errors or omissions; or any loss, damage, or disruptions in your travels for any reason.

Contents

17.3
PER
COP

PUBLIC LIBRARY
DANVILLE, ILLINOIS

7. The Southwest   155

8. The West   220

9. The Northwest   237

10. Beyond the Continental U.S.   259

Index   277

Maps

National Parks with Kids

National Parks
with Kids

1. INTRODUCTION

National Park. Just the words bring to mind family vacations: loading up the car and traveling to the natural wonders of the country; mugging for the camera at some of the best recognized landmarks in America; learning about the men and women who shaped the United States. For almost a century, travelers have set their sights on American national parks.

Since our own childhood, we've loved these national parks. Both of us remember childhood trips to see the places for which America is known: Grand Canyon, Yosemite, Yellowstone, Carlsbad Caverns.

Each of those trips started with months of family preparations: talking about where we'd visit, what we'd see there, writing off for brochures, highlighting maps with the route we'd take.

Once there, memories that have lasted for decades were formed. Paris recalls a cold summer sunrise on the rim of Grand Canyon, huddled in a sleeping bag as the glowing orb marked another day at this incredible park. John remembers the excitement of traveling with his parents to Carlsbad Caverns, touring the world-class cave and imagining the secrets its dark recesses held.

The investment of even the shortest family excursion, even a day trip to a local national park site, will reward you and your family with experiences and memories for a lifetime.

What we've included in this guide are the parks we think will be of special interest to families. This is not a comprehensive book of all the national park sites; you'll find other guides that cover this very well. Rather, this is a selective look at family-oriented sites in just about every state. On these pages, you'll find parks where you and your children can hike, camp, swim, and explore.

Whether your interests are mountains, lakes, seashores, or historic sites, you'll find parks to suit your interests.

So settle down and have a look at some of our favorite places in this vast country. Imagine you and your family planning an excursion to one or more of these beautiful and fascinating parks.

Talk it over with the whole family so everyone will be excited about the trip, then head off down the road. Like America's earliest explorers, you've got an incredible journey ahead of you.

Chapter 2

OVERVIEW

Parks, Parks, Parks

You've now looked at the list of national parks and seen not just parks but national monuments, national seashores, national lake shores, national memorials, national battlefields, and more. Confused?

There are nearly 400 sites in the national park system. Of these, about 1/8th are considered "national parks," the real bigness. Think of all the favorites you dreamt about when you were growing up: Yellowstone, Grand Canyon, Yosemite, Great Smoky Mountains–these are a few of the designated national parks.

But there are plenty of other jewels in the national park system, places that are also well known (or not so well known) and offer great family getaways. Here's a look at the different types of parks in the system and what you might expect to find:

National Monuments. These are historic sites or sites of scientific interest. Muir Woods, Arizona's Montezuma Castle, Devil's Postpile, and other parks are designated national monuments.

National Preserves. These are natural places that are maintained like the national parks but with the exception that hunting, oil and/or gas exploration or extraction are allowed. Some examples of national preserves are Big Thicket, Big Cypress and over a dozen other parks are considered national preserves.

National Historic Site. These are, like their name suggests, a site (usually a single one) of historic importance. There are over 70 national historic sites in the system including parks that honor Jimmy Carter, Martin Luther King, Jr. and Harry S. Truman.

National Historic Park. OK, here's where things get tricky. A national historic park is usually larger than a national historic site with multiple buildings. There are close to 40 national historic parks including the Boston National Historic Park, Chico Culture in New Mexico, the Lyndon B. Johnson Park, and Harper's Ferry.

National Memorial. This is a memorial either honoring a person or an event. There are close to 30 national memorials in the nation and, unlike national historic sites, they may or may not be located at the site associated with the person or event. Some examples of national memorials include Mount Rushmore and the USS Arizona Memorial in Hawaii.

National Battlefield. There are various types of park that fall under this designation: national battlefields, national battlefield parks, national battlefield sites, and national military parks. You'll find these parks in Gettysburg, Richmond, Vicksburg, and other sites.

National Cemetery. There are over a dozen national cemeteries in the park system; the best known is Arlington.

National Recreation Area. These parks emphasize fun in the sun. Waterspouts are the top attraction at these parks which include Amistad in Texas, Glen Canyon, Lake Mead, and others.

National Seashore. Another sun and fun destination, these national seashores are found on all the coasts. In all there are nearly a dozen national seashores such as Padre Island, Cape Cod, and Assateague Island.

National Lakeshore. These are all found along the Great Lakes. There are four national lake shores: Apostle Islands, Indiana Dunes, Pictured Rocks, and Sleeping Bear Dunes.

National River. You'll find national scenic rivers, national wild and scenic rivers, and other designations in this category. The Mississippi National River and Recreation Area is one example of this park.

National Parkway. These parkways are for car travelers and wind along scenic drives such as the Blue Ridge Parkway and the Natchez Trace.

National Trail. These trails wind through multiple states and are popular with hikers. The Appalachian National Scenic Trail is the best known of these beautiful walks.

Youth Conservation Corp

An interesting program for teens is the Youth Conservation Corp. A summer employment program for teens ages 15-18, the program operates throughout the country. Work includes duties ranging from trail construction to litter collection to offering information to park visitors.

Teens need to apply for the jobs between January 1 and April 15. For some locations, participants commute to the park from home; for other locations, residential camps are offered (Yellowstone and Yosemite). For information on the Yellowstone program, contact **YCC Coordinator**, PO Box 168, Yellowstone National Park, WY 82190; for information on Yosemite, contact **YCC Coordinator**, PO Box 577, Yosemite National Park, CA 95389.

Trivia Quiz

Here's a little trivia quiz for you and your family during that next long car trip:

• *When did the National Park System start?*
1916
• *What was the first national park?*
Yellowstone National Park, which became a park in 1872.
• *What's the most visited site in the National Park System?*
Blue Ridge Parkway
• *What's the second most visited park site?*
Golden Gate National Recreation Area in San Francisco
• *How many people visit the National Park System every year? a. between 100 and 200 million, b. between 200 and 300 million, or c. between 300 and 400 million?*
b. Between 200 and 300 million
• *What is the symbol of the National Park Service?*
An arrowhead
• *What is the biggest site in the National Park System?*
The Wrangell-St. Elias National Park and Preserve in Alaska

The pay is minimum wage (or state minimum wage if that's higher) and participants are selected at random. Most of the programs run for eight weeks.

Using This Guide

As we mentioned, this is a selective list of what we feel are the most family-oriented properties in the National Park System. Some are selected for their beauty, others for their rich history. At the back of this book you'll find a complete list of all sites in the park system with addresses and phone numbers for more information.

This guide is divided geographically, starting on the east coast and working westward to some of the grandest and oldest parks in the system. You'll also find an index by state as well as an index of parks by interest so you can quickly find all the parks that offer cave tours, good swimming beaches, or boat excursions.

Each park description begins with a section called **Are We There Yet?** which offers directions to the park site. If you'll be visiting many of the parks during the winter months, we also recommend calling the park ahead of your visit to make sure roads are open and clear.

What's There To Do Here? takes a look at the various activities in each park, from hiking trails to visitors centers to mule trips. We've selected activities with family travelers in mind and included information on Junior Ranger programs at many of the parks, a fun way for young travelers to learn about the special attractions of a region. Following each of these sections, we've included a selection of suggested books about the park as well as the region, time period, or historical figure. These books, offer material for a variety of reading levels and are a great way to introduce your child to the park and to get the whole family involved in the trip before you ever leave home. Most books in the lists are still in print and can be found at your local library or ordered from your bookseller or on-line bookstore such as a.m.*azon.com* or *barnesandnoble.com.*

When Are We Going? gives you tips about the best time to visit the park. Unfortunately, the best time to visit the park is usually also the most popular time for a visit, so we'll warn you about the crowds if that's a problem. We'll also give you a clue as to the weather conditions during that time of year.

How Long Are We Staying? offers a suggested time so you can budget for your visit. Keep in mind that this is an average visit, however, and if your family wants to enjoy long hikes, would like to participate in many of the ranger-led programs, or would like to explore back country areas, you'll want to plan for additional time at the park.

No one wants to get to a destination without the right equipment, whether that means a bottle of insect repellent or a pair of hiking shoes. We've included a section called **What Should I Bring?** offering tips on specific items you'll want to pack for your trip or for specialized tours such as cave excursions or mule trips.

Once you've come all the way to the park, you'll also want to see what else is of interest to your family in the area and that's where **What Are We Doing Next?** comes in. This section points out other national park sites within driving distance as well as family attractions in the nearby cities.

Which One Is My Room? looks at campgrounds and overnight lodging in each of the national parks, where available. Many national park sites don't offer overnight accommodations (or, if they do, they often fill up fast) so we've also included phone numbers for the local Chamber of Commerce and Convention and Visitors Bureaus in the area so you can find out about area motels, hotels, and campgrounds near the parks.

Each park section is followed by a **Practical Information** section that gives you all the nuts and bolts you'll need to plan your trip: the mailing address, phone number, operating season, hours, and cost.

Chapter 3

PLANNING YOUR TRIP

Before You Visit

Planning your trip is part of the fun. After you decide on a park, contact the **Department of the Interior, National Park System: Office of Public Inquiries,** P.O. Box 37127, Room 1013, Washington, DC 20013-7127, *Tel. 202/208-4747*. The office can answer your specific questions or provide you with park brochures to help you plan your trip.

Another good source of information is the National Park Service's internet site, **ParksNet**. Check out *www.nps.gov* for information, maps, and activities at all the parks in the system. While you're on the site, have a look at the Learn NPS section as well, *www.nps.gov/learn/*. Designed for teachers, the section is a great tool for parents as well, offering lots of information and online activities.

On the site, you'll also find forms for emailing your questions to each of the parks.

What to Pack

When it comes to packing, there's no doubt that less is more. This axiom is especially true for a summer vacation, where the order of the day is casual and cool. Most guests are comfortable in shorts and T-shirts in the days.

Here's a look at what we bring on summer trips:

His
• 1 pair casual slacks
• 2 T-shirts
• 1 pair jeans

- 2 polo or short sleeve shirts
- 2 pair of shorts
- 2 swimsuits
- 1 pair walking shoes or hiking boots
- 1 pair walking sandals
- 3 pair socks
- light jacket

Hers
- 1 pair casual slacks
- 2 pair jeans or casual pants
- 1 T-shirt
- 2 short sleeve/sleeveless blouses
- 2 pair of shorts
- 2 swimsuits
- 1 pair walking shoes or hiking boots
- 3 pair socks
- 1 pair sandals or tennis shoes
- light jacket

Kids
- 3 pair shorts
- 1 pair jeans
- 3 T-shirts
- 1 old t-shirt to wear while swimming
- 2 swimsuits
- 1 pair walking shoes or hiking boots
- 3 pair socks
- 1 pair sandals
- 1 pair sneakers
- light jacket

Other gear we never leave home without includes:
- film and camera, extra camera battery
- insect repellent
- all prescriptions (in prescription bottles)
- 2 pairs of sunglasses each
- paperback book or two
- antiseptic for bug bites
- aloe vera lotion for sunburn
- first aid kit with aspirin, stomach medicine, bandages, children's aspirin, etc.
- mini-address book for postcard writing
- hat

For beach parks, we also carry:
- sunscreen (usually two bottles of different strengths)
- snorkel gear (and certified divers must bring a "C" card)
- aqua shoes
- beach toys
- towels

How Much Longer?

For most families, a trip to a national park means a car trip. As American as apple pie, the summer car trip to the national parks inevitably means a long car ride. How can you keep the kids happy (and yourself sane) during the trip?

- Designate jobs. Give each child an age-appropriate job: navigator, accountant, postman, grocery clerk, travel agent. Whether the job is as simple as collecting brochures or as complicated as keeping track of vacation finances and receipts, the responsibility will be a learning experience.
- Stop often. Patience runs thin in all travelers when the journey gets too long. Plan for stops and take them.
- Minimize your luggage. You'll travel lighter (remember the "lug" in luggage!) and loading and unloading at motels or campgrounds every night will be that much simpler.
- Pack some special activities in a secret "goody bag" or two you keep out of the child's hands until the trip is underway.
- Bring extra batteries for children's electronic games and headsets.

Capturing Your Trip in Photos

All too often, photographs come back from the developer looking nothing like the planned picture. Scenics are just a blur in the distance; the sun has washed out half of the print; people look posed. But you can capture your national park trip on film with a little pre-trip preparation. With today's high-tech cameras and some practice before the trip, you can improve your photos and return with pictures that will bring back memories for years to come. All it takes is a little practice and knowledge of some of the techniques used by professional photographers. Here are a few helpful hints:

Know Your Equipment. It has happened more than once that a vacationer buys a new camera, sets off on his trip and comes back with rolls of black film.

The best camera in the world isn't worth having if you don't know how to use it. First, read your owner's manual. If you have any questions, visit your camera store.

Next, shoot several rolls of film as a test. Shoot some pictures inside and outside in conditions such as bright sunshine, clouds and night skies. Get the film developed and then analyze it to see what you did right and wrong.

Get Close. Many photos fail because the point of interest is just a spot in the center of the picture. Get in close for successful photos.

First, try to fill the frame with your subject. Now, move in even closer! Most cameras will focus up to a distance of three feet with no special equipment. Don't be afraid to let the center of interest pour out over the edges of the frame.

Use the Rule of Thirds. Professional photographers make use of the "rule of thirds" to improve the composition of their pictures. To use this rule, imagine your camera's viewer is covered by a tic-tac-toe board.

The rule of thirds says that the center of interest in your photo should lie at any place where two lines intersect. Never place the subject in the middle square, which is the natural tendency. Moving the subject to one side will create tension within the picture.

Photograph Scenery Carefully. Ever notice how those sweeping landscapes look like shrunken fields when captured on film?

The problem lies in the small portion of the landscape your camera photographs. Most lenses see only a portion of the scene before you, producing a picture with only a fraction of the landscape.

To avoid this disappointment, change to a wide angle lens, if you're using a camera with interchangeable lenses. A 24mm or 28mm lens will portray the scene as you witnessed it, without distortion that plagues wider angle lenses, such as the 18mm.

Another problem is often a lack of perspective. When viewing a landscape, you know its approximate size by your position in the scene. When it comes time to snap a picture, you need to include an object in the foreground to give your pictures a sense of proportion. Placing a person in the picture can make a mediocre photo more engaging. You can try the same with nearby trees and other objects instead of people.

Use Fill Flash. Sometimes there's plenty of light to take a shot, but shadows make the light uneven. Or the background is well lit but your subject isn't quite as bright. You'll especially have this problem in forest-covered parks such as Yosemite or Moiré Woods. The solution: use your flash.

Put People in the Picture. People can make a vacation picture truly special, one to return to for many years. But while people can add greatly to a photograph, they can also ruin a picture if not photographed correctly.

Too many vacationers stand the kids in the middle of a scene, order them to smile, and then snap the shutter, producing an obviously staged picture.

Next time move the subject to the side of the frame. Have them look into the distance, touch a statue, walk in a brook, smell a flower. People in vacation pictures are interesting only if they look as if they are participating in, rather than blocking out, the scene.

Don't Be Afraid of Indoor Shots. Taking photos indoors isn't an easy task. Artificial lighting plays havoc with color films, often producing colors far different from the ones you saw.

There are two kinds of color film- daylight and tungsten film. Daylight film is for outdoor use, and tungsten film is for indoor shots. If you use daylight film under artificial lights, the photos will have a warm yellow cast, a sometimes desirable side effect. If you use tungsten film outdoors, your pictures will have a greenish tinge.

If you use a flash, you may use daylight film indoors without changes in color. Flash bulbs used by small cameras and flash units used by single lens reflex cameras are easy to use with today's automatic cameras and can produce excellent photos that would be unattainable in any other way.

Watch Out for Motion. How many pictures have you eagerly waited for, only to be disappointed because everything was a blur? Motion, caused by either the photographer or the subject, has ruined countless vacation pictures.

One of the first ways to guard against blur is to make sure you are steady. Brace your body against your car, a tree, a building, or even another person when photographing in dim or windy conditions. If you want to take a photo from your moving car, do so from the rear or front window, watching out for reflections.

Second, check the film speed you're using. The lower the number, the slower the film, and the more light necessary. Film speeds such as 24 ASA require bright sunlight or the use of tripods. Faster films such as 200 or 400 ASA require less light for clear pictures.

Sometimes you will want to photograph a moving subject. If your camera allows you to choose the shutter speed, you can freeze or blur the motion. A fast shutter speed of 1/500 will freeze falling water to the point that drops are isolated. A slow shutter speed of 1/60 or lower photographs falling water as a solid mass much like flowing hair.

Move To Your Child's Level. Your child looks at life from a different perspective than you see. As an adult, you've become accustomed to looking down at your child, or rather, at the top of your child's head.

Unfortunately, most people photograph their preschoolers from the same viewpoint. This results in photos of children gazing up at the camera. For a more professional look, kneel or sit so the camera is at the same level as your child's head. For an unusual perspective, try getting even lower and photographing from the ground up at your child!

Check All Corners. Frequent photographers always check every corner of the viewfinder before pressing the shutter. This "once over" will force your eye to cover all the outside edges of the future photograph, an area where telephone poles, garbage cans and litter often hide.

In this last step, look for anything that distracts from the subject. Check for a telephone pole that appears to be growing from someone's head. Beware of wires and signs which distract. Change positions before taking the picture to remove these distractions.

Photography on the road can be fun, exciting and worth all the trouble when you look back on the finished product months and years later. With a little preparation, you may find that travel photography can be a "snap!"

Entry Passes
Admission Costs
The cost for admission at the national park sites varies by the popularity of the park. Many are free; most range from free to $4-$10 per car, with a few of the most popular parks reaching $20 per car.

National Parks Pass
If you might be visiting many parks within the year, consider a National Parks Pass. The pass costs $50 and is valid for one full year after its first use in a park. The pass covers the assignee and accompanying passengers in a private car. It doesn't reduce camping fees.

You can obtain a National Parks Pass several ways:
•Call the toll-free number: *Tel. 888/GO-PARKS*
•Online at *www.nationalparks.org*
•Send $50 (plus and additional $3.95 for shipping and handling) to National Park Foundation, PO Box 3410, Washington, DC 20043-4108

Golden Age Passports
If you are 62 years or older you can obtain a lifetime entrance pass for the national parks. The **Golden Age Passport** is available for a one-time fee of $10; this entitles you to entrance (along with your passengers) in parks under the National Park Service. It has to be obtained in person and can be purchased at any of the parks. You'll need to show proof of age and also you must be a citizen or permanent resident of the United States.

The passport also gives you a 50% discount on federal use fees–camping, tours, boat launching, and other activities.

Golden Eagle
A Golden Eagle Pass is a hologram adhered to your National Parks Pass which gives you access not only to national parks sites, but also those run by the US Fish and Wildlife Service, the US Forest Service, as well as the Bureau of Land Management. The hologram, which costs an additional $15, expires on the same date as the National Parks Pass.

You can buy a Golden Eagle Passport at any of the park sites or through the mail by writing:

National Park Service
1100 Ohio Drive, SW
Room 138
Washington, DC 20242
Attention: Golden Eagle Passport

What does the Golden Eagle cover? Admission fees for yourself and your passengers and if the park charges per person instead of per vehicle it provides admission for yourself, spouse, children and parents. The hologram doesn't provide for reduced fees for camping, tours, and other services.

Golden Access Passports

Blind or permanently disabled travelers qualify for free lifetime entrance at the national parks through the Golden Access Passport. You must be a citizen or permanent resident of the United States. To obtain a passport, apply at one of the parks with proof of disability and eligibility for obtaining federal benefits. The passport is good for you and your passengers and also provides a 50% discount for camping, tours, etc.

Central Reservation Service

A central reservation service handles campground and tour reservations at several of the most popular parks. You can call up to a year in advance of your visit and reserve your family a spot at a campground or a place on a tour.

Toll-free Park Reservation Phone Numbers

The following numbers, operated by Biospherics Inc. of Beltsville, Maryland, take reservations for the following parks:

• *Tel. 800/436-PARK:* Yellowstone National Park

• *Tel. 800/365-CAMP*: Acadia National Park, Assateague Island National Seashore, Cape Hatteras National Seashore, Channel Islands National Park, Chickasaw National Recreation Area, Death Valley National Park, Everglades National Park, Glacier National Park, Grand Canyon National Park, Great Smoky Mountains National Park, Greenbelt Park, Gulf Islands National Seashore, Joshua Tree National Park, Katmai National Park, Mount Rainier National Park, Rocky Mountain National Park

• *Tel. 800/967-CAVE*: Carlsbad Caverns National Park, Mammoth Cave National Park, Frederick Douglass National Historic Site

෮

When to Visit

At almost every park in this book, you'll soon see that the busiest season is summer. From late May through August, visitation numbers soar.

There's good reason for those booming numbers. Not only do the summer months coincide with most families' vacation times, but these months also represent the best time in terms of weather at many of the parks. Many parks in the mountains and the North close certain sections during the winter months so for full access the only time to visit is during warm weather.

However, spring and summer months are great times to visit many parks. While southern locations such as San Antonio may suffer 100 degree temperatures in August, the spring and fall usually offer beautiful days to sightsee without worrying about climbing into a stifling hot car. Even mid-winter days are comfortable at many of the southern and western parks.

And winter can be a unique time to visit even cold weather parks. Yellowstone takes on a completely different atmosphere during the winter months, when wildlife can more easily be spotted, crowds are nil, and activities mean snowmobiling or snow shoeing.

Camping

Camping is a great way to enjoy most of the national park sites. We've provided information on park campgrounds and included reservation numbers if applicable. Always keep in mind that during summer months the national park campgrounds fill up fast. Some take reservations and some don't.

Junior Ranger Program

Many parks offer Junior Ranger programs either year around or during peak months. These programs are a fun way for children, usually ages 5-12, to learn more about the unique aspects of the park.

You'll need a whole day in the park to participate in the Junior Ranger program because most require kids to attend a ranger-led activity.

Check in at the visitors center when you arrive at the park for details on any Junior Ranger programs.

Getting the Kids Ready

One of the best ways to build excitement about an upcoming trip is to start the vacation before you ever leave home. Read about the park. Rent movies that feature park locales. Surf the internet and look for news, notices, and even photos of your destination.

In each park description, we've included a list of books for different ages, from preschool through teens. Introducing your children to the park's rich natural and social history through books can be a way to enrich your experience.

Help Your Child Bring Home Vacation Memories

Every vacationer wants to return home with memories of the experience that will help him relive the trip time after time. Adults rely on cameras to capture these memories, but children all too often fall prey to overpriced souvenirs as a poor substitute.

There is a way to help your child bring back vacation memories – without breaking your trip budget. No matter where you travel, free (or low cost) souvenirs are yours for the asking. Your children can collect everything ranging from postcards to matchbooks and placemats. They are available in restaurants, campgrounds, motels, tourist attractions, and service stations, potentially every place your family might stop. By showing your child the fun of searching for (not just buying) souvenirs, you can involve him in the excitement of seeking out free souvenirs and keep him away from the trinket stands which plague so many tourist attractions.

Your first step begins before the vacation at your neighborhood five-and-dime. Buy each child an inexpensive photo album ($1-2) with adhesive pages. These pages allow small fingers to stick memorabilia in the book, and they will survive several rearrangements before you have to resort to glue.

Keep an eye out for these souvenirs:

Restaurants – You'll find special children's placemats in many family restaurants, often with pictures or a map of local attractions. Free children's menus, containing a game or a puzzle, are available in many restaurants. And don't overlook tiny sugar packets with the restaurant's name or picture on it. These can act as miniature postcards, ready to assume a place in your child's scrapbook.

Postcards – For about a quarter each, you can carry home a professional photo of almost any attraction in the world. These are a great bargain, and a much better buy than the slides sold at many places, which have often faded under fluorescent lights. And if you've heard your child complain "I never get any mail," encourage them to send a postcard to themselves! They'll act as miniature vacation diaries when they return home, and give returning vacationers a little something to look forward to as well.

Matchbooks – Many restaurants and hotels give away free matchbooks. Minus the matches, of course, these make good additions to the scrapbook. Also, your young travelers may want to start a matchbook collection in a jar once they return home.

Chapter 4

THE NORTHEAST

Abraham Lincoln's Birthplace National Historical Site
Kentucky

Abraham Lincoln's parents settled on this farm just a couple of months before his birth in a log cabin. Today part of that farm is preserved in this national historic site. The park is also home to a log cabin that was once believed to be his birthplace; today scholars generally believe that it is not the original cabin. The park still makes an interesting visit and a good place to learn more about this important president.

Are We There Yet?

The park is located near Hodgenville, Kentucky. If you are traveling I-65 north, take the Sonora exit and travel east on KY 84 to KY 61. Take a right on KY 61 and continue three miles to park.

If you are traveling south on I-65, take the Elizabethtown exit to Hwy. 61 (Lincoln Parkway). Continue south for 13 miles to park.

What's There To Do Here?

The cabin was located near the Sinking Spring and today you can take a walk down to this natural spring. Over two miles of hiking trails wind through the park.

At the park you'll find a visitors center with exhibits showcasing the life and times of Lincoln and his family, including the Lincoln family Bible and farming implements used to work the land, as well as a film playing throughout the day titled "Lincoln: The Kentucky Years".

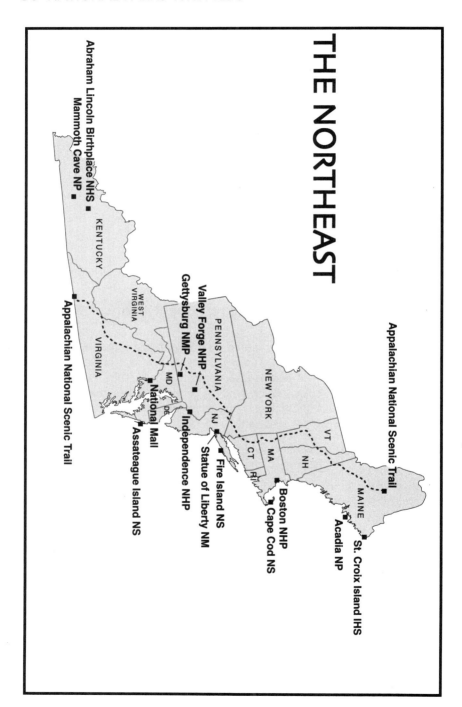

THE NORTHEAST

Abraham Lincoln Birthplace NHS
Mammoth Cave NP
KENTUCKY
WEST VIRGINIA
VIRGINIA
Appalachian National Scenic Trail
Gettysburg NMP
Valley Forge NHP
PENNSYLVANIA
NEW YORK
MD
DE
National Mall
Independence NHP
Assateague Island NS
NJ
Statue of Liberty NM
Fire Island NS
CT
RI
MA
Boston NHP
Cape Cod NS
NH
VT
Appalachian National Scenic Trail
MAINE
Acadia NP
St. Croix Island IHS

Fifty-six steps, each one marking a year in the life of the nation's sixteenth president, lead to the Memorial Building, a grandiose neoclassical structure of granite and marble which was dedicated in 1911 by then President William H. Taft. The building's opulent exterior is a sharp contrast to the simple log cabin housed within. Once believed to be the actual home in which young Abraham was born, its preservation was accomplished by a group known as the Lincoln Farm Association, which included Mark Twain and William Jennings Bryan among its notable members. Although now known to be a reproduction, the cabin provides insight into the humble origin of a man who would one day see the nation through its darkest hour.

When Are We Going?

The summer months are the peak time for visitors, a time of year when the weather is hot and generally humid. Dress coolly.

In the winter months, visitation is at an all-time low and the park is very quiet. Winter days can be chilly so dress in layers.

How Long Are We Staying?

You'll want a couple of hours to see the Lincoln film, view the displays, and enjoy the hiking trail.

What Should I Bring?

Comfortable walking shoes are probably the most important accessory.

Which One Is My Room?

You won't find any lodging or camping in the park, but overnight accommodations are available in the communities of **Dale**, *Tel. 812/937-4445*, and **Santa Claus**, *Tel. 812/937-2848*. **Lincoln State Park**, adjacent, offers campground facilities, *Tel. 812/937-4541*.

Where Are We Going Next?

Lincoln Statue and Lincoln Museum. Only three miles away in downtown Hodgenville a bronze depiction of the sixteenth president presides over the town square, and at the Lincoln Museum twelve wax figures bring to life in dioramas various events, from Lincoln's childhood, the signing of the Emancipation Proclamation, to his untimely death. The museum also offers a look at rare Lincoln memorabilia, including newspaper clippings and campaign posters, as well as a 21-minute film covering his life. The museum, which is listed on the National Register of Historic Places, is open daily year round. Open Monday through Saturday 8:30am-5pm and Sunday 12:30pm- 5pm, *www.noinkmedia.com/lincolnmuseum/index.htm*.

Lincoln's Boyhood Home At Knob Creek. Lincoln's earliest ,and perhaps fondest, memories were of his boyhood days spent at Knob Creek, located only ten miles from the visitors center. The logs used for the faithful reproduction of Lincoln's home are said to have come from the cabin of his childhood friend, Austin Gallaher, who once saved the future president from drowning. Address: Lincoln's Boyhood Home, 7120 Bardstown Road, Hodgenville, KY 42748.

The Mary Todd Lincoln House. The early life of Abraham Lincoln bore little resemblance to that of his future wife, Mary Todd. Born and raised in Lexington, (a five 1/2 hour drive from Hodgenville), the woman destined to become first lady spent her adolescence as one of sixteen siblings in a two-story, Georgian-style brick structure which is open to the public from March 15 through November 30. From family portraits hanging on the walls to authentic furnishings once owned by both the Todds and the Lincolns, this fourteen room home offers a unique glimpse into Mary Todd's younger days. Address: 578 West Main St. in Lexington, Kentucky; *Tel. 859/233-9999, www.mtlhouse.org.*

Fun Facts

• At six feet four inches in height, Abraham Lincoln holds the record as America's tallest president.

• Abraham Lincoln loved animals, and during his time in the White House his family kept as pets two goats named Nanny and Nanko and a wild turkey that answered to the name of Jack.

• More national parks have been named in honor of Lincoln than any other president.

• "Honest Abe" grew his famous beard at the suggestion of an 11-year-old girl! Young Grace Bedell of Westfield, NY wrote to the presidential hopeful, stating her opinion that Lincoln would win more votes in the upcoming election if he grew whiskers. Lincoln took her advice, and the newly elected president even stopped in Grace's hometown on his way to begin his term in office to tell her so. Today there is a statue of Lincoln and Grace Bedell in Westerfield, NY to commemorate the event.

Practical Information

Address: Abraham Lincoln Birthplace National Historic Site, 2995 Lincoln Farm Rd., Hodgenville, KY 42748

Telephone: *270/358-3137*

Operating Season: year round; closed Thanksgiving, Christmas Day and New Year's Day

Hours: Memorial Day through Labor Day: 8 am-6:45 pm; other months 8 am-4:45 pm

Cost: free
Website: *www.nps.gov/abli/index.htm*

Learning About Abraham Lincoln

Bracken, Thomas. *Abraham Lincoln (Overcoming Adversity)*. Chelsea House Publishing, 1998. Ages 9-12.

Crenson, Victoria. *Abraham Lincoln: An Adventure in Courage* (Pop-Up Book).Troll House, 1991. Ages 9-12.

D'Aulaire, Ingri and Edgar D'Aulaire. *Abraham Lincoln*. Dell Picture Yearling, 1987. Ages 4-8.

Greene, Carol and Steven Dobson (Illustrator). *Abraham Lincoln: President of a Divided Country* (Rookie Biographies). Children's Press, 1990. Ages 4-8.

Marrin, Albert. *Commander in Chief : Abraham Lincoln and the Civil War*. Dutton Books, 1997. Young Adult.

Smith, A. G. *Abraham Lincoln Coloring Book*. Dover Publications, 1987. Baby-preschool.

Stevenson, Augusta and Jerry W. Robinson (Illustrator). *Abraham Lincoln: The Great Emancipator*. Aladdin Paperbacks, 1988. Ages 9-12.

Acadia National Park
Maine

This park was the first national park east of the Mississippi River, founded in 1916 as Lafayette National Park. A decade later the name was changed and today visitors can enjoy 40,000 acres of coastline here.

Are We There Yet?

To reach the park, take I-95 north to Bangor, then take Route 1A to Ellsworth. From Ellsworth, take Route 3 east to Mount Desert Island.

What's There To Do Here?

Along with a visitors center with information about this wilderness area including an orientation film, there is also the Sieur de Monts Spring Nature Center, with exhibits concentrating on Acadia's natural history and The Isleford Historical Museum at Little Cranberry Island, which takes a look at the history of the people of this area.

With over 120 miles of trails, hiking is one of Acadia's most popular activities. Bar Harbor Shore Path offers impressive island scenery, while Cadillac Summit takes you to Frenchman Bay. View nature's ever-changing palette of colors on Jordan Pond Nature Trail, while Wonderland takes you through the forest to the rocky shoreline. All of these paths are easy to maneuver and are only two miles or less in length.

Children will love the clip-clop of horses hooves as you ride along on a carriage tour offered by Wildwood Stables. One- and two-hour tours run from mid-June through early October. From June-October call *207/276-3622*, while throughout the winter months call *859/356-7139* or email *carriages@wildwood.acadia.net,* or write Acadia National Parks, Wildwood Stables, Box 241, Seal Harbor, ME 04675.

If you would rather get see the park from the comfort of motorized transportation, ride The Island Explorer Shuttle Bus, a free service. Call *207/667-5796, email info@exploreacadia.com* or see *www.exploreacadia.com.*

When Are We Going?

Summer is the peak time at this park and, during busy weekends, you might find portions of the loop drive very busy. Fall is another excellent time to plan a visit.

How Long Are We Staying?

You can do the journey as a day trip but, to get a real feel for the park, plan an overnight visit.

What Should I Bring?

You'll definitely want a jacket just about any time of the year you visit this northerly park.

Which One Is My Room?

The park is home to the Blackwoods and Seawall campgrounds. Blackwoods is open year around, although Seawall closes from October until mid-May. You can make reservations for **Blackwoods** by calling *800/365-2267 (international calls Tel. 301/722-1257)* or write **NPRS**, *PO Box 1600, Cumberland, Maryland 21502.*

Where Are We Going Next?

During your stay in Bar Harbor, be sure to visit the **Abbe Museum**, which is dedicated to the lives of Maine's first inhabitants, the Wabanaki. Over 50,000 objects ranging from primitive stone tools to elaborate jewelry and intricately woven baskets bring to life the tribe known as "The People of The Dawn". For further information on the museum's two locations (exhibits can be seen at downtown Bay Harbor and Sieur de Monts), write to PO Box 286, Bar Harbor ME 04609, call 207/288-3519, email: abbe@midmaine.com or see www.abbemuseum.org.

The inviting red, two story house overlooking peaceful waters dotted by drifting sailboats was close to the heart of one of America's most respected presidents, and you can tour this idyllic summer retreat at Roosevelt Campobello International Park, located 140 from Acadia. FDR's family life comes into focus as you stroll through the room where his son was born, Mrs. Roosevelt's writing room, and the former president's bedroom.

There are eight miles of trails from which to choose, or simply meander through the picturesque garden. This site is free to the public. Call 506/752-2922 or send an email to info@fdr.net. Write to either Executive Secretary, P.O. Box 97, Lubec, ME 04652 or Superintendent, P.O. Box 9, Welshpool, NB Canada E0G 3H0.

Practical Information

Address: Acadia National Park, PO Box 177, Bar Harbor, ME 04609-0177
Telephone: *207/288-3338*
Operating Season: year around although some sections of park close in winter. Closed Thanksgiving, Dec. 24, Dec. 25, Jan. 1
Cost: $10 per vehicle for 7-day pass
Web address: *www.nps.gov/acad/index.htm*

Did You Know.....?

- More blueberries are grown in Maine than in any other state.
- The official state bird is the chickadee.
- The state insect is the honeybee.
- Maine's nickname is The Pine Tree State.
- The state motto is "Dirigo," which means "I lead."
- Many famous people hail from Maine or make their home here, including children's author E.B. White, who wrote *Charlotte's Web*, former President George Bush, artist Andrew Wyeth and actress Liv Tyler.
- The white pine cone and tassel is the state flower.
- The state capital is Augusta.
- The official state cat is the Maine coon cat.

Learning about Acadia

Fazio, Wende. *Acadia National Park* (True Book). Children's Press, 1998. Ages 4-8.

Scheid, Margaret. Discovering *Acadia : A Guide for Young Naturalists.* Acadia Publishing Company, 1987. Ages 4-8.

Tallant, Robert and Corinne Boyd Dillon (Illustrator). *Evangeline and the Acadians.* Pelican Publishing Company, 1998. Ages 4-8.

Appalachian National Scenic Trail

The following states are part of the Appalachian National Scenic Trail: Maine, New Hampshire, Vermont, Massachusetts, Connecticut, New York, New Jersey, Pennsylvania, Maryland, West Virginia, Virginia, Tennessee, North Carolina and Georgia.

The Appalachian Trail runs over 2,000 beautiful miles and is the best-known hiking trail in the country. Families enjoy short day hikes and weekend excursions all along its length.

Are We There Yet?

Because the trail has so many access points (over 500!) you'll need to contact the Appalachian Trail Conference (see below) for directions depending on your starting point. The Conference is a non-profit body that provides visitor information.

What's There To Do Here?

Hiking, hiking, and more hiking! The trail has all levels of difficulty and plenty of scenic beauty. You'll also have the chance to do some bird watching and some wildlife viewing along the way.

When Are We Going?

The trail is open year around but late spring and early autumn are some of the best times to enjoy its beauty.

How Long Are We Staying?

The length of your visit is totally up to you, depending on how far you want to walk. Most families spend a night or two along the trail if they're camping but you can also come as a day visitor and just enjoy a brief walk.

What Should I Bring?

Good walking shoes are a must. We'd also recommend binoculars to help with your wildlife viewing.

Which One Is My Room?

There are campgrounds and overnight accommodations scattered throughout the trail; contact the Appalachian Conference for details on sites close to where you'll be hiking. There are also three-sided shelters along the trail every 10 miles or so.

What Are We Doing Next?

Two locales which helped to forge the shape of the nation are close by. Learn about a turning point in the struggle against slavery at **Harpers Ferry National Historical Park**, where you can take guided tours of the sites associated with John Brown, including the one story brick building where he spent his final moments after the Harpers Ferry raid. A number of historic figures have a connection to this 2,300 acre park which spreads across West Virginia, Maryland and Virginia, including George Washington, Thomas Jefferson, Frederick Douglass, and Meriwether Lewis, and guided tours of the sites associated with this legendary explorer are also available. Admission is $6 for a 3-day pass. Harpers Ferry National Historical Park, PO Box 65, Harpers Ferry, WV 25425, *Tel. 304/535-6298.*

An air of sadness still hangs over **Antietam National Battlefield**, where in a single day over 23,000 soldiers were either killed or wounded. At the visitors center view "Antietam Visit", a 26-minute film which helps to illustrate the events which took place on September 17, 1862, and at noon each day a documentary narrated by renowned actor James Earl Jones is shown. To better understand the battle which pitted brother against brother drive past the 8 1/2 mile road which winds past the sites— audio tapes which help to conjure up mental images of the event can either be purchased or rented. $5 admission fee for a family. Antietam National Battlefield, PO Box 158, Sharpsburg, MD 21782-0158, *Tel. 301/432-5124.*

Practical Information
Address: Appalachian Trail Conference,, PO Box 807, Harper's Ferry, WV 25425-0807
Telephone: *304/535-6331*
Operating Season: year round
Cost: free (although fees are collected in Shenandoah National Park and Great Smoky Mountains National Park where the trail comes through)
Website: *www.nps.gov/appa/index.htm*

Assateague Island National Seashore
Maryland & Virginia
Assateague Island, managed by the National Park Service as well as other agencies, is home to the famous wild horses. These pony-size horses are descendants of horses brought to the barrier islands in the 17th century and roam wild in two herds found on the Virginia and the Maryland sides. Your odds of seeing the wild horses are good.

Are We There Yet?
You can enter the park at the north from Route 611, eight miles south of Ocean City, Maryland. From the south, enter off Route 175, two miles from Chincoteague, Virginia.

Wild Horse Warning

The National Park Service warns visitors not to feed or pet the wild horses. Not only is there a danger of being bitten or kicked, but feeding encourages the horses to stay near the roads, putting them at risk.

What's There To Do Here?

Along with searching for the wild horses, you'll find plenty of outdoor fun in the park. Beach combing and swimming are the top activities during summer months. The island has beautiful white sand beaches, some accessible only by four-wheel drive vehicle (you'll need a special permit to drive on these beaches so check at the visitors center first).

The park is home to three visitors centers:

Barrier Island Visitor Center. Located near the Maryland entrance, this center has an aquarium where kids can touch some of the marine life found in this region. Open all year from 9 am - 5 pm except Thanksgiving and Christmas Day. *Tel. 410/641-1441.*

Chincoteague Refuge Visitors Center. This center is in the Virginia section of the park and also has exhibits on beachcombing. Open all year from 9 am- 4 pm with the exception of Christmas Day and New Year's Day. *Tel. 757/ 336-6122.*

Toms Cove Visitors Center. Also in Virginia, this center has lots of information on the beaches and wildlife of the area. Open all year with the exception of Thanksgiving and Christmas Day, hours vary according to season. *Tel. 757/336-6577.*

When Are We Going?

Summer months are the peak time for this park as well as the best time to visit to enjoy swimming and beach combing.

How Long Are We Staying?

You'll want to plan on a full day in the park to see the exhibits, try to see the horses, and enjoy those beaches!

What Should I Bring?

Sunscreen! During the summer months, bring the full beach kit: swim shoes, towels, sunscreens, lotions, beach toys, etc. Insect repellent is also an important item, especially if you'll be camping.

What Are We Doing Next?

The island is close to many additional attractions such as:

Ocean City, Maryland, Chamber of Commerce, *Tel. 410/213-0552.* Ocean City is home to a large boardwalk with plenty of family fun.

Chincoteague, Virginia, Chamber of Commerce, *Tel. 757/336-6161.* This small town is still a fishing village with an authentic atmosphere.

From March through December families can see up close the wild ponies which have wandered the island since the 1600's, along with the possibility of spotting a bald eagle or dolphin on the Pony Express Tour in Ocean City. Admission is $20, and children under 11 receive a discount. Call toll free 1-866-PONY or contact by email at tours@assateagueisland.com.

The Island Aquarium at Chincoteague offers a view of life under the sea, and children can hold area sea life such as a horseshoe crab, starfish or turtle at the touch tank. Open Memorial Day through Labor Day from 10 am - 9 pm at the Landmark Plaza on North Main Street. Admission: $4 for adults, $3 for children under 12. For more information, call *757/336-2212.*

Which One Is My Room?

There is year-around camping in the national park at Oceanside and Bayside. Tent and trailer sites are available. Facilities include cold showers, chemical toilets, drinking water, picnic tables and grills. (At the Bayside campground you'll also have ground fire rings.)

Camping is on a first-come, first-served basis from mid-October through mid-April; during those months camping fees are $16 per night. During peak season from mid-April through mid-October, reservations are taken for the campsites and the prices rise to $20 per night. Call for reservations, *Tel. 800/365-2267* or online at *http://reservations.nps.gov* up to five months in advance of your visit.

Over three hundred campsites are available from April through October at the Assateague State Park in Maryland, *Tel. 410/641-2120 ext. 22 or 410/641-2918.*

Commercial camping is also available on the island of Chincoteague, Virginia. For more information contact the **Chincoteague Chamber of Commerce**, *Tel. 757/336-6161).*

Practical Information

Address: Assateague Island National Seashore, 7206 National Seashore Lane, Berlin, MD 21811

Telephone: *410/641-1441*

Operating Season: year round

Hours: 24 hours daily in Maryland; 5 am to 10 pm during daylight savings time in Virginia (shorter hours during winter). Visitors center open 9 am-5 pm

Cost: $10 per vehicle for one week pass
Website: *www.nps.gov/asis/index.htm*

Did You Know.....?

• Maryland was named after the wife of King Charles I of England, Henrietta Maria.

• In 1696 the first school in the United States, King Williams School, opened in Maryland.

• The state flower is the black-eyed susan.

• The state capital is Annapolis, which is considered the sailing capital of the world.

• The state bird is the Baltimore Oriole.

• *Maryland, My Maryland* is the official state song.

• Cecil Calvert founded the state as an English colony in 1634. His black and gold family crest is emblazoned upon the state flag, as is the red and white crest of the Crossland family.

• Many famous people have called Maryland home, including baseball legend Babe Ruth, Muppet creator Jim Henson, and author Edgar Allan Poe.

• Maryland was admitted into the union on April 28, 1788.

• The state nickname is the Old Line State.

• The movies "Tuck Everlansting" and "Runaway Bride" were both filmed in the town of Berlin, where the Assateague Island National Seashore is located.

• The official tree of Maryland is the white oak.

• It is believed that Francis Scott Key penned the national anthem while watching the battle of Fort McHenry in Baltimore Harbor.

• Maryland's motto is "fatti maschii parole femine," which is loosely translated as "strong deeds, gentle words."

Learning About Assateague

Points, Larry et al. *Assateague Island of the Wild Ponies*. Sierra Press, 1997. Young adult.

Boston National Historical Park
Massachusetts

A great place to learn about the history of the United States is this popular park. Kids can learn more about the American Revolution at sites in the park, most connected by the three-mile Freedom Trail.

Are We There Yet?

From Route 1 South and Route 93 North and South, you'll find signs to the Charleston Navy Yard, home of the USS Constitution. Most sites are within walking distance. There is some parking at the Navy Yard.

What's There To Do Here?

The three-mile Freedom Trail begins at **Boston Common**, then makes its way to the Massachusetts State House, where the state legislature resides today. Standing watch over the gold-domed building is the monument erected in honor of Robert Gould Shaw and the 54th Massachusetts Regiment.

The hymn "America" was sung for the first time at **Park Street Church**— its steeple was once a travelers' first glimpse of Boston. The house of worship looks out **on Granary Burying Ground**, which is the final resting place of such notable figures as Paul Revere, John Hancock and Samuel Adams.

King's Chapel and Burying Ground is a Georgian-style church which holds the gravestone that was the inspiration for an American literary masterpiece, The Scarlet Letter.

The **Franklin Statue** and **First School Site** is located in the courtyard of Old City Hall. The likeness of this American icon was Boston's first statue, and it stands guard over the school where Benjamin Franklin, Samuel Adams and John Hancock were educated. The decision to launch the Boston Tea Party was made **at Old South Meeting House**. There is a small admission fee for this site, which showcases the exhibit "Voices of Protest".

Now home to The Boston Globe Store, the **Old Corner Bookstore** once brought such authors as Henry Wadsworth Longfellow, Harriet Beecher Stowe, Ralph Waldo Emerson and Louisa May Alcott to prominence.

The Old State House is now a museum dedicated to Boston's history. A cobblestone circle within the building marks the site of The Boston Massacre. Open from 9 am - 5 pm, there is a small admission fee for this site. The voices of such legendary figures as Samuel Adams and Frederick Douglass have rung out in **Faneuil Hall**. Park rangers offer talks at this site. Open from 9am-5pm daily. Call *617/242-5675 or 617/242-5642* for more details.

Next see the **Paul Revere House**, where the famous midnight ride began. In the courtyard stands a 900 lb. bell, mortar and bolt from the USS Constitution which bear the stamp of Paul Revere and Sons. A small fee is charged to tour the house. Hours of operation are 9:30am-4:15pm from November through mid-April and 9:30 - 5:15 from mid April through October. Call *617/523-2338* for more information.

Boston's oldest place of worship, **Old North Church**, is still in use today. You can imagine the glow from the steeple as lanterns were hung to warn that the British were coming. The church is open from 9am-5 pm. Call *617/523-6676* for more information.

At **Copp's Hill Burying Ground** the man who built the USS Constitution was laid to rest, as was many men of color who once worked in the shipyards. The first battle for American independence is commemorated at **Bunker Hill Monument**, a 221-foot granite structure which is open to the public daily from 9am-5pm. Call *617/242-5641* for further details. Take a guided tour of the world's oldest warship, **the USS Constitution**—"Old Ironsides" is open from 9:30-3:50 daily, led by the US Navy.

When Are We Going?
Summer months are the busiest times at this park, although spring days can get busy with school field trip groups as well.

How Long Are We Staying?
You'll need a full day to see the major sites, more if you want to visit all areas of the park and do the tours.

What Should I Bring?
Good walking shoes are a must.

Which One Is My Room?
For information on rooms in the Boston area, contact the **Massachusetts Tourism Office**, *Tel. 800/227-6277*, or *www.mass-vacation.com*.

What Are We Doing Next?
The **Boston African American National Historic Site** recognizes the historic figures and events which have helped to unite all ethnicities. Walk the Black Heritage Trail, a 1.6 mile stretch which takes you past 14 sites including the homes of early African American leaders, the first schoolhouse built for the education of African American children, the oldest American Black church, and the African Meeting House, whose halls have been graced by the likes of Harriet Tubman, Frederick Douglass and Sojourner Truth.

The tour begins at the Robert Gould Shaw and 54th Regiment memorial, a moving bronze relief tribute to the first all African American regiment to fight for freedom in the Civil War. A map and site brochure of the area are available at the African Meeting House, located at 8 Smith Court. Ranger-guided tours are also available. To find out more, write to Boston African American National Historic Site, 14 Beacon St., Suite 503, Boston, MA 02108, or call *617/742-5415*.

Practical Information
Address: Boston National Historical Park, Charlestown Navy Yard, Boston, MA 02129-4543
Telephone: *617/242-5642* or *617/242-5601*

Operating Season: *year round*
Hours: *hours vary by visitors center and site*
Cost: *no fee for federally owned sites or tours; fee for sites privately owned such as the Paul Revere House*
Website: www.nps.gov/bost/index.htm

Cape Cod National Seashore
Massachusetts

This popular getaway is a great summer destination. With six swimming beaches, 11 nature trails, and more, there are plenty of reasons to visit.

Are We There Yet?

From Boston, follow Route 3 south to the Sagamore Bridge in Bourne then take Route 6 east to Eastham and Provincetown.

What's There To Do Here?

Start your visit with a stop at the **Salt Pond Visitor Center.** Here you can tour the museum with exhibits about the Cape and its flora and fauna. You can also see four short films here covering the formation of the Cape, its maritime history, Thoreau's Cape Cod, and the story of Marconi's use of the Cape as the location for the first wireless radio station.

After a look at the museum, you can take a walk on one of the nature trails outside: a one mile **Nauset Marsh Trail** or the 1/4 mile **Buttonbush Trail**, a multisensory trail with Braille panels and a guide rope.

Rent a bike in town and head out on one of the three bike trails. For a level ride, try Head of The Meadow Bike Trail, a two mile trek each way which takes you past both marshes and dunes. By law, children under the age of 13 must wear a safety helmet.

The park is also home to another visitors center, the **Province Lands Visitor Center**, on the northern end of the park about a mile from Provincetown. It is perched on a sand dune and offers good views of the surrounding dunes from an observation deck. Stop by the ranger desk for maps and brochures that outline trails. The center is also home to a museum with exhibits on the area's history including the Pilgrim's landing in Provincetown Harbor.

When Are We Going?

Summer months are definitely the most popular and with good reason. You'll find beautiful days in the 70s and 80s, perfect for a day of beachcombing.

How Long Are We Staying?

You'll probably want a full day to see the visitors centers and enjoy the beaches.

What Should I Bring?

Bring along the full beach kit: towels, swimsuits, sunscreen, swim shoes, etc. Insect repellent is also a good idea.

What Are We Doing Next?

Don't miss the **Boston National Historic Park**, which is detailed in this book, as well as Minute Man National Historic Park, the birthplace of the American Revolution. The legendary "shot heard round the world" was fired in this wooded area on April 19, 1775, and your family can walk in the footsteps of history on the Battle Road Trail, which takes you through the areas where fighting took place and past historic structures such as Brooks House, Hartwell Tavern, where volunteers dressed in period garb reenact daily life in the 1700's, the Captain William Smith House, and The Wayside, which in later years would be the home of several prominent authors including Nathaniel Hawthorn and Louisa May Alcott. The author of "Little Women" drew her inspiration from her childhood days spent in this home.

Minute Man National Historic Park is located within the confines of Lexington, Lincoln and Concord. For further information write to Minute Man National Historic Park, 174 Liberty Street, Concord, MA 01742 or call *Tel. 978/ 369-6993*.

Which One Is My Room?

For overnight accommodations, contact the **Cape Cod Chamber of Commerce**, Hyannis, MA 02601, *Tel. 508/362-3225*.

Practical Information

Address: Cape Cod National Seashore, 99 Marconi Station Site Rd., Wellfleet, MA 02667

Telephone: *508/349-3785* (headquarters); *508/255-3421 or 508/487-1256* (visitor information)

Operating Season: year round

Hours: Parking 6 am to midnight; Salt Pond Visitor Center 9am-4:30pm with extended summer hours; Province Lands Visitor Center 9am-5pm daily from early May to late October; headquarters open daily 8am 4:30pm except on weekends and holidays

Cost: $10 per vehicle daily fee at the park's lifeguard-protected swimming beaches during summer months

Website: *www.nps.gov/caco/index.htm*

Learning About Cape Cod

Adkins, Jan. *A Storm Without Rain*. 1993.

Coleman, Kay et al. *The Cape Cod Collection: Stories and Poems for Children*. 1998.

Hill, Donna. *Shipwreck Season*. 1998.

Murphy, T. M. *Secrets of Belltown* (Belltown Mystery Series ; No. 1) . 1995.

Murphy, Ted M. *The Secrets of Cranberry Beach* (A Belltown Mystery ; No. 2). 1996.

Taylor, Courtney. *Cape Cod Adventure*. 1995.

Tresselt, Alvin R. and Duvoisin, Roger (Illustrator). *Hide and Seek Fog*. 1988.

Weller, Francis Ward. *Riptide*. 1990.

Fire Island National Seashore
New York

This scenic area off of Long Island is a great trip to combine with a visit to New York City.

Are We There Yet?

This park has five units:

Fire Island Light Station: Take Long Island Expressway to Sagtikos State Parkway south (Exit 53) or Southern State Parkway to Robert Moses Causeway (Exit 40) south. Follow signs for Robert Moses State Park. At traffic circle, park in Field 5 and then walk one mile down the dirt road or boardwalk nature trail to Lighthouse.

Sailors Haven: Take Sunrise Highway (Route 27) to Lakeland Avenue exit (to Sayville). At intersection with Main Street (Montauk Highway), turn east then turn south on Foster Avenue and follow signs to Sayville Ferry. Walk to Sailors Haven ferry terminal; the ferry takes foot traffic only.

Watch Hill: Take Long Island Expressway (495) or Sunrise Highway (Route 27) to Route 19 (Waverly Avenue). Waverly Avenue forks about a mile south of Sunrise Highway. Take the left fork to Main Street (Montauk Highway). Cross Main Street (the road becomes West Avenue now). Continue past railroad tracks and a traffic light, and look for a sign for Fire Island National Seashore. The Watch Hill Ferry Terminal is on the right. Park for the ferry which takes foot traffic only.

Smith Point. Take Long Island Expressway (495) or Sunrise Highway (27) to William Floyd Parkway south. At end of parkway, bear left at traffic circle to go to Smith Point County Park lot. Park in the county lot, then walk west to Fire Island National Seashore visitor contact station.

William Floyd Estate. Take Long Island Expressway (495) to William Floyd Parkway south. Turn left on Neighborhood Road and follow signs for William Floyd Estate.

What's There To Do Here?

Each unit has its own distinct attractions which include nature trail and exhibits at the Fire Island Light Station. Visitors can tour the Fire Island Lighthouse in the daytime or evening hours. Fee is $5 for adults and $3.50 for children under 12. However, children under 42" in height are not permitted to make the climb.

Other attractions include a visitors center and boardwalk nature trail and marina and lifeguarded beach at Sailors Haven; nature trail and visitors center and lifeguarded beach at Watch Hill; sports fishing, nature trail and ocean beach at Smith Point; guided house tours at William Floyd Estate, William Floyd was a general in the Revolutionary War, and his signature can be found on the Declaration of Independence. This colonial home was lived in by generations of the Floyd family, and the influence of each era can be seen in the house.

When Are We Going?

Summer months are the peak times. We'd recommend weekdays to avoid the worst crowds.

How Long Are We Staying?

You'll want a day to visit the park and this means visiting just one unit. Schedule more time if you want to visit several units.

What Should I Bring?

Swimwear, insect repellent, and sunscreen are musts.

What Are We Doing Next?

While you are in the New York area, don't miss the Statue of Liberty and Ellis Island National Historical Park. There are a variety of National Park sites in the area including the following:

The General Grant National Memorial, the final resting place of the man who led the Union troops to victory in the Civil War and led his country through two terms as President of the United States, is an imposing 150 foot tall monument composed of over 8,000 tons of granite which is located 60 miles from Fire Island. Inside the tomb are bronze likenesses of the many generals who served Grant in battle, including Sherman, Sheridan, and MacPherson, while on the structure's outside is a plaque carved with the words " Let us have peace". Ranger-guided tours are available, as are reenactors in period garments who give talks on Grant's life. General Grant National Memorial, Riverside Drive and 122nd Street, New York, NY 10027, *Tel. 212/666-1640.*

Two nearby establishments offer insight into the life of the nation's 26th president, Theodore Roosevelt. A lesson in the life of the man known fondly as "Teddie" in his childhood can be learned at the **Theodore Roosevelt Birthplace National Historic Site**, which is 59 miles away from Fire Island. Although the original home was demolished in 1916, the structure was faithfully reconstructed and the furnishings were donated by Roosevelt's sisters and wife. An introductory video is also available at the site, which is open to the public Tuesday- Saturday from 9am-5pm. Admission is $3 per person. 28 East 20th Street, New York, NY 10003, *Tel. 212/260-1616.*

Did You Know.....?

• Four Presidents were born in New York: Martin Van Buren, Millard Fillmore, Theodore Roosevelt, and Franklin Delano Roosevelt.
• The world's smallest church can be found in Oneida.
• New York City was the nation's first capital.
• The state capital is Albany.
• The New York Post is the nation's oldest running newspaper—the first edition was published in 1803.
• The rose is the state flower.
• The bluebird is the state bird.
• "Excelsior" is the state motto.
• New York was admitted into statehood on July 26, 1788.
• "I Love New York" is the state song.
• Many famous personalities were either born or raised in New York including:
  basketball player Kareem Abdul-Jabbar
  comedian Lucille Ball
  actor Humphrey Bogart
  singer Sean "P Diddy" Combs
  actor Tom Cruise
  actress Claire Danes
  entertainer Sammy Davis Jr.
  baseball player Henry Louis Gehrig
  actress Sarah Michelle Gellar
  composer George Gershwin
  singer Billy Joel
  basketball player Michael Jordan
  comedians The Marx Brothers
  actor Christopher Reeve
  artist Norman Rockwell
  singer Barbra Streisand
  poet Walt Whitman

For a glimpse into Roosevelt's later days, tour **Sagamore Hill National Historic Site**, which is only 15 miles from Fire Island. This abode was referred to as the "Summer White House" during his presidential years. Roosevelt's hobbies are evident throughout the house—an avid reader in English, French and German, thousands of books line the bookshelves, and the skins of animals from his many hunting expeditions line the floors and walls. Guided tours are offered every hour from 10am-4pm, but each tour has a limit of 14. A five-minute drive from the home takes you to Young Memorial Cemetery and the gravesite of the 26th president. Admission for the home tour is $5 for adults, while 16 and under are admitted free. Sagamore Hill Road, Oyster Bay, NY 11771-1809.

Which One Is My Room?

There's a campground at the **Watch Hill** unit. You can select from 26 sites from mid-May through Mid-October. Campsites are $15 per night. For reservations, call *516/597-6633*.

For lodging in the area, contact the Fire Island Tourism Bureau, *Tel. 631/563-8448* or visit their website at *www.fireisland.com*.

Practical Information

Address: Fire Island National Seashore, 120 Laurel St., Patchogue, NY 11772

Telephone: *631/289-4810* (headquarters;) *631-399-2030* (William Floyd Estate); *631/321-7028* (Fire Island Lighthouse); *631/281-3010* (Wilderness Visitors Center); *631/597-6183* (Sailors Haven Visitors Center)

Operating Season: most units are open year round except the Sailors Haven and Watch Hill, which are open only from mid-May to mid-October)

Hours: vary with season

Cost: free

Website: *www.nps.gov/fiis/index.htm*

Learning About Fire Island

Farrell, Vivian, et al. *Robert's Tall Friend: A Story of the Fire Island Lighthouse.* Tracy Logan Publications, 1997. Ages 9-12.

Martin, Ann M. *Eleven Kids, One Summer.* Apple, 1996. Ages 9-12.

Shub, Elizabeth. *Cutlass in the Snow.* William Morrow and Company Library, 1986.

Gettysburg National Military Park
Pennsylvania

The site of the largest battle of the Civil War later became the location for President Lincoln's famous Gettysburg Address. The park is also a cemetery, remembering the thousands who died in the Civil War. The park is dotted with over 1,400 monuments and memorials, making it one of the largest outdoor sculpture gardens in the world.

Are We There Yet?

The park is located 50 miles north of Baltimore between the Taneytown Road (State Rt. 134) and Steinwehr Avenue (Bus. Rt. 15). The park is about a mile south of the town of Gettysburg.

If you are on US15, you'll find park signs to the visitors center. If you are on State Route 30, take the exit for US15 South and look for the park signs. If you are on State Route 30 driving east, travel into Gettysburg to Washington Street and turn right. Continue for one mile to the visitors center.

What's There To Do Here?

Start your visit at the Visitor's Center which includes the Gettysburg Museum of The Civil War, the home of one of the largest collections of Civil War items in the world. Personal items from shaving kits to cards and dominoes allow a battle of epic proportions to be seen on a more basic human level. One of the most interesting exhibits (and there is a separate admission charge of $4 for adults and $3 for children 6-16) is the Electric Map, a giant map of the battle.

The Gettysburg Cyclorama is a circular painting at the Cyclorama Center which spans 360 degrees and portrays the peak of the skirmish. The painting was created in 1884; there's also a 20-minute sound and light program that accompanies the Cyclorama. The center also shows a film on the battle. Unfortunately, due to restoration efforts, after the summer of 2004 the painting will not be on view again until 2006.

When you're ready to go out and see the park, you'll find 26 miles of roads and also walking trails. Ranger-led walks and tours are offered through the park during peak months; check with the visitor's center for times, *Tel. 717/ 334-1124.*

If you would rather venture out on your own, the Gettysburg National Military Park brochure found at either the visitor's center or Cyclorama Center has a map which will direct you. An audio tape of the tour route is also available to buy or rent. Contact The Gettysburg Convention and Visitors Bureau.

When Are We Going?

The summer months are the peak times at this park, which can get busy. Summer months can be hot and humid. Spring and fall months are pleasant and preferable, but winter months can be cold (and the park occasionally closes due to bad weather).

How Long Are We Staying?

You'll need about half a day to see the exhibits (a full day if you're really interested in the history and want to learn more about the site).

What Should I Bring?

Bring along cool clothes if you come during the summer months.

Which One Is My Room?

There are no accommodations in the park but you will find plenty of facilities in Gettysburg. Contact the **Gettysburg Convention and Visitors Bureau**, *Tel. 717/334-2100.*

What Are We Doing Next?

The bus shuttle from Gettysburg Battlefield to Eisenhower National Historic Site will transport you on a journey through time from the Civil War to the 1950's . The home of the 34th president was used as a weekend haven, and you can get a feel for the time period on a tour of his home which contains all original furnishings

Affairs of state were often run from his small office, and you can see the desk built of floorboards which had been removed from the White House during remodeling, and the portrait of a young Abraham Lincoln which decorates the office wall.

The 16th president was an inspiration to Eisenhower, and his likeness can be found on statues, portraits and books throughout the house. On a tour of the grounds you can see the PGA putting green, guest house, and the former president's station wagon, along with his jeep and golf cart, which are still parked in the garage.

Be sure to visit the reception area, displaying items which span Eisenhower's life, and view a 10-minute video which is continuously run on the first floor of the barn and in the reception area during the winter months. Admission is $7 for adults, $4 for children 13-16, and $3 for kids 6-12. Eisenhower National Historic Site, 97 Taneytown Rd., Gettysburg, PA 17325-2804, *Tel. 717/338-9114.*

Practical Information

Address: Gettysburg National Military Park, 97 Taneytown Road, Gettysburg, PA 17325

Telephone: *717/334-1124*

Operating Season: year round; closed Thanksgiving, Dec. 25, Jan. 1

Hours: grounds open 6am-10pm; visitors center open 8am-5pm (until 6 pm during summer months)

Cost: free; Cyclorama Center admission is $4 for adults, $3 for children 6-16

Restrictions: As the Visitor's Center and Cyclorama Center are both Federal facilities, security measures have been implemented and items such as back packs, large handbags and packages are forbidden. Anyone who enters these buildings are subject to a search.

Website: *www.nps.gov/gett/index.htm*

Battle of Gettysburg Facts

Over a period of three days 51,116 men lost their lives at Gettysburg.

Mary Virginia "Jennie" Wade was the only civilian to die during the battle. The 20 year old woman was shot through the heart while making bread in her sister's kitchen. The musket ball tore a hole through the door of the house, which can still be seen today. The American flag flies over her grave at Evergreen Cemetery—the only other woman to receive such an honor is Betsy Ross.

Russel C. Mitchell, the grandfather of *Gone With The Wind* author Margaret Mitchell, fought in the battle.

Corporal Cyrus W. James is believed to be the first Union soldier to die at Gettysburg, and it is thought that Private Henry Raison was the first fallen Confederate soldier in the battle.

"Faugh A Ballaugh", a Gaelic phrase uttered by many fighting men of Irish descent which is translated as "Clear The Way", is found carved on the Monument for the 28th Massachusetts Infantry.

The woman hovering over a dead soldier on the Louisiana State Memorial is said to be "The Spirit of The Confederacy."

The name David Diffenbaugh appears on the back of the 8th Illinois Cavalry monument. He was the only man in the regiment to die at Gettysburg.

There is a sculpture of the troop's mascot found on the 11th Pennsylvania Infantry Monument. The tiny dog was named Sallie, and she was killed at the Battle of Hatcher's Run in Virginia. The infantrymen asked that she be remembered in the Gettysburg monument.

Learning About Gettysburg

Beller, Susan Provost. *To Hold This Ground: A Desperate Battle at Gettysburg.* 1995.

Gauch, Patricia Lee. *Thunder at Gettysburg.* 1990.

Kallen, Stuard A. and Terry Boles (Illustrator). *The Gettysburg Address* (Famous Illustrated Speeches and Documents). 1994.

Kantor, MacKinlay. *Gettysburg* (Landmark Books).1987.

Morris, Gilbert. *The Gallant Boys of Gettysburg* .1996.

Murphy, Jim. *The Long Road to Gettysburg*. 1992.

Reef, Catherine. *Gettysburg*. 1992.

Richards, Kenneth G. *The Gettysburg Address* (Cornerstones of Freedom). 1992.

Weinberg, Larry. *The Drummer Boy*. Avon, 1996.

Wilhelm, Doug and Tom LaPadula (Illustrator). *Gunfire at Gettysburg* (Choose Your Own Adventure, No. 151) . 1994.

Independence National Historic Site
Pennsylvania

The birthplace of the nation is an educational and fun trip. Families can see the Liberty Bell and Independence Hall as well as enjoy all of the other things Philadelphia has to offer, such as excellent museums, shops and restaurants.

Are We There Yet?

From the north, take the New Jersey Turnpike to exit 4. Turn onto Route 73 north to Route 38, continue west to US 30. Follow US 30 west over the Benjamin Franklin Bridge then, at the base of the bridge, look for signs to Sixth Street. Take Sixth Street to Market Street then take a left on Market. Follow Market to Second Street and turn right on Second, continuing to the intersection of Chestnut Street. Cross Chestnut and look for the parking garage in the next block.

If you are coming in from the south, take I-95 north and follow the signs for "Central Philadelphia/I-676." Take the exit for 6th Street and follow Sixth Street to Market Street. Take a left on Market. Follow Market to Second Street and turn right on Second, continuing to the intersection of Chestnut Street. Cross Chestnut and look for the parking garage in the next block.

If you are coming in from the west, take PA Turnpike (I-76) and exit at interchange 24 (the Schuykill Expressway, I-76). Take Schuykill Expressway (I-76) to I-676 exit and follow the signs for Independence Hall. Take Eighth Street south to Market Street, turn left on Market Street. Follow Market to Second Street and turn right on Second, continuing to the intersection of Chestnut Street. Cross Chestnut and look for the parking garage in the next block.

What's There To Do Here?

There are 24 sites in the park. A few of the "must-see" spots are:

- **Visitor's Center**—(6th and Market Streets) Kids will enjoy the interactive computer exhibits and parents can obtain tickets and information.
- **Independence Hall**—(Chestnut Street between 5th and 6th Streets) The Georgian-style building has witnessed some of the nation's most historic events, including the adoption of the Declaration of Independence and

the signing of The Constitution of the United States. The design for the nation's first flag was also decided at this location.

- **Liberty Bell Center**—(on Market Street between 5th and 6th Streets). This symbol of the nation, viewed with Independence Hall as its backdrop, is a moving sight. Open to the public year round, a video and exhibits are also on hand to illuminate the history of the bell from its inception to its present day status.
- **Congress Hall**—(6th and Chestnut Streets). George Washington's second inauguration was held here. Open to the public year round, free tours are on a first-come, first-served basis.
- **New Hall Military Museum**—(4th and Chestnut). Learn about the origins of the Army, Navy and US Marine Corps.
- **Franklin Court**—(Market Street between 3rd and 4th Streets). A steel structure outlines the spot where Benjamin Franklin's brick, three story home once stood. Underground is a museum dedicated to Franklin's life and times, filled with reproductions of his inventions. A 22-minute video presentation, "The Real Benjamin Franklin" is also shown. Other buildings in the area include the US Postal Service Museum and the Franklin Print Shop.
- **Christ Church**—(2nd and Market Streets). Still in use today, this Episcopal house of worship, which was built between 1727 and 1754, was once attended by the likes of Benjamin Franklin and George Washington. Although the cemetery on 5th and Arch is not open to the public, Benjamin Franklin's grave can be seen from outside the fence.
- **Todd House**—The home of lawyer John Todd and his wife, Dolley Payne. Todd's widow would later become the nation's fourth first lady upon her marriage to James Madison. This home is shown in conjunction with the Bishop White House, the home of Christ Church's pastor.
- **Declaration House**—(7th and Market Streets). It was on the second floor of this home that Thomas Jefferson penned the Declaration of Independence. These rooms are decorated today with furnishings typical of the era, and the first floor displays exhibits and a video presentation.
- **City Taver**n—(2nd and Walnut Streets). This is a reconstruction of the Revolutionary-era tavern and a good place for lunch on your tour.

When Are We Going?

You'll find the park busiest during the summer months but look for school field trip crowds during April and May as well.

How Long Are We Staying?

You'll want almost a whole day to see the highlights, even longer if you'll be touring most of the sights.

What Should I Bring?

Good walking shoes are a must.

Which One Is My Room?

There's one accommodation in the park: the **Thomas Bond House**, 129 S. 2nd Street, *Tel. 800/845-2663 or 215/923-8523*. This bed-and-breakfast is housed in a colonial-period building and is within walking distance of most park sites.

Within the city, you'll find a full range of accommodations. contact the **Philadelphia Convention and Visitors Bureau**, 1515 Market Street, Suite 2020, Philadelphia, PA 19102, *Tel. 215/636-3300*.

What Are We Doing Next?

Continue exploring the birth of this nation with a stop at the Betsy Ross House, located at 239 Arch Street. Strips of cloth are still tucked away in the storage room, and you can view the room where the flag was sewn and see her final resting place in the courtyard. Open from 10am to 5pm daily from April through October and 10am-5pm Tuesday through Sunday form November through March. *Tel. 215/686-1252*.

The Please Touch Museum at 210 N. 21st Street is a child's paradise where they can step into a favorite storybook like Where The Wild Things Are or Alice In Wonderland, or simply have a story read to them in the Story Garden. For children 3 and under there is the Barnyard Babies exhibit, where toddlers can pet toy sheep and chicks and play dress-up as a scarecrow. Admission is $8.95 per person. Open 7 days a week from 9am-4:30pm, until 5pm during summer months. *Tel. 215/963-0667*.

Did You Know.....?

• The Liberty Bell was shipped to America from England aboard the Hibernia.

• The now famous crack on the bell occurred the first time it was rung.

• From 1777 to 1778 the Liberty Bell was hidden from British troops beneath the floorboards of Zion's United Church of Christ in Allentown, Pennsylvania. Today the church, located at 622 Hamilton Mall, is home to The Liberty Bell Shrine Museum.

• "Pennsylvania" is misspelled as "Pensylvania" on the bell.

• The tone of the bell, which is no longer rung, is E- flat.

Practical Information
Address: Independence National Historical Park, 143 South Third Street, Philadelphia, PA 19106
Telephone: *215/597-8974*
Operating Season: year round; some sites closed Thanksgiving, Dec. 25, Jan. 1
Hours: 9am-5 pm (extended hours during some periods)
Cost: free
Website: *www.nps.gov/inde/index.htm*

Mammoth Cave National Park
Kentucky
Ready, set, cave! This is the longest known cave system in the world so don't worry about hearing "been there, done that" when it comes to this site.

Are We There Yet?
Mammoth Cave National Park is located in south central Kentucky about 90 miles from either Nashville or Louisville. Coming South from Louisville, take I-65 South to exit 53 at Cave City. A 15-minute drive will lead you to the visitors center. From the north, take I-65 North to exit 48 at Park City. You will reach the visitors center in 10 minutes.

What's There To Do Here?
Over 336 miles of cave have been mapped so far and you've got a full menu of cave tours to choose from, depending on your interest level:
Discovery Tour. This 1/2-hour tour is the shortest look at the cave. You'll walk about 3/4 mile to see the largest of the cave rooms. The tour is considered moderately strenuous because of a long stair climb but the good news is that this tour is just about always available (maximum numbers limit availability of some tours). The cost is just $4 for adults, $2.50 for children. There is also a ranger-guided Discovery tour, which costs $5 for adults and $3.50 for children.
Trog Tour. If you've got a child age 8 to 12 ready to take off and explore a little without the rest of the family, the Trog Tour is a great option. This two-hour excursion is for kids only and offers young visitors a look at areas of the cave not seen on most tours. Parents accompany the children for the first 15 minutes of the tour as rules are discussed. Your young traveler will need to bring along jeans and good walking shoes; kneepads are recommended and the ones used for rollerblading work perfectly. (Helmets and lights are provided.) The tour takes a peek at the historic section of the cave (when young tourists can wriggle along on their bellies a little) and White's Cave for

a look at formations. The tour is offered daily in the summer months and some weekends in the spring and fall months; the cost of the 2 1/2 hour tour is $12..

Travertine Tour. This is an easy tour and runs a little over an hour in length. You'll ride a bus to the Frozen Niagara entrance to see many of the cave formations. There is some stair climbing but basically this tour is very easy going and is recommended for families with young children. The cost $9 adults and $4.50 for children; reservations are recommended because the tour is limited to 39 visitors.

Introduction to Caving Tour. Any spelunkers in your family age 10 and over will enjoy this introduction to the basics of caving. The park provides helmets and lights but you'll need to bring gloves, long pants, and boots. Visitors age 10-15 need to be accompanied by an adult on this tour which includes plenty of opportunities to get down and crawl along narrow passages. Reservations are required for this 20-person tour; the cost is $22 adult and $17 for children.

Wild Cave Tour. Only visitors age 16 and over can take part on this extremely strenuous tour that involves lots of crawling through very tight spaces. Bring along gloves and boots as well as water and a lunch for this six-hour trip. Reservations are required for the 14-person trip; the cost is $45.

Strenuous Tours. Families with older children ready for a challenge will find plenty of tours to keep even the most active visitors busy. The **Making of Mammoth Tour** ($10 for adults, $5 for children) is considered strenuous with many steps and even a tower to climb as visitors have a look at the cave's origins. The **Frozen Niagara Tour** ($10 for adults, $5 for children) also includes a lot of step climbing and steep walks as it has a look at the beautiful formations of the cave. The **Historic Tour** ($10 for adults, $5 for children) is a two-hour look at the cave and its use by native Americans, miners, and early visitors.

Once you decide on your visit dates, make your tour reservations; these are critical for the tours that limit participation. You can reserve a tour by calling the **National Park Reservation Service**, *Tel. 800/967-2283*. Payment can be made with a major credit card. If you have questions on a specific tour and would like to talk with a park ranger, call *Tel. 502/758-2328* on weekdays between 8am and 4:30pm.

Other activities are also available at the park besides caving. Six miles of hiking trails are available near the Visitor's Center and many trails are available near the Green River.

When Are We Going?

The summer is the peak visitation time, when outside temperatures can be warm and humid but inside, the cave remains 54 degrees.

How Long Are We Staying?

A minimum of half a day is required to have a look at the visitors center, sign up for the Discovery Tour, and take the most basic tour. If you would like to take additional tours, plan on at least one full day at the park.

What Should I Bring?

Packing will vary by the type of tour you select. At the very least, bring along good walking shoes, long pants and a jacket or sweater. If you'll be taking one of the more adventurous tours, be sure to bring along leather or heavy canvas gloves, boots, and even kneepads as well as water.

Strollers are not permitted in the cave.

What Are We Doing Next?

Abraham Lincoln Birthplace National Historic Park is located about 45 minutes from Mammoth Cave (see heading for more information on this national park site).

For information on local attractions, contact the **Cave City Convention Center**, *Tel. 800/346-8908*.

The echo of a cappella singing still rings out at **Shaker Village of Pleasant Hill**, where a religious community devoted to a simple way of life once lived. A video presentation, hands-on exhibits and costumed interpreters making brooms, weaving and gardening help to bring an understanding of the Shaker existence as you stroll through fourteen restored buildings.

You can also take a relaxing one-hour ride down the Palisades river on the riverboat **Dixie Belle** from late April through October, and see the remnants of other Shaker sites along the village's many trails. This attraction is located only 75 miles away from Mammoth Cave in Harrodsburg. For further information call *800/734-5611*.

A trip to **The Kentucky Horse Park** will be a hit with any equine enthusiast in the family. A bronze sculpture of the legendary Man O' War greets you at the entrance of this 12,000-acre Lexington horse farm, and within are two museums celebrating man's relationship with the horse. At the Hall of Champions racing legends are presented to the public from March through October, and also during these months you can witness a Parade of Breeds at the Breeds Barn. No one can resist the Draft Horse barn, where you can see up close such gentle giants as Suffolks, English Shires, and Clydesdales, and no visit would be complete without an actual horseback or pony ride. For further information call *800/678-8813*.

Which One Is My Room?

Several campgrounds are available at the park. The **Headquarters Campground** offers 111 sites with hot showers, a laundry and more. This campground is open from spring to fall. **Houchins Ferry** has 12 primitive sites for $12 per night and is open year around. **Maple Springs**, open seasonally, accepts reservations, *Tel. 800/967-2283*.

Motel accommodations are available nearby. Contact the **Cave City Convention Center**, *Tel. 800/346-8908*.

Practical Information
Address: Mammoth Cave National Park, P.O. Box 7, Mammoth Cave, KY 42259
Telephone: *270/758-2180*
Operating Season: open year round; closed Christmas Day
Hours: vary by season
Cost: Admission to the park is free; fees for cave tours vary from $4 to $45 (for a wild cave tour)
Website: *www.nps.gov/maca/index.htm*

Did You Know.....?

• Both of America's Presidents during the Civil War, Abraham Lincoln and Jefferson Davis, were born in Kentucky, less than 100 miles apart .

• The tune sung at every birthday party, "Happy Birthday To You", was written by Louisville, Kentucky sisters Mildred and Patricia Hill.

• The state capital is Frankfort.

• The state bird is the cardinal.

• Kentucky's nickname is "The Bluegrass State."

• The name Kentucky was derived from a Cherokee word meaning "meadowland."

• Kentucky's motto is "United we stand, divided we fall."

• The Kentucky Derby is the oldest continuously held horse race in the United States.

• The state song is "My Old Kentucky Home."

• Cheeseburgers were served for the first time at a restaurant in Louisville, Kentucky.

Learning About Mammoth Cave
Radlauer, Ruth. *Mammoth Cave National Park*. 1987.

National Mall
Washington, DC

The National Mall is a mega-park, the strip of 46 acres between the Washington Monument and Capitol Hill. Here you'll find numerous sites of interest to families.

Are We There Yet?

Trains, planes and automobiles all make their way to this government hub. If you're coming by car, you'll find that I-66 and I-395 arrive from the south; I-494 as well as New York Avenue, Rock Creek Parkway, George Washington Memorial Parkway and the Cabin John Parkway all arrive from the north; I-66, Rt. 50 and Rt. 29 from the west; and Rt. 50, Rt. 1, Rt. 4 from the East. If you do arrive by car, know that parking is tough to find. There are two-hour lots at the Washington Monument and Jefferson Memorial and parking on Ohio Drive. For security reasons visitors must enter the Washington Monument from the 15th Street access point.

By train, several metro routes come in from the outlying areas. The Smithsonian Metro stop is on the National Mall.

If you're arriving by air, you can come in via Reagan National, Dulles, or Baltimore-Washington Airport with a quick taxi ride into the city.

What's There To Do Here?

The National Mall isn't one park but a collection of monuments and memorials including:

Lincoln Memorial. Built like a Greek parthanon with 36 Doric columns representing the states in the Union at the time of Lincoln's passing, this monument to the nations' 16th president has the Gettysburg Address inscribed along its south wall.

Washington Monument. This memorial to the first president is an obelisk that soars 555 feet above the city streets. A landing at 500 feet offers visitors an unbeatable view of the city. Although the monument is open to the public, the grounds are closed for the foreseeable future. The monument is open daily from 9 am - 4:30 pm For information, call *Tel. 202/426-6841*. The monument is slated for an upcoming restoration so call before you visit.

Jefferson Memorial, *Tel. 202/426-6821*. Modeled after the Roman Pantheon, this memorial is open from 8 am-11:45 pm daily. Check out the displays on the lower level and get information on ranger-led programs.

Vietnam Veterans Memorial. The 58,226 names carved on this moving monument, along with The Three Servicemen Statue and Vietnam Women's Memorial, are solemn reminders of the ultimate sacrifice made by the men and women in the armed forces. Open to the public daily from 8 am to midnight.

Korean War Veterans Memorial. This touching testament to the 54,246 men and women who lost their lives and those who came home includes the United Nations Wall and Pool of Remembrance. The site is open to the public daily from 8 am to midnight.

Franklin Delano Roosevelt Memorial. There are four outdoor galleries to pay tribute to the man who guided the nation through twelve turbulent years. Water is a recurring theme, and pools and cascades run throughout this peaceful memorial.

One of the best ways to see all the sites is aboard a guided tour operated by **Tourmobile Sightseeing.** These tours visit 24 sites in the National Mall and Arlington National Cemetery. You'll buy a ticket and have unlimited on and off privileges so you can stop at the sites that interest your family. You can make arrangements through **Ticket Master**, *Tel. 800/551-SEAT* (outside DC, Maryland and Virginia); locally call *202/432-SEAT*.

Stops include Arlington Cemetery, the Kennedy Gravesites, Tomb of the Unknowns, Arlington House, Kennedy Center, Lincoln, Vietnam and Korean War Memorials, White House, Washington Monument, Arts and Industries Building and, Smithsonian Castle, Air and Space Museum, US Botanic Gardens, Union Station and National Postal Museum, US Capitol, Library of Congress and Supreme Court, National Gallery of Art, Museum of Natural History, Museum of American History, Bureau of Engraving and Printing and US Holocaust Memorial Museum, Jefferson Memorial, Franklin Delano Roosevelt Memorial, Old Post Office Pavilion, Ford's Theatre and FBI, National Archives and US Navy Memorial, National Law Enforcement Memorial, National Museum of American Art, National Portrait Gallery and MCI Center.

When Are We Going?

Summer months are the peak visitation time for the city. During the summer, expect temperatures to be hot and humid so dress coolly. If you visit during the winter, expect very cold temperatures.

How Long Are We Staying?

The National Mall requires at least a full day to explore, more if you'll be visiting all the sites.

What Should I Bring?

Bring your cameras! Even young visitors can capture memories that will last forever with point and shoot cameras. Good walking shoes are a must.

What Are We Doing Next?

The National Mall is near many other parks in the national park system such as the White House, the Ford's Theater National Historic Site, the George Washington Memorial Parkway and others. While you're in Washington, don't miss the **Smithsonian Museum**, *Tel* 202/357-2700, or for a recorded message, *202/633-1000*. The Smithsonian is adjacent to the National Mall and includes numerous museums: Arthur M. Sackler Gallery, the Arts and Industries Building, the Freer Gallery of Art, the Hirshhorn Museum and Sculpture Garden, the National Air and Space Museum, the National Museum of African Art, the National Museum of American History, the National Museum of Natural History and the affiliated National Gallery of Art. *Most museums are open daily from 10 am-5:30 pm.*

Practical Information
    Address: The National Mall, 900 Ohio Drive, S.W., Washington, D.C 200242
    Telephone: *202/426-6841*
    Operating Season: year round, closed Dec. 25
    Hours: 8am until 11pm daily – The Washington Monument is open daily from 9am-4:30pm – All monuments are closed Christmas Day
    Cost: Free
    Website: *www.nps.gov/nama/index.htm*

Did You Know.....?
    • Washington DC's official motto is "Justitia Omnibus," which means "Justice to all."
    • The official song is The Star-Spangled Banner.
    • The district was named in honor of Christopher Columbus.
    • The official bird is the Wood Thrush.
    • The official flower is the American Beauty Rose.
    • Some of the famous personalities who were either born or raised in Washington DC include TV journalist Connie Chung; Carl Bernstein, the reporter who helped to bring the Watergate scandal to light; Sugar Ray Leonard, boxer; Benjamin Oliver Davis, the first African-American general in the United States Army; J. Edgar Hoover, the first director of the FBI.

~

Learning About Washington, DC
    Brill, Marlene Targ. *Building the Capital City* (Cornerstones of Freedom). Children's Press, 1996. Ages 9-12.
    Clark, Diane C. *A Kid's Guide to Washington, D.C.* (Gullivers Travels). Gulliver Books, 1996. Ages 9-12.
    Debnam, Betty et al. *A Kid's Guide to the White House*. Andrews and McMeel, 1997. Ages 9-12.
    Doherty, Craig and Katherine M. Doherty. *The Washington Monument* (Building America). Blackbirch Marketing, 1995. Ages 9-12.

Guzzetti, Paula. *The White House* (Places in American History). Dillon Press, 1995. Ages 9-12.

Kent, Deborah. *The Lincoln Memorial* (Cornerstones of Freedom). Children's Press, 1997. Ages 9-12.

Steins, Richard. *Our National Capital* (I Know America). Milbrook Press, 1994. Ages 4-8.

Warner, Gertrude Chandler and Charles Tang (Illustrator). *The Mystery in Washington, DC.* Albert Whitman and Company, 1994. Ages 9-12.

Waters, Kate. *The Story of the White House*. Demco Media, 1992.

St. Croix Island International Historic Site
Maine

You've heard of Jamestown, you've heard of Plymouth, but you may not have heard of St. Croix Island. This was one of the first sites developed by Europeans in the Americas, founded by Pierre Dugua Sieur de Mons in 1604. Called l'Acadie (Acadia), this site was later abandoned in favor of a settlement in Nova Scotia.

The park is unique in the US: this is the only international historic site in the US National Park System.

Are We There Yet?

The park is located on U.S. Route 1 six miles south of Calais, Maine. You can travel Route 9 from Bangor or U.S. Route 1 from Portland.

What's There To Do Here?

To be honest, there's not a lot to do at this park, although it is a good place to learn more about early colonization and think about those first settlers. The park includes a shelter with an interpretive panel; other facilities include picnic tables and a vault toilet. The park is only staffed during peak season.

When Are We Going?

Any time of year, this park is pretty darn quiet. Throughout the whole year, visitation only tops 15,000, most during the summer months. Compare this to five million visitors a year at Grand Canyon and you'll see that the lines–if any–will be short.

In the summer, look for comfortable, warm days in the 70s and sometimes in the 80s. Winter is another story, however, with chilly conditions and a cold wind.

How Long Are We Staying?

You won't need long at this park: even a half hour will give you a chance to have a look around. Bring along a picnic lunch and stay a couple of hours for a real feel of the quietness of this historic site.

What Should I Bring?

Whatever you'll want for your visit, including water, you'll want to bring with you. There is no drinking water or food at the park. The closest facilities are in the town of Calais.

Practical Information

Address: Saint Croix Island IHS, c/o Acadia National Park, PO Box 177, Bar Harbor, Maine 04609-0177
Telephone: *207/288-3338*
Operating Season: year round
Hours: dawn to dusk
Cost: free
Website: *www.nps.gov/sacr/index.htm*

Statue of Liberty National Monument & Ellis Island New York & New Jersey

Every schoolchild is familiar with the Statue of Liberty, a symbol of the US and a gift from France. A visit to this national monument can be a special vacation that combines a visit to the statue as well as nearby Ellis Island as a way to learn more about the freedoms that attracted immigrants here from around the globe.

Are We There Yet?

The park is located in Lower New York Harbor about a mile from Lower Manhattan. You'll reach the park via ferry service from either New York or New Jersey. From New York, take the ferry from Battery Park in Lower Manhattan.

From New Jersey, purchase your ferry tickets at the Railroad Terminal Building and Museum in Liberty State Park in Jersey City. Parking is available at the state park for a fee. The park is located off Exit 14B on the New Jersey Turnpike. Advance ferry tickets can be purchased by calling *800/600-1600* or *301/784-9023* for those living outside of the US or Canada.

Both ferries operate round trip loops that include stops at both Liberty Island and Ellis Island.

What's There To Do Here?

Due to increased security concerns, the interior of The Statue of Liberty closed after 9/11 but, at press time, is rescheduled to reopen following an extensive renovation in Summer 2004. Guests will be able to explore the Statue of Liberty museum, peer into the intricate inner structure through a glass ceiling near the base of the statue and enjoy the 360 degree views from the observation deck on top of the 16-story pedestal. Also, a new reservations ticketing system will help eliminate long lines further enhancing the visitor experience.

Ellis Island is also home to a museum, the **Ellis Island Immigration Museum**. Housed in the main building through which thousands of immigrants once passed between 1892 and 1954, the three story museum now contains many exhibits, historic photographs, and a 30-minute film called *Island of Hope, Island of Tears* continuously throughout the day. Free 45-minute ranger tours are available throughout the day.

When Are We Going?

Summer months are definitely the peak time for a visit but if you come during the summer (a) dress coolly, (b) bring water for everyone and drink it and (c) be prepared for lines. Remember, we warned you.

How Long Are We Staying?

Plan to spend the day to do both attractions. Our recommendation is to come early, especially during summer months. The lines at the Statue can especially get long (up to three hours during peak times) so if that's the focus of your visit we suggest departing from the NY ferry since the statue is the first stop.

What Should I Bring?

Don't forget your camera! We also suggest bringing water. A wide brimmed hat and sunglasses are important in summer months as well.

Which One Is My Room?

For nearby accommodations contact the New York City Convention and Visitors Bureau, or visit their website at www.nycvisit.com.

What Are We Doing Next?

From museums to theatrical extravaganzas, New York City offers something to appeal to everyone. For more information, visit the New York City Convention and Visitors Bureau at www.nycvisit.com.

Practical Information

Address: Statue of Liberty National Monument and Ellis Island, Liberty Island, New York, NY 10004

Telephone: *212/363-3200*

Operating Season: year round; closed Dec. 25
Hours: Park hours are 9:30 am-5 pm; Ellis Island: 9:30 am-5 pm
Cost: free; fee for ferry ride is $10 for adults, $4 for kids 4 - 12
Website: *www.nps.gov/stli/index.htm*

Statue of Liberty Quiz

Questions:
1. What is the name of the man who sculpted The Statue of Liberty?
2. The Statue of Liberty is a gift from which country?
3. What is the name of the ship which bore the statue to America?
4. What do the rays on the crown symbolize?
5. How many windows are in the crown?
6. How tall is The Statue of Liberty from the ground to the tip of the torch?
7. What is the size of Lady Liberty's waist?
8. How many steps lead up to the crown?
9. How many pounds of copper are in the statue?
10. What is the amount of steel in the statue?

Answers:
1. Frederic Auguste Bartholdi
2. France
3. Isere
4. The seven rays stand for both the seven seas and the seven continents of the world
5. Twenty-five
6. 305 feet 1 inch
7. The waist is 35 feet
8. 354 steps
9. 62,000 pounds
10. 250,000 pounds

Learning About the Statue of Liberty

Doherty, Craig A. et al. *The Statue of Liberty* (Building America). Blackbirch Marketing, 1996. Ages 9-12.

Kallen, Stuart A. *The Statue of Liberty, "The New Colossus."* Abdo, 1994. Ages 9-12.

Maestro, Betsy C. and Giulio Maestro (Illustrator). *The Story of the Statue of Liberty*. Mulberry Books, 1989. Ages 4-8.

Miller, Natalie. *The Statue of Liberty* (Cornerstones of Freedom). Children's Press, 1992. Ages 9-12.

Penner, Lucille Recht and Jada Rowland (Illustrator). *The Statue of Liberty* (Step into Reading : A Step 1 Book, Preschool-Grade 1). Random House, 1995. Ages 4-8.

Quiri, Patricia Ryon. *The Statue of Liberty* (True Book).Children's Press, 1998. Ages 4-8.

Ross, Alice et al. *The Copper Lady.* Carolrhoda Press, 1997. Ages 4-8.

Smith, A. G. *Statue of Liberty and Ellis Island Coloring Book.* Dover Publications, 1985. All ages.

Stevens, Carla and Deborah Kogan Ray (Illustrator). *Lily and Miss Liberty.* Little Apple, 1993. Ages 9-12.

Zimelman, Nathan et al. *How the Second Grade Got $8,205.50 to Visit the Statue of Liberty.* Albert Whitman and Company, 1992. Ages 4-8.

Valley Forge National Historical Park
Pennsylvania

Every young schoolchild has heard of Valley Forge and the terrible winter the early troops endured. A visit to this site is a good place to learn more about colonial history and George Washington.

Are We There Yet?

The park is located 18 miles west of Philadelphia. From the Pennsylvania Turnpike, take exit 24.

What's There To Do Here?

The visitors center includes exhibits on this historic site as well as a film called *Valley Forge: A Winter Encampment* which is shown throughout the day. Bus tours of the park are available through **Valley Forge Bus Tours** from May through September; call *610/783-1077* for reservations and a schedule of tour times.

Some of the sites viewed along the way include **Memorial Arch**—a granite, Romanesque-style structure which was erected in 1917 as a tribute to the tenacity of the soldiers of Valley Forge; the **Wayne Statue**, a bronze depiction of General Anthony Wayne, this statue was the first to be erected in Valley Forge National Historical Park; **Washington's Headquarters**; the **Washington Memorial Chapel**, where visitors can see a bronze statue of Washington, carvings of Valley Forge soldiers, and a reproduction of the Liberty Bell in the Bell Tower. There are a number of historical markers found within the park as well, including the **Unknown Soldiers** memorial marker, placed by The Daughters of The American Revolution.

One of the best ways to see the site is on the trails and the roads that wind through the park. You can hike along miles of walking trails or take a 10-mile self-guided car tour; we'd recommend buying the cassette tape to play along the way which will explain more about the history of the site.

The park also conducts a **Living History Program**. You can see interpreters in period clothes at Washington's Headquarters; encourage the kids to go up to them and talk to learn more about General Washington. If you visit on a Saturday afternoon, you can see a musket firing demonstration at the second tour stop, **Muhlenbuerg's Brigade**.

When Are We Going?

Summer months are the peak time for visitors, a time when you should plan on the days being warm and humid. Dress coolly.

During the winter months, though, the weather can be brutal (and storms can occasionally even close the park).

How Long Are We Staying?

You'll want at least a couple of hours to see the film and exhibits and have a look at the battlefield. If you'll be doing the driving tour and talking with the costumed interpreters, allow for a about a half day visit.

What Should I Bring?

Bring along good walking shoes so that you can get out and enjoy the walking trails and really get a sense of these battlefields. During the winter months, be sure to bring along a heavy coat and sturdy shoes for walking in snow or ice.

What Are We Doing Next?

Independence National Historical Park, which is detailed in this book, is a good choice to see in conjunction with Valley Forge.

If you are looking for a historic site away from the hustle and bustle of Philadelphia, the **Daniel Boone Homestead** is a quiet retreat only 32 miles from Valley Forge in Birdsboro. The birthplace of a true American icon, guided tours of Boone's childhood home are available, and several other 18th century establishments, such as a blacksmith shop and log cabin designed with a German influence are on display. Set on 579 sprawling acres, it is a serene setting with lakeside picnic areas available. Admission $4 for adults, $2 for children 6-17. Open Tuesday through Saturday from 9am-5pm and on Sunday from noon to 5pm. Located at 400 Daniel Boone Road. *Tel. 610/582-4900.*

Which One Is My Room?

While you're at the visitors center, you can stop by the information desk run by the Valley Forge Convention and Visitor Bureau for information on area hotels and attractions. The desk operates from May through Labor Day daily and on weekends at other times.

There are no accommodations in the park, but you'll find facilities in King Of Prussia and Phoenixville. For information, call the **Valley Forge Convention and Visitors Bureau**, *Tel. 610/834-1550.*

Special Events

Children can further their knowledge of Valley Forge at **the Saturday Morning Kids Corner**, a park program which offers storytelling and nature walks along with a variety of other entertaining activities. Programs differ each weekend.

Practical Information

Address: Valley Forge National Historical Park, PO Box 953, Valley Forge, PA 19482- 0953

Telephone: *610/783-1077*

Operating Season: year round; closed Thanksgiving, Christmas and New Year's Day

Hours: Dawn to dusk daily; visitors center and Washington's Headquarters open 9 am-5 pm

Cost: park free$3 for adult admission to Washington's Headquarters from spring through fall months

Website: *www.nps.gov/vafo/index.htm*

Learning About Valley Forge

Gregory, Kristiana. *The Winter of Red Snow: The Revolutionary War Diary of Abigail Jane Stewart*. Scholastic Parade, 1996. Ages 9-12.

Hughes, Libby. *Valley Forge* (Places in American History). Dillon Press, 1993. Ages 9-12.

Kelly, Frances. *Paul Revere - Valley Forge - Molly Pitcher - Nathan Hale* (Living Adventures from American History) Vol. 2, Audio Cassette. Independent Publishers Marketing, 1995.

Stein, Richard Conrad. *Valley Forge* (Cornerstones of Freedom). Children's Press, 1997. Ages 9-12.

Chapter 5

THE SOUTHEAST

Cape Hatteras National Seashore
North Carolina

Sun, sand, and kids are a sure-fire combination. Cape Hatteras National Seashore offers a lot more than the traditional beach fun, though, and you'll find that, while the beaching is fun here, the swimming can be hazardous. Anglers in the family will love this park as will those who are interested in the romance of the candy-striped lighthouse for which this park is often recognized.

Are We There Yet?

The national seashore is located on the Outer Banks. North Carolina Highway 12 is the main drive through the park. You can also reach the Outer Banks from the north via North Carolina Highway 158 then connect with NC12 at the north entrance to the park. From the West, US 64 intersects NC 12.

One of the most fun ways to reach the park is aboard the ferries operated by the state. These come into the park's southern entrance at Ocracoke Island; departures are from Swanquarter, North Carolina (2-1/2 hours) and Cedar Island, North Carolina (40 minutes). For information and times, call *800/BY-FERRY*.

What's There To Do Here?

Hatteras Island Visitor Center. Make your first stop here and don't worry about missing it–the center is located at the Cape Hatteras Lighthouse. You'll find lots of exhibits on the history of this area, its lighthouses, and the ecology of the region. The center is open from 9am to 6pm during the summer months, and 9am to 5pm the rest of the year.

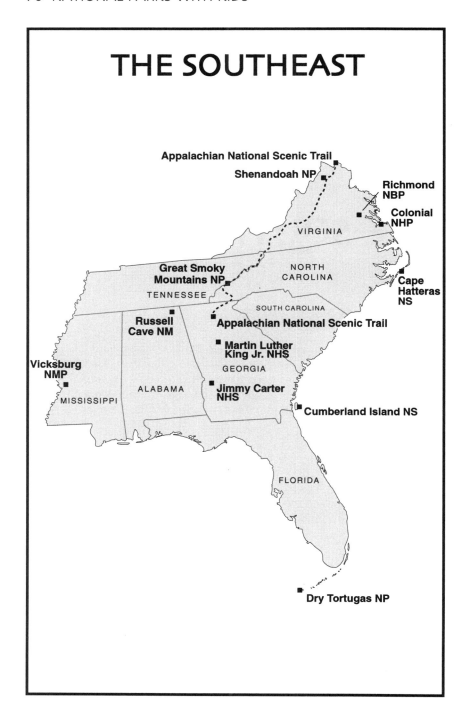

THE SOUTHEAST

Appalachian National Scenic Trail

Shenandoah NP

Richmond
NBP

Colonial
NHP

VIRGINIA

Great Smoky
Mountains NP

NORTH
CAROLINA

TENNESSEE

Cape
Hatteras
NS

SOUTH CAROLINA

Russell
Cave NM

Appalachian National Scenic Trail

Martin Luther
King Jr. NHS

Vicksburg
NMP

GEORGIA

ALABAMA

Jimmy Carter
NHS

MISSISSIPPI

Cumberland Island NS

FLORIDA

Dry Tortugas NP

Climb the Lighthouse. Put on your best walking shoes and make the spiral climb up the Cape Hatteras Lighthouse, the tallest lighthouse in North America. Your reward at the end of the climb (20 to 30 minutes round trip) is a spectacular view of the sand dunes and marshes below. For safety reasons children under 38 inches in height are not permitted to make the trip. Admission $6 for adults and $3 for children under the age of 12.

Swimming. This may be the seashore, but Cape Hatteras isn't the ideal swimming spot for families because of currents and waves. You will find beach lifeguards during the summer months at several beaches but keep a close eye on children and just allow them to go into the water a little ways–this area was once named the "Graveyard of the Atlantic" because of the many ships that went down due to currents along this shoreline.

Fishing. If you've got an angler in the family, this is the place to be, especially in the fall and spring months. Don't worry about packing everything; tackle is available in stores and you can even take a charter fishing trip if you like. Surf and pier fishing are very popular.

Hiking. Several nature trails wind along the seashore and point out more about the delicate ecology of this area.

When Are We Going?

The summer months are definitely the peak season for this seaside park. The summer days are hot and humid but usually tempered by sea breezes.

Winter months are the low time for visitors, a time when the sea breezes can make the shoreline feel even colder than it is. Spring and fall can be pleasant times to visit.

How Long Are We Staying?

You'll want to allow a minimum of half a day to check out the exhibits, walk on the beach, and have a picnic. If you're interested in climbing the lighthouse or doing some fishing, allow longer.

What Should I Bring?

If you visit during the summer months, don't forget to pack the mosquito repellent. Sunscreen, sunglasses, and a hat are other important accessories. Bring good walking shoes for climbing the lighthouse and all the beach essentials for the seashore itself–bathing suit, swim shoes, and beach toys!

Which One Is My Room?

Cape Hatteras National Seashore has four campgrounds open from early April (although Point doesn't open until late May) through early to mid-October. Each campground includes rest rooms, water, unheated showers, grills and tables. Reservations can be made online at *http://reservations.nps.gov.*

The campgrounds are:

Oregon Inlet. This campground has 120 sites. Reservations are not accepted. The campground can accommodate trailers and RVs as well as tents.

Cape Point. This site has 202 campsites and includes trailers and RVs. Reservations are not accepted.

Frisco. This 127-site campground accommodates trailers and RVs as well as tents. Reservations are not accepted.

Ocracoke. This 136-site campground accepts reservations through the central reservations number, *Tel. 800/365-CAMP.* Reservations can be made starting in mid-April for the following year and can be held with a major credit card.

Accommodations are also available in area motels. For information, contact the **Dare County Tourist Bureau**, 704 S. Hwy 64/264, Manteo, NC 27954, *Tel. 252/473-2138* or *800/446-6262* and the **Outer Banks Chamber of Commerce**, P. O. Box 1757, Kill Devil Hills, NC 27948, *Tel. 252/441-8144.*

What Are We Doing Next?

The Wright Brothers National Monument is only eight miles away, and on Kill Devil Hill there stands a 60-foot tall granite tribute erected to the two pioneers of aviation. Granite markers show the length of the four successful flights made on December 17, 1903, and at the visitors center there are reproductions of Wilber and Orville Wright's wind tunnel, 1902 glider and 1903 flyer. Admission is $3 for adults, free for children age 16 and under. Call *Tel. 252/441-7430* or visit the website at *www.nps.gov/wrbr/index.htm.*

Practical Information

Address: 1401 National Park Drive, Manteo, NC 27954

Telephone: *252/473-2111* (headquarters); Bodie Island visitor information: *252/441-5711;* Hatteras Island visitor information: *252/995-4474;* Ocracoke Island visitor information: *252/928-4531*

Operating Season: year round

Hours: Hatteras Visitor Center is open daily 9am to 5pm(extended hours from 9am - 6pm in summer); closed Christmas.

Cost: free

Website: *www.nps.gov/caha/index.htm*

Learning About North Carolina

Charlet, James D. et al. North Carolina: *Our People, Places and Past.* Carolina Academic Press, 1987. Baby-Preschool.

Marsh, Carole. *North Carolina: A Kid's Look at Our States, Chiefs, Tribes, Reservations, Powwows.* Gallopade Publishing Group,1995. Ages 9-12.

Marsh, Carole. *North Carolina: Indian Dictionary for Kids.* Gallopade Publishing Group,1995. Ages 9-12.

Did You Know.....?

• The Wright Brothers made history in 1903 with man's first flight at Kill Devil Hill near Kitty Hawk.

• North Carolina produces more sweet potatoes than any other state.

• Pepsi was invented in New Bern in 1898.

• Baseball fans in Fayetteville were lucky enough to see Babe Ruth's first professional home run.

• Bath, which was founded in 1705, is North Carolina's oldest town.

• The state flower is the dogwood.

• The state dog is the Plott Hound.

• The first miniature golf course was built in Fayetteville .

• Krispy Kreme Doughnuts was founded in Winston-Salem.

• The state motto is "esse quam videri", which translates as "to be rather than to seem."

• North Carolina has two nicknames—Old North State and Tar Heel State.

• The cardinal is the state bird.

• Raleigh is the state capital.

• Famous North Carolinians include:

David Brinkley—TV commentator (Wilmington)

Howard Cosell—sports commentator (Winston-Salem)

Roberta Flack—singer (Black Mountain)

Ava Gardner—actress (Smithfield)

Billy Graham—evangelist (Charlotte)

Andy Griffith—actor (Mount Airy)

O. Henry—writer (Greensboro)

Andrew Johnson—17th president (Raleigh)

Charles Kuralt—TV commentator (Wilmington)

Dolley Payne Madison—first lady (Guliford County)

Ronnie Milsap—country singer (Robinsville)

Thelonious Monk—pianist (Rocky Mount)

Richard Petty—race car driver (Level Cross)

James K. Polk—11th president (Mechlenburg)

Earl Scruggs—bluegrass musician (Flint Hill)

Randy Travis—country singer (Charlotte)

Marsh, Carole. *North Carolina Dingbats! A Fun Book of Games, Stories, Activities and More About Our State That's All in Code! for You to Decipher.* Gallopade Publishing Group, 1991. Ages 9-12.

Marsh, Carole. *North Carolina Facts and Factivities.* Gallopade Publishing Group, 1996. Ages 9-12.

Marsh, Carole. N*orth Carolina History!: Surprising Secrets About Our State's Founding Mothers, Fathers & Kids!* Gallopade Publishing Group, 1996. Young Adult.

Marsh, Carole. *North Carolina State Greats.* Gallopade Publishing Group, 1990.

Colonial National Historical Park
Virginia

When English pioneers arrived in the New World and prepared to make their first settlement, they selected a site in what is now Virginia with tall trees, temperate weather, and miles of beautiful waterfront. They called their new home Jamestown.

Those first American tourists knew a good thing when they saw it. Today Jamestown and neighboring Yorktown battlefield, site of the last battle of the American Revolution, comprise the Colonial National Historical Park.

Located 75 miles south of Richmond on a fertile peninsula nestled between the James River and Chesapeake Bay, this region is home to the communities of Jamestown, Yorktown, Williamsburg, Hampton and Newport News.

Are We There Yet?

Colonial National Historical Park is tucked along the James and York rivers about 50 miles southeast of Richmond near Williamsburg and Newport News.

To reach the park from Richmond, take I-64 to Route 199, taking exit 242A for Jamestown and 242B for Yorktown. This exit leads to the Colonial Parkway; follow this drive to the park.

If you're traveling from Virginia Beach or Norfolk, take I-64 westbound to Route 105 East (Fort Eustis Boulevard east). Take exit 250B to Route 17 (George Washington Memorial Highway) then turn north (left) on Route 17 to reach Yorktown. To reach Jamestown, take Route 199, exit 242A to the Colonial Parkway.

What's There To Do Here?

Yorktown was the site of the final skirmish of the American Revolution, and walking through the town you can almost imagine you can hear the sounds of battle. A park ranger tour (30 minutes in length) of the Siege Line helps to conjure up mental images of the 1781 Siege of Yorktown, while a 45 minute Yorktown tour takes you past buildings which have stood the test of time for over 300 years.

A 25 minute non-firing artillary demonstration is also held between mid-June and mid-August. Two dwellings which witnessed historic events are Nelson House, where a dramatic reenactment is performed at noon on the second floor of the home of Thomas Nelson Jr., whose signature can be found on the Declaration of Independence, and Moore House, where the terms for British surrender were agreed upon. Both houses are open to the public from 10am-5pm from mid-June through mid-August, with shortened hours in the spring and fall.

Stop at the Yorktown Visitors Center for a 15 minute video presentation entitled " The Siege At Yorktown". While there you can rent an audio tape to accompany you on self-guided auto tours of the battlefield and encampment. The Battlefield Tour is 7 miles in length and takes you past Overlook Surrender Field, while the Encampment Tour is 9 miles long and takes you past Washington's headquarters.

Jamestown was the site of the first English settlement, and today you can witness glassblowing demonstrations by interpreters in period garb, mirroring the techniques used by glassblowers in the 1600's. Men and women in costume help to reconstruct the past in the mind's eye as they tell tales of 17th century life on the Living History tour, which is held daily in the summer months and weekends in September and October.

Children will enjoy the Pinch Pot Program, where rangers teach young-sters the technique for making pottery in the manner of the early Native Americans. The presentation lasts 20 minutes, and children will have some-thing hand-made to remember their trip to Jamestown. Rent an audio tape at the visitors center, which will illuminate facts along the Loop Drive, a 5 mile driving tour where the "Gallery In The Woods" (roadside murals) depicts colonial life.

Also in Jamestown you can take a walking tour of New Towne and Old Towne and visit the statue of Pocahontas.

When Are We Going?

The summer months are the busiest at this park and summer days are generally warm and humid. We've visited the park during the winter months as well, when temperatures average about 50 degrees, although it can be colder.

How Long Are We Staying?

The combined parks easily fill a full day, especially considering the one hour driving time between the two parks. If you'll just be visiting one of the sites, budget about two hours to go to the visitors center and see the nearby sites on foot; if you want to do a driving tour schedule another 45 minutes.

What Should I Bring?

Don't forget to bring good walking shoes. During the summer months, mosquito repellent is a good idea as well.

What Are We Doing Next?

The northern area of the Virginia Peninsula is home to two terrific amusement parks – **Busch Gardens, the Old Country** and **Water Country U.S.A.** Each park deserves an entire day's visit, and if you're a fast ride fanatic, better make that two days!

Busch Gardens, the Old Country, is the sister park to Busch Gardens, the Dark Continent in Tampa, Florida. The Virginia park takes as its theme nine European hamlets, each featured in a section of the park. In Oktoberfest you can see an Oompah band, take a ride on a suspended roller coaster, or shop for German steins. In San Marco, Italy listen for screams from DaVinci's Cradle, a stomach-flipping, 360-degree ride, or relax to Italian opera and fresh pasta. And Hastings, England will take you back to the days of King Arthur with its costumed storytellers, renaissance games, and wizardry shows.

Just a few miles away, you can cool off at **Water Country USA**, a water park with shows, fast rides, and plenty of chances to lounge in the sun. Thrill seekers will enjoy the Sonic Whip, with its 180 degree turn, and Double Rampage, where riders on plastic sleds shoot down the 75 foot slide and, like a stone skipped over water, skim across the landing pond for over 100 feet!

Virginia Living Museum. Virginia is home to a wide variety of plant, bird and animal life, many of which are difficult to see if you're just in the area a few days and if you're not out in the woods at night. You'll have your chance to see these creatures at the **Virginia Living Museum** 524 J. Clyde Morris Blvd., Newport News, *Tel. 757/595-1900*, a combination wildlife park, aquarium, planetarium, botanical garden, and aviary. Start your visit with the indoor exhibits, where you can hold a horseshoe crab or see a bat who's fooled into thinking it's nighttime. When you step outside, you'll be surrounded by free-flying birds in the two-story aviary, with songbirds and waterfowl. The large wildlife park contains 150 species, most animals who have been injured and could not live in the wild. You'll see bobcats, fox, deer, and even a couple of busy beavers who constantly build a dam for their pond.

Colonial Williamsburg. Many visitors start their trip in the town of Williamsburg, best known as the home of Colonial Williamsburg, 1800 History Exit 238 off I-64, *Tel. 800/HISTORY*. This town was the capital of Virginia in the 1770's, and the historic district has been restored to the days of the American Revolution. Tour historic homes, dine in recreated colonial taverns, and shop in 18th century style stores on Merchants' Square at the end of Duke of Gloucester Street. Colonial items such as reproductions of pewter plates, iron hooks or hats are made by craftsmen. Wigmakers, blacksmiths, gunsmiths, printers and even shoe makers ply their trades here as they did over two centuries ago.

Fort Monroe. Fort Monroe, still in use, is the largest stone fort ever built in the United States. After a driver's license check at the security gate, you are welcome to drive onto the base where many famous Americans once served. At the base's Casemate Museum, housed within the thick walls of the old fort, you'll see exhibits on some of Ft. Monroe's most famous visitors and employees, such as sergeant major Edgar Allen Poe, Ulysses S. Grant, and Harriet Tubman, a nurse at the separate "Colored Hospital." Many escaped slaves sought refuge in the union fort, earning it the nickname "Freedom's Fortress."

As you walk through the old fort, with its cool damp stone walls, it's easy to imagine the tension here over a hundred years ago when Lincoln directed the amphibious assault on Norfolk from the casemates, or chambers inside the thick rock walls. Later, Jefferson Davis, former president of the Confederacy, was imprisoned in this facility, accused of plotting the assassination of President Lincoln. There's even a legend that the ghost of Mrs. Jefferson Davis' widow walks the walls at night, waiting for the release of her husband.

Virginia War Museum. If these forts have piqued your interest in the military, don't miss the Virginia War Museum, 9285 Warwick Blvd., *Tel. 757/ 247-8523*, in Newport News. This excellent museum chronicles the role of warfare in American history from 1775 to the present. Its over 60,000 artifacts include everything from Gatling Guns to atomic cannons, from a Revolutionary War commission to barbed war from World War II concentration camps.

Which One Is My Room?

There are no camping or motel facilities in the park but you'll find many options in the area including:

Williamsburg. Here you'll find plenty of options. Contact the **Williamsburg Convention and Conference Bureau**, *Tel. 757/253-0192* or *800/368-6511*, *www.wacc.com/wacc* or the **Williamsburg Hotel and Motel Association**, *Tel. 800/999-4485*.

Hampton Tourist Visitors Center, *Tel. 757/727-1102* or *800/800-2202*.

Newport News Tourist Visitors Center, *Tel. 757/886-7912* or *800/ 333-7787*.

You'll find excellent camping facilities at the **Newport News Park**, *Tel. 800/333-RSVP*, the largest municipal park east of the Mississippi River. Open 365 days a year, the park features 180 sites. The park also includes an interpretive center with nature and historical exhibits, two golf courses (nine and 18 holes), pier fishing, paddleboats, canoes, and row boat rental.

Practical Information

Address: Colonial National Historical Park, PO Box 210, Yorktown, Virginia 23690-0210

Telephone: *757/898-3400*

Operating Season: year round

Hours: Open 9am-5pm daily

Cost: Yorktown alone: $4 for adults, children 16 and under free; Jamestown alone: $5 for adults, children 16 and under free. Jamestown-Yorktown joint ticket: $7 for adults, 16 and under free (this ticket is good for a seven day period).

Website *www.nps.gov/colo/index.htm*

Learning About Jamestown & Yorktown

Ferrie, Richard. *The World Turned Upside Down : George Washington and the Battle of Yorktown.* Holiday House, 1999. Ages 9-12.

Jassem, Kate. *Pocahontas, Girl of Jamestown.* Troll Communications, 1979. Ages 9-12.

Kent, Zachary. *The Surrender at Yorktown.* Children's Book Press, 1994. Ages 9-12.

Knight, James E. and David Wenzel (Illustrator). *Jamestown New World Adventure* (Adventures in Colonial America) .Troll Associates, 1998. Ages 9-12.

Sakurai, Gail. *The Jamestown Colony.* Children's Press, 1997. Ages 9-12.

Weber, Michael. *Yorktown* (Battlefields Across America). Twenty First Century Books, 1997. Ages 9-12.

Cumberland Island National Seashore
Georgia

This 17.5 mile-long island is a favorite with those travelers looking for a seashore that's filled with birds, marine turtles, dunes, marshes, and an unspoiled atmosphere.

Note: only 300 visitors are permitted in the park every day.

Are We There Yet?

The seashore is located 7.3 miles east of St. Marys, Georgia (located about 32 miles north of Jacksonville, Florida). From I-95, take State Road 40 to the National Park Service visitors center in St. Marys. Here you'll get information on the passenger ferry that takes visitors out to the island. The ferry travels to the island twice a day from mid-March to the end of November.

What's There To Do Here?

Ranger-guided tours of Plum Orchard Mansion, a 1898 Georgian Revival style structure are offered every second and fourth Sunday of the month. Access by ferry costs $6 per person, or you can hike to the site.

Swimming during the summer months is the top activity. You can also enjoy hiking trails that run the whole length of the island.

When Are We Going?
Summer is the peak time for visiting so come with cool clothing during these hot, humid months.

How Long Are We Staying?
Because of the ferry schedule, you'll want to budget at least a half day to see the island.

What Should I Bring?
Don't forget your swimsuit and sunscreen! Swim shoes, beach toys, towels and other beach accessories are must-haves as well.

You'll also want to bring your food for the day. The island does not have any concession, just drinking water, so don't forget a picnic lunch or snacks.

Which One Is My Room?
The park has a developed campground with restrooms, cold showers and drinking water as well as a picnic table and fire ring. The park also offers several back country sites but these do not offer facilities and campfires are not permitted. Camping fees are $4 per person per night for the developed sites at Sea Camp; $2 per person per night for primitive sites. Reservations are required and can be made up to 6 months in advance.

Where Are We Going Next?
The Hofwyl-Broadfield Plantation Historic Site, once a thriving rice plantation, is only an hour away in Brunswick. This 1800's antebellum home, filled with a family's heirlooms, takes you back to a bygone era. Be sure to walk the nature trail which winds along the edge of the marsh. Tours are self-guided. Open Tuesday-Saturday 9am-5pm and Sunday 2pm-5:30pm. Admission from $2 to $5 Located at 5556 US Hwy 17 N, *Tel. 912/264-7333*.

Also in Brunswick is the Mary Miller Doll Museum, with over 3,000 intricate doll houses, dolls and toys representing over 90 countries. Located at 209-211 Gloucester St. Adults $4, $3 children. Call *912/267-7569* for further information.

Practical Information
Address: Cumberland Island National Seashore, PO Box 806, St. Marys, GA 31558

Telephone: *912/882-4335* or *888/817-3421*

Operating Season: year round

Hours: 8:15am-4:30pm daily but closed Christmas Day

Cost: $4 adult; ferry passes are $12 adults, $9 seniors, $7 children under 12

Website: *www.nps.gov/cuis/index.htm*

Did You Know.....?

- The late John F. Kennedy Jr. and Carolyn Bessette were married at the First African Baptist Church on Cumberland Island.
- The remnants of the Carnegie estate, Dungeness, can still be seen at Cumberland Island National Seashore.
- Georgia was named after King George II of England.
- Coca-Cola was invented in the city of Atlanta in May 1886 by John S. Pemberton.
- The state motto is "Wisdom, justice, and moderation."
- The official state song is "Georgia On My Mind."
- Cordele is considered the watermelon capital of the world.
- Georgia has many nicknames—The Peach State, The Cracker State, and Empire State of The South.
- The state flower is the Cherokee Rose.
- The official state tree is the live oak.
- The state fish is the largemouth bass.
- St. Marys, Georgia is the second oldest city in the United States.
- The state capital is Atlanta.
- The Okefenokee swamp received its name from an Indian word meaning "trembling earth."
- Georgia is the nation's largest producer of peanuts, peaches and pecans.
- The state bird is the Brown Thrasher.
- Macon's Wesleyan College was the first university in the US to award degrees to women.
- The International Poultry Trade Show, held every year in Georgia, is the largest poultry convention in the world.
- Celebrities either born or were raised in Georgia, including:

Jimmy Carter—the 39th president of the United States
Martin Luther King, Jr.—civil rights leader
Gladys Knight—singer
James Brown—"The Godfather of Soul"
Trisha Yearwood—singer
Jackie Robinson—first major league African-American baseball player
Margaret Mitchell—author of Gone With The Wind
Little Richard—singer
Travis Tritt—country singer
Alice Walker—author of The Color Purple
Ray Charles—singer
Amy Grant—singer
Oliver Hardy—part of comedy team Laurel and Hardy
Hulk Hogan—wrestler
DeForest Kelley—actor in TV classic Star Trek
Brenda Lee—singer
Otis Redding—singer
Burt Reynolds—actor
Joanne Woodward—actress

Dry Tortugas National Park
Florida

Located 70 miles from Key West, this park is an isolated enclave of coral reefs. A great destination for snorkelers and scuba divers, this park is remote.

Are We There Yet?

Now here's something different: you can reach this park only by boat or seaplane! Several private operators offer trips out to the park. For information on the operators, contact the city from which you'll be departing:

Marathon. 12222 Overseas Highway, Marathon, FL 33050, *Tel. 800262-7284, 305/743-5417*

Key West. 402 Wall St., Key West, FL 33040, *Tel. 305/294-2587*

Naples. 895 Fifth Ave. South Naples, FL 34102-6605, *Tel. 239/262-6141*

What's There To Do Here?

Snorkelling and scuba diving are top activities, and be sure to take your binoculars as up to 200 species of birds are seen in the area each year. April and May are the most promising months to view migrating birds.

The park is also home to Fort Jefferson, a hexagon-shaped fortress composed of over 16 million bricks, which held military deserters during The Civil War. Dr. Samuel Mudd, found guilty of conspiracy in the assassination of Abraham Lincoln, was among the many to be incarcerated here.

When Are We Going?

The warm climate means that any time of year is a good time to visit the Dry Tortugas. The remoteness of the park also ensures that you won't have to fight off crowds, regardless of when you visit.

How Long Are We Staying?

Because you must enter by boat or seaplane, plan for a whole day to visit the park.

What Should I Bring?

Bring all your beach items, including snorkel gear.

Which One Is My Room?

There are a few primitive campsites in the Garden Key area. Most visitors stay in Key West. For information on accommodations in Key West, contact the **Key West Chamber of Commerce**, *Tel. 305/294-2587*, *e-mail info@keywestchamber.*

What Are We Going To Do Next?

Harry S. Truman's **Little White House** was used by the nation's 33rd leader as a getaway from the pressures of presidency, and can also boast that Presidents Eisenhower, Kennedy, and Carter have also been beneath its roof. A film, *Truman in Key West*, and fully narrated tours are offered of the home, which is still decorated with the same furnishings used by the former president. Located at 111 Front Street., *Tel. 305/294-9911.*

Whitehead Street was once home to two American legends. At 205 Whitehead is the **Audubon House and Tropical Gardens**, where the noted ornithologist and artist found inspiration for many of his drawings for the birds of Key West. In fact, the Geiger tree standing in the front yard can be seen in one of his paintings. Audio tours of the 19th century abode and gardens, festooned with a multitude of orchids, a lily pond, and nursery, are available. Call either *305/294-2116 or 877/281-BIRD (2473).*

907 Whitehead Street was home to one of the literary world's most colorful characters, **Ernest Hemingway**. Papa lived at the residence for ten years, and during this time he wrote many of his masterpieces, including *To Have and Have Not and For Whom The Bell Tolls.*

Take a guided tour of the house with its Spanish influenced decor, and imagine the pounding of typewriter keys as you make your way to the writing studio, where Hemingway could be found most mornings. While strolling through the grounds pay special attention to the many cats that will surely cross your path. Over 60 felines live on the premises, many the direct descendants of Papa's cat, given to him by a ship's captain. As unique as the American icon who lived here, half of these cats has the distinct characteristic of possessing extra toes! The house and museum are open from 9am - 5pm year round. Price of admission for adults $10, $6 for children and those under the age of 5 free.

Discovery Undersea Tours offers a glimpse at life below sea level. This glass bottom boat ride takes you on a narrated tour of both the harbor and the coral reef, where you can see a multitude of rainbow- colored tropical fish in their native habitat. Three trips daily. For the morning trip, admission is $30 for adults, $16 for children 8-12 and children under 7 free. For the midday excursion, the price is $30 for adults, $16 for those age 5-12 and children under 5 admitted free. Located at 251 Margaret St. Call either *800/262-0099* or *305/293-0099.*

Practical Information

Address: Dry Tortugas National Park, PO Box 6208, Key West, FL 33041
Telephone: *305/242-7700*
Operating Season: year round
Hours: day use only

Cost: $5 for 7 days for those 17 and older
Website: *www.nps.gov/drto/index.htm*

Did You Know.....?

- The state reptile is the alligator.
- The Sunshine State is Florida's nickname .
- The state beverage is orange juice.
- Venice, Florida is known as the Shark Tooth Capital of The World.
- The state motto is "In God We Trust."
- Along with Arkansas, Mississippi, Tennessee and Texas, Florida chose the mockingbird as the official state bird.
- "Swanee River" is the state song.
- Florida was named on Easter 1513 by Ponce de Leon, who called the land Pascua Florida, or "Flowery Easter."
- The orange blossom is the state flower.
- The Cabbage Palmetto is the state tree.
- The state capital is Tallahassee.
- Among the many famous people who have called Florida home are:

  John James Audubon—orthinologist and artist (Harte)
  Pat Boone—singer (Jacksonville)
  Howie Dorough—member of the group The Backstreet Boys (Orlando)
  Faye Dunaway—actress (Bascom)
  Dwight Gooden—baseball player (Tampa)
  A.J. McLean—member of the group The Backstreet Boys (West Palm Beach)
  Butterfly McQueen—actress who starred in Gone With The Wind (Tampa)
  Jim Morrison—singer (Melbourne)
  Sidney Poitier—actor (Miami)
  Ben Vereen—actor (Miami)

Learning About Florida

Clark, Margaret Goff. *Save the Florida Key Deer*. Cobblehill, 1998. Ages 9-12.

Robinson, Jacky. *Saltwater Adventure in the Florida Keys: An Introduction to Fishing for Kids*. White Heron Press, 1994. Young adult.

Warner, Gertrude Chandler and Charles Tang (Illustrator). *The Mystery of the Hidden Beach* (The Boxcar Children Mysteries, No. 41). Albert Whitman and Company, 1994. Ages 9-12.

Great Smoky Mountains National Park
Tennessee & North Carolina

The stone corn grinder turns slowly, sometimes picking up tempo a little as the water-driven paddlewheel outside gets an extra push. Before the water reached the moss-covered paddles, it traveled down the hills, past deer, cattle and people alike, and finally into a slippery and sometimes leaky flume.

Sound like a scene from the 1800's? It might well have been. But for 20th century travelers, the old mill and an entire settlement from a century ago lies deep in the Great Smoky Mountains National Park.

This park, the most visited in the national park system, has something for everyone, whether your family's interests are nature, history, backpacking, hiking, or crafts.

Are We There Yet?

Many travelers will be coming in on the Tennessee side. From I-40 take exit 407, the Sevierville exit, to TN Route 66 South. Continue to US441 South and follow it to the park.

If you are arriving from North Carolina, from I-40 take US 19 West through Maggie Valley. Take US 441 north at Cherokee and follow it to the park.

What's There To Do Here?

This park really has something for everyone, and plenty of room so that you can get a feel for the natural setting even on crowded days. Start your visit with a stop at the **Sugarlands Visitor Center** near Gatlinburg for an orientation to the park with information on the animals and natural history of the region. You'll also find the **Oconaluftee Visitor Center** near Cherokee, North Carolina if you are coming in from that direction; it contains historic exhibits about life in the region during the 1800s. The **Mountain Farm Museum** with historic buildings is located next door.

Our favorite family stop in the park is **Cades Cove**. It lies about 42 miles from the Gatlinburg entrance, or 11 miles from Townsend, a trip filled with winding roads, small mountainside streams, and a more than occasional glimpse of some furry creature. But unlike most of the dense, wooded park, Cades Cove is a quiet pastureland set inside a ring of forest.

The community began around 1819 when settlers entered the area. The pastures were not native to this land; they had to be chiseled out of the forest by many hands. Once this was accomplished, corn, oats and wheat were planted along with an apple orchard. This wilderness became a settlement and home for many settlers, with a population of over 600 by the 1850's.

With the onset of the Civil War, the population began decreasing. The U.S. Park Service established the park in the 1920's, and the residents left for other areas.

Today Cades Cove remains as an example of what life was like in a community secluded from the world by a range of bluish mountain peaks. Visitors can take an 11 mile drive through the cove, past the homes, businesses and churches of the former community.

Frequent reminders of a life filled with backbreaking labor appear as your car noisily winds down the one-way road. Hand-split fences surround the homes. Sparks Lane, a road built in the early days of the settlement, stretches across the cove. The **Cooper Road Trail**, named after Joe Cooper who upgraded the road and made it passable by wagon, cuts through the untamed land. The echoes of hoofbeats seem to linger on in the ruts of trails carved long ago.

Several cabins show visitors what life was like in the cove. The **Tipton House** sports a stone fireplace, a large front porch, small windows, and a shingled roof. Near the home are bee hives, a blacksmith's shop, a corn crib and a cantilever barn much like the original.

Other interesting homes in the cove include the **John Oliver Cabin** and the **Elijah Oliver Place**. Many members of the Oliver family lived in the cove, and these two houses were built with split logs cemented by clay.

Wildlife in the cove is varied. Deer, wild turkey, wild hogs, and an occasional bear populate the nearby woods. Early mornings and evenings are the best times for spotting animals.

Other activities include over 800 miles of trails and hundreds of miles of backroads for quiet exploration of the park.

Two local programs are popular with families who are interested in learning more about everything from mountain music to local flora and fauna. **The Great Smoky Mountains Institute at Tremont**, *Tel. 865/448-6709,* operates year around; this residential educational center accepts all ages from children to grandparents. **The Smoky Mountain Field School**, *Tel. 865/974-0150,* also offers education programs for families and adults in cooperation with the National Park Service and the University of Tennessee. Programs include weekend workshops, hikes, and more.

There are a few "must see" sites in the park including **Abrams Falls** and **Clingmans Dome**. Clingmans Dome is one of the most popular sites in the park, the highest point in the park (as well the highest in Mississippi and the second highest point east of the Mississippi River.) There's a paved trail up to an observation tower (take your time–it's steep!) for great views.

When Are We Going?

Summer months are definitely the peak time to visit the park and it can get very busy, especially on weekends. Fall is also a popular time with autumnal color. Spring makes a great time for a getaway here. Winter brings the quietest days although you may find some areas of the park closed due to weather.

How Long Are We Staying?

At the very least, you need a full day to see the highlights of the park. A two or three day visit is preferable.

What Should I Bring?

Good walking shoes, a jacket, and insect repellent during summer months are good to pack.

What Are We Doing Next?

You'll find a full vacation worth of fun in Gatlinburg and nearby Pigeon Forge, home to **Dollywood**, the theme park owned by Dolly Parton. The theme park is well known for its Smoky Mountain theme and filled with local crafts as well as rides for the kids. The theme park is open from April through December. Call *865-428-9488*.

Other Smoky Mountain attractions include **The Museum of The Cherokee Indian**, which teaches the history of the tribe through both ancient artifacts and the latest technology. Located at Highway 441 and Drama Road in Cherokee, NC. Admission is $8 for adults, $5 for children and those under the age of 6 are admitted free. *Call 828/497-3481.*

For a true western experience, explore the countryside on a guided horseback ride offered by **Walden Creek Stables**. There are a variety of rides to accommodate both the equine novice and the experienced rider. Wagon rides are also provided, and you can choose from the simplicity of an Amish buggy, stagecoach, or a surrey with the fringe on top. At the end of the buggy ride you can enjoy a supper show filled with cowboy songs, Native American dancing, and trick riding. Located at 2709 Walden Creek Road in Pigeon Forge. Call either *865/429-0411* or *865/429-0607*.

Escape into an exotic jungle at **Rain Forest Adventures**, an indoor rain forest that is home to over 500 animals, from comical lemurs to a seven foot long King Cobra. Open all year with the exception of Christmas. Admission is $11.99 for adults, $6.99 for those age 3-12, and children under 3 are admitted free. 109 NASCAR Drive, Sevierville, TN 37862. Call *865/428-4091* for further information.

Which One Is My Room?

There are 10 developed campgrounds in the park, two open year around. For just $12 to $20 a night, you can enjoy staying in the park. For reservations, call *800/365-CAMP.* You'll also find all types of lodging in nearby Gatlinburg.

Practical Information

Address: Great Smoky Mountains National Park, 107 Park Headquarters Rd., Gatlinburg, TN 37738

Telephone: *865/436-1200* (recorded message)

Operating Season: Year round, although some areas may close due to weather
Cost: free
Hours: daily year round (call park for hours). Cades Cove Visitors Center has limited winter hours
Website: *www.nps.gov/grsm/index.htm*

Did You Know.....?

- Tennessee was the 16th state to enter into the union.
- Tennessee was the first state to be readmitted into the union after the Civil War.
- Bristol is considered The Birthplace of Country Music.
- The iris is the state flower.
- Tennessee's nickname is The Volunteer State.
- The raccoon is the state animal.
- The name Tennessee comes from the Yuchi tribe, whose word "Tana-see" means "The meeting place."
- Agriculture and Commerce is the state motto.
- The mockingbird is the official state bird.
- Tennessee has five official state songs: The Tennessee Waltz; Tennessee, My Homeland; Tennessee; When It's Iris Time In Tennessee; and My Tennessee Rocky Top.
- From entertainers to presidents, many famous personalities were either born or raised in Tennessee, including: Andrew Jackson (7th President of the United State), James K. Polk (11th President of the United States), Andrew Johnson (17th President of The United States), Davy Crockett (frontiersman), Aretha Franklin (blues and gospel singer), Dolly Parton (country singer/songwriter), Morgan Freeman (actor), Lester Faltt (bluegrass musician), Tina Turner (singer), Cybill Shepherd (actress), Sgt. Alvin C. York (the most decorated WWI soldier), Wilma Rudolph (athlete), Alex Haley (author), Bill Monroe (The Father of Bluegrass music), and Kenny Chesney (country singer).

Learning About the Great Smoky Mountains

Petersen, David. *Great Smoky Mountains National Park* (A New True Book). 1993.

Cleaver, Vera and Bill Cleaver. *Where the Lilies Bloom*. 1989.

Petersen, David. *Great Smoky Mountains National Park*. (A New True Book). 1993.

In addition, the Great Smoky Mountains Natural History Association sells several good kids' books on the park (to order, call *423/436-0120* or send check or money order to 416 Cherry St., Gatlinburg, TN 37738:

Great Smoky Mountains National Park Coloring Book ($2.29)

Let's Explore the Southern Appalachian Mountains ($2.95) Recommended for ages 6-12.

Connecting People and Nature ($12.95). This is a guide for parents about environmental education.

Jimmy Carter National Historic Site
Georgia

The hometown of the 39th president of the United States is the focus of this historic site. It also offers a good look at a small Southern town that still continues to rely on agriculture for much of its economy.

Are We There Yet?

This national historic site is located in Plains, Georgia, about 40 miles from Albany. To reach the park, take exit 33 off I-75 in Cordele. Travel on Georgia Highway 280 to Americus and continue 10 miles to Plains. In Plains, travel north on North Bond Street and follow the signs.

This park is unique: the Plains High School serves as the visitors center and the park museum. Here you'll find park rangers to direct you to other historic sites in Plains.

What's There To Do Here?

Begin at the visitor's center, housed in the former Plains High School from which both Jimmy and Roslynn Carter graduated. Here you'll find a museum dedicated to the 39th president, a 25-minute video presentation about the president's life and a video tour of the Carter's home. Park rangers at the center can direct you to other sites, such as:

Depot: Built in 1888, the depot is the oldest structure in Plains. Used as the headquarters for Carter's presidential campaign, it is filled with memorabilia from the 1976 bid for the presidency.

Boyhood Home: The former president moved into this house in 1928, and it was occupied by his family until 1949.

Present Home. This home is closed to the public and is still the private resident of President and Mrs. Carter.

Smiling Peanut. Ready for a great photo op? Here it is: a smiling peanut. This peanut, complete with a giant smile, came from a campaign rally and today is *the* place to get the family photo made in Plains.

When Are We Going?
The busiest times for this park are the months of March and April.

How Long Are We Staying?
You'll want to budget about half a day to visit all the sites.

What Should I Bring?
This park is an easy one and mostly involves popping in and out of your car. You won't find many facilities along the way so some water in the car is a good idea.

What Are We Doing Next?
About 40 miles from Plains you'll find a living history village in Westville, Georgia. The park recreates an 1850s village and is open Tuesday through Sunday (closed New Year's Day, Thanksgiving, and Christmas); hours are 10am-5pm Tuesday through Saturday and 1pm-5pm Sunday. Admission is $8 for adults and $4 for school age children. For information, write **Westville**, PO Box 1850, Lumpkin, GA 31815, *Tel. 229/838-6310* or toll free at *888/733-1850*.

In Americus, about 10 miles east of Plains, you'll find the International Headquarters for the Habitat for Humanity.

Find out more about the life of the 39th president at the Jimmy Carter Library and Museum in Atlanta. On display are an array of items from his years at the White House, gifts from heads of state, a replica of the Oval Office, and Carter's Nobel Peace Prize. Located at 441 Freedom Parkway. Open Monday-Saturday from 9am-4:45pm and Sunday from noon to 4:45pm. Admission $7 for adults, children 16 and under admitted free. *Tel. 404/865-7100*.

Jimmy Carter Trivia

• A speed reader, Jimmy Carter can read up to 2,000 words per minute.

• Carter attended the US Naval Academy in Annapolis, where he studied nuclear physics.

• A devoutly religious man, Jimmy Carter can often be found teaching Sunday School at Marantha Baptist Church in Plains, GA.

• Jimmy Carter was the first president who was born in a hospital.

• The former president has written a number of books over the years including An Hour Before Daylight: Memoirs of a Rural Boyhood; Christmas In Plains: Memories; Always A Reckoning: and other poems; Why Not The Best?; An Outdoor Journal: adventures and reflections; and Little Baby Snoogle-Fleejer, a children's tale with illustrations by daughter Amy Carter.

❧

The Plains Peanut Festival
The biggest event of the year in Plains is the Plains Peanut Festival, held the last Saturday in September. The event includes arts and crafts, races, and plenty of country fun.

Which One Is My Room?
There is no lodging available in the park. Most accommodations are found in nearby Americus, including:

Americus Days Inn, 1007 Martin Luther King Jr. Blvd., *Tel. 229/924-3613*

Jameson Inn Americus, 1605 East Lamar St., *Tel. 229/924-2726*

Holiday Inn Express Americus, 1607 Hwy 280 East, *Tel. 229/928-5400*

Ramada Inn Americus, US 19 South, *Tel. 229/924-4431*

Jimmy and Roslynn Carter had a hand in the design of the **Plains Historic Inn and Antiques Mall**, located on Main Street in Plains. The inn is a time capsule of American culture, with each of the seven rooms available decorated with a motif from decades past, from the roaring '20's to the '80's. An antiques mall is stationed on the first floor. Call *229/824-4517* for more information.

Practical Information
Address: Jimmy Carter National Historic Site, 300 North Bond St., Plains, GA 31780

Telephone: *229/824-4104*

Operating Season: year round, closed Christmas and New Year's Day

Hours: 9am-5pm daily

Cost: Free

Website: *www.nps.gov/jica/index.htm*

Learning about President Jimmy Carter
A good biography for readers age 9-12 is *Jimmy Carter: Beyond the Presidency,* by Pamela Dell and Mellonee Carrigan (Children's Press, 1995).

Martin Luther King Jr. National Historic Site
Georgia
The legacy of Martin Luther King Jr. is remembered on a daily basis in Atlanta, the home town of the slain civil rights leader. Families can visit the birthplace of Reverend King, tour his old neighborhood, and learn more about the life and goals of this important leader.

Are We There Yet?

The historic site is located at 450 Auburn Avenue. From I-75/85 North or South, take exit 248C Freedom Parkway. Get in the right lane and turn right at the first traffic light on Boulevard. Follow the signs.

Another option is to take the public transportation system, MARTA. Bus 3 from the Five Points station in downtown Atlanta provides transportation to the site.

What's There To Do Here?

The historic park isn't really one site but several:

Visitor Center. Make your first stop here to learn more about Dr. Martin Luther King, Jr. The center features exhibits and audio programs on his life and the Civil Rights Movement. Here you'll also pick up a map to all the sites.

The King Center. The Martin Luther King Jr. Center for Nonviolent Social Chance was established by the Reverend's widow, Mrs. Coretta Scott King. The Center is home to exhibits on MLK as well as Mahatma Gandhi. Here, too, is the burial place of Dr. King.

Ebenezer Baptist Church. Still a working church, this church was attended by Dr. King as a child. Later he and his father, "Daddy" King, were co-pastors from 1960 until 1968. You'll find the church closed when its congregation is using the facility.

Birthplace. This two-story Victorian home was the birthplace of MLK. Park rangers offer guided tours of the home.

Fire Station No. 6. This station, built in 1894, was used until 1991. Today you can learn about the desegregation of the fire department, see an historic fire engine, and visit a bookstore with an emphasis on African-American history at the site.

Birth Home Block. Not only the birthplace of MLK is being preserved, but homes all along this block of Auburn Avenue are being purchased and restored to their 1930s look on the exterior. The houses are still homes and are rented to local residents.

Peace Plaza. This is a good place to stop and think about the contributions of Dr. King. Located between the Visitor Center and Auburn Avenue, the plaza is home of the Peace Rose Garden and waterfalls and the "Behold" statue.

When Are We Going?

The busiest months for this park are January, February, and the summer months. Anytime of year makes a good time to visit this park, however, because of its many indoor exhibits.

How Long Are We Staying?

The park recommends a minimum of two hours to visit the site; allow longer if you'll be taking the trails.

What Should I Bring?

Don't forget good walking shoes for strolling from site to site; layers are also recommended.

Which One Is My Room?

You'll find plenty of motels, hotels, and even a few campgrounds nearby.

What Are We Doing Next?

For sheer entertainment, spend a day at **Six Flags Over Georgia** or **Zoo Atlanta**. Those who want to delve into Atlanta's history should check out **Atlanta Cyclorama and Civil War Museum**, where lights and sound catapult you back to a time when the nation was divided. Located at 800 Cherokee Ave SE in Grant Park. Open daily from 9:30am-4:30pm; admission is $6 for adults, $4 for children 6-12 and those under 6 admitted free.

Kids will be able to unleash their creativity at **The Children's Museum of Atlanta,** filled with hands-on exhibits. Open seven days a week from 10 am - 5pm Located at 275 Centennial Olympic Park Drive NW. For more information call *404/659-KIDS (5437)*.

Special Events at MLK Historic Site

Several significant days in Dr. King's life are remembered through-out the year with special events:

• **January 15, Dr. King's Birthday**. Both the federal holiday (the third Monday in January) and the actual birth date are celebrated at the park and throughout Atlanta as well.

• **February, Black History Month**. Many special events occur throughout the month of February; check with the park for times and details.

• **April 4, Assassination Remembrance**. The date of Dr. King's assassination in Memphis is a solemn day at the site with wreaths laid on his grave.

• **October 2, Mahatma Gandhi Birthday Celebration**. Because of the influence Gandhi had on Dr. King, the Indian leader's birthday is recalled at the park.

• **October 10, National Historic Site Birthday**. The park was created on this day in 1980, a date remembered with special ceremonies.

• **December, Evening Birthplace Tours**. Candlelight tours of the birth home are held two evenings in December. This is a magical time to visit the home when it is decorated like it would have been for a 1930s Christmas.

Practical Information
    Address: Martin Luther King, Jr. National Historic Site, 450 Auburn Avenue, NE, Atlanta, GA 30312-1525
    Telephone: *404/331-5190;* (for a recorded message call *404/331-6922)*
    Operating Season: year round; closed Jan. 1, Thanksgiving, and Dec. 25
    Hours: 9am-5pm in the winter, 9am-6pm in the summer
    Cost: free; fee for parking of $3.
    Website*: www.nps.gov/malu/index.htm*

Words of Wisdom from Martin Luther King Jr.

• "Injustice anywhere is a threat to justice everywhere."
• "The ultimate measure of a man is not where he stands in moments of comfort and convenience, but where he stands at times of challenge and controversy."
• "Even if I knew that tomorrow the world would go to pieces, I would still plant my apple tree."
• "Faith is taking the first step even when you don't see the whole staircase."
• "A right delayed is a right denied."
• "Almost always, the creative dedicated minority has made the world better."
• "Darkness cannot drive out darkness; only light can do that. Hate cannot drive out hate; only love can do that."

Learning About Martin Luther King, Jr.
    Adler, David A. and Robert Casilla (Illustrator). *A Picture Book of Martin Luther King, Jr.* Holiday House, 1991. Ages 4-8.
    Boone-Jones, Margaret. *Martin Luther King, Jr.: A Picture Story.* Children's Press, 1986. Ages 9-12.
    Colbert, Jan (Editor), Ann McMillan Harms (Editor), Ernest C. Withers, Roy Cajero (Photographer). *Dear Dr. King: Today's Children Write to Dr. Martin Luther King, Jr.* Disney Press, 1998. Ages 9-12.
    De Rubertis, Barbara, Gershom Griffith (Illustrator), Barbara Derubertis. *Martin Luther King Day: Let's Meet Dr. Martin Luther King, Jr.* Kane Press, 1996. Ages 4-8.
    Greene, Carol, Steven Greene (Illustrator), Steven Dobson (Illustrator). *Martin Luther King Jr.: A Man Who Changed Things* (Rookie Biographies). Children's Press, 1989. Ages 4-8.
    Hakim, Rita. *Martin Luther King Jr. and the March Toward Freedom.* Millbrook Press Trade, 1994. Ages 4-8.

Haskins, Jim. *I Have a Dream: The Life and Words of Martin Luther King, Jr.* Milbrook Press Trade, 1994. Ages 9-12.

McDonnell, Janet , Helen Endres, Lydia Halverson (Illustrator). *Martin Luther King, Jr.* (Circle the Year With Holidays Series). Children's Press, 1994. Baby-preschool.

Tate, Eleanora E. *Thank You, Dr. Martin Luther King, Jr.!* Yearling Books, 1992. Ages 9-12.

Richmond National Battlefield Park
Virginia

Richmond was once the capital of the Confederacy and during the Civil War the city saw a great deal of battle. This national battlefield is actually a series of battlefields in the Richmond area, a good place to learn more about the war between the states.

Are We There Yet?

If you are traveling north or south on I-95, take exit 74 and follow the signs to the visitor center at 3215 East Broad Street.

If you are traveling east or west on I-64, take the intersection of I-95 south then take 74. Follow the signs to the visitor center.

What's There To Do Here?

You'll want to start your visit at the **Visitors Center** at 470 Tredegar Street. Here your family will see exhibits and audiovisual programs on the Civil War and its effect on Richmond.

The main visitors center will be your home base for a visit to the park which is actually 10 battlefields spread out over an 80 mile route. At the main visitors center you can pick up maps to the other sites which include:

Chickahominy Bluff. This bluff overlooks the Chickahominy River Valley. Here you'll find self-guided trails and audio stations that explain more about this site from where General Robert E. Lee watched the battles.

Gaines Mill. Here you can take a self-guided walk near the Watt House, an 1835 home that served as a battle headquarters. Union headquarters were set up during the skirmish near Watt House, an 1835 home. Take a self-guided walk in the footsteps of the Texas and Georgia soldiers who broke through Union lines. Glendale—Confederate troops were unable to take hold of the crossroads near Frayer's Farm, which was known as Glendale.

Glendale (Frayser's Farm).

Malvern Hill. There's a short walking trail here to the battle site with audio stations that explain more about the battlefield where the final clash in the Seven Days Battle occurred. Audio stations explain more about the battlefield and how the Confederate troops had to attack on open ground.

Drewry's Bluff. This bluff has several exhibits along a self-guided trail. This site guarded Fort Darling. Audio stations explain more about the battle.

Cold Harbor. There's a visitors center with a one-mile walking trail at this site. There's a visitor's center with an electric map detailing the skirmish. Trenches dug by the Confederate soldiers can still be seen along the one-mile walking trail.

Garthright House. You can't go inside this restored house that was once a Union field hospital. Although tours are not offered of this restored house which was once a Union hospital, you can see the exterior.

Fort Harrison and Vicinity. A self-guided trail winds through Fort Harrison; there's also a good overlook from which to view the James River. Audio stations explain more about the battle.

When Are We Going?

The peak months are May (with lots of school groups) and July. These summer months are hot and humid so dress cool, bring sunscreen, and take it easy.

How Long Are We Staying?

The length of time you'll want to budget for this park depends on the depth you want to explore Civil War history. If you are interested in learning about the battlefields and want to visit most sites along the route, plan for a full day's visit. If you just want to look at the main visitors center and perhaps one battlefield, budget a couple of hours.

What Should I Bring?

Good walking shoes are a must if you'll be taking the self-guided walks at the battlefields. Also, there's a cassette tape available for the auto tour so if your vehicle doesn't have one, it's a good idea to bring along a portable audio player.

What Are We Doing Next?

Jamestown and Yorktown are about an hour's drive from Richmond. Also in the area is Williamsburg, best known as the home of **Colonial Williamsburg**, *Tel. 800/HISTORY*. This town was the capital of Virginia in the 1770's, and the historic district has been restored to the days of the American Revolution.

Tour historic homes, dine in recreated colonial taverns, and shop in 18th century style stores on Merchants' Square at the end of Duke of Gloucester Street. Colonial items such as reproductions of pewter plates, iron hooks or hats are made by craftsmen. Wigmakers, blacksmiths, gunsmiths, printers and even shoe makers ply their trades here as they did over two centuries ago.

For a day of family fun visit **Paramount's Kings Dominion** theme park, located 20 miles away from Richmond in nearby Doswell. There are eleven roller coasters to choose from for the family thrill-seeker, and little ones can enjoy rides featuring their favorite contemporary cartoon characters, then take a spin on one of the few remaining wooden carousels which dates from the early 1900s. The whole family will love the view from the 275-foot-high platform of a recreation of The Eiffel Tower. Open in the summer months from 10:30am-8pm and periodically in the spring and fall. 16000 Theme Park Way, *Tel. 804/876-5561.*

Which One Is My Room?

Richmond has a full host of accommodations, from budget motels to high-rise hotels. For more information, contact the **Richmond Convention and Visitors Bureau**, *Tel. 888/RICHMOND.*

Practical Information

Address: Richmond National Battlefield Park, 3215 East Broad St., Richmond, VA 23223

Telephone: *804/226-1981*

Operating Season: year round, closed Thanksgiving, Christmas, New Year's Day

Hours: 9am-5pm daily

Cost: free

Website *www.nps.gov/rich/index/htm*

Learning About Richmond

Evans, Lynn. Richmond, *Virginia: The Travel Guide for Kids.* 1993.

Russell Cave National Monument
Alabama

Russell Cave is far more than just another cave–it's a look back 8,000 years to some of the earliest days of human habitation in North America. This is an archaeological site where your family can learn more about Archaic, Woodland, and Mississippian periods.

Are We There Yet?

The cave is located seven miles north of Bridgeport, Alabama. From Bridgeport, follow County Road 75 north for four miles, turn on County Road 98.

What's There To Do Here?

The park includes a visitors center with displays on the early residents of this region, including ancient tools. Slide shows and films explain more about these early people. You'll find the cave shelter extremely fascinating, the place where the prehistoric people of these parts took shelter from the weather. You'll also find a hiking trail and a horse trail.

Learn more about the prehistoric man who once roamed the area through a 30-minute movie as well as through demonstrations of ancient weapons and tools. The exhibits illustrate man's progress, from the crude implements made by the Archaic Indians (7,000 BC–1,000 BC) to the more elaborate tools and shards of pottery left behind by the Woodland Indians (1,000 BC–800 AD).

When Are We Going?

The busiest time of year is the summer, when you can expect temperatures to be high, right along with the humidity. Fall and spring are excellent times to visit but in the winter temperatures can be chilly.

How Long Are We Staying?

You'll want to budget a minimum of one hour which will give you time to check out the exhibits and walk to the mouth of the cave.

What Should I Bring?

Bring along comfortable walking shoes for this trip.

Which One is My Room?

There are no campsites or accommodations in the park. Meals and lodging available in South Pittsburgh, Tennessee, and Stevenson, Alabama.

What Are We Doing Next?

Over 300 species of fish, from the intimidating bonnethead shark and southern stingray to the tiny wonders of the deep like seahorses and the fish which were the inspiration behind *Finding Nemo* are on display at the **Tennessee Aquarium**, located 35 miles from Russell Cave in Chattanooga along the banks of the Tennessee River. Other animals, from birds to reptiles are also on view, and next door to the aquarium is an IMAX theater. Both the aquarium and IMAX theater are open every day from 10 am- 6pm with the exceptions of Thanksgiving and Christmas. *Tel. 800/262/0695.*

Practical Information

Address: Russell Cave National Monument, 3729 County Road 98, Bridgeport, AL 35740

Telephone: *256/495-2672*

Operating Season: year round; closed Thanksgiving, Christmas, New Year's Day

Hours: 8:30 am- 5pm daily; during daylight savings time 8 am - 4:30 pm

Cost: free

Website: *www.nps.gov/ruca/index.htm*

Did You Know.....?

• Huntsville is considered the Rocket Capital of The World, and workers from the state built the first rocketship to carry men to the moon.

• The name Alabama derives from a Creek Indian word meaning "tribal town" "Audemus jura nostra defendere", a Latin phrase meaning "We dare defend our rights" is the state motto.

• The Yellowhammer is the official state bird, and Alabama is referred to as The Yellowhammer State.

• The Camellia is the state flower.

• Alabama was admitted as the 22nd state in the union on December 14, 1819.

• Montgomery is the state capital.

• From athletes to civil rights leaders, many famous personalities were either born or raised in Alabama including:

baseball legend Hank Aaron—Mobile

civil rights activist Ralph Abernathy—Linden

actress Tallulah Bankhead—Huntsville

singer Nat "King" Cole—Montgomery

writer Zelda Fitzgerald—Montgomery

singer Emmylou Harris—Birmingham

"Charlie's Angels" actress Kate Jackson—Birmingham

author/educator Helen Keller—Tuscumbia

civil rights leader/ wife of Dr. Martin Luther King Coretta Scot King—Marion

"To Kill A Mockingbird" author Harper Lee—Monroeville

athlete Carl Lewis—Birmingham

boxer Joe Lewis—Lexington

baseball player Willie Mays—Westfield

actor Jim Nabors—Sylacauga

athlete Jesse Owens—Danville

civil rights leader Rosa Parks—Tuskegee

singer Jimmie Rodgers—Geiger

politician George Wallace—Clio

Miss America Heather Whitestone—Dothan

singer Hank Williams—Georgiana

≈

Learn More About Caves

Some good books to introduce young travelers to caves are:

Davis, Wendy. *Limestone Cave*. Children's Press, 1998. Good for readers age 9-12.

Hoare, Stephen. *The Amazing Underworld of Caves, Mines and Tunnels*. Simon and Schuster Young Books, 1997. Good for readers age 4-8.

Shenandoah National Park
Virginia
"Oh Shenandoah, I long to see you..."

If you long to see this beautiful park on the Blue Ridge Mountains, pack up the kids and go. You'll find plenty to do.

Are We There Yet?
Located about 75 miles west of Washington, DC or four miles east of Luray, Virginia, the park is easy to reach on US 211.

What's There To Do Here?
If your family likes to hike, Shenandoah offers over 500 miles of trails, many with spectacular wooded views. Fishing is another popular activity as well as camping.

When Are We Going?
Fall colors bring the greatest number of visitors to the park. You'll also find it busy during summer weekends, due, in part, to its proximity to Washington, DC.

How Long Are We Staying?
At a minimum, you'll want to budget a day to visit the park, take a hike, and enjoy a picnic.

What Should I Bring?
Bring along some picnic supplies, good walking shoes, and insect repellent if you are visiting during the summer months.

Which One Is My Room?
Several overnight accommodations are available in the park: Skyland Lodge, Big Meadows Lodge, and Lewis Mountain Cabins. For reservations or information on these properties, call *800/999-4714* or write for reservations at Skyland, Big Meadows Lodge and Lewis Mountain Cabins write to ARAMARK Sports and Entertainment, Inc.. PO Box 727, Luray, VA 22835.

Several campgrounds also offer space on a first-come, first-served basis. Matthews Arms, Big Meadows, Lewis Mountain, and Loft Mountain offer numerous sites. **Big Meadows** takes reservations during summer months; call *800/365-CAMP.*

What Are We Doing Next?
Virginia was home to the man regarded as the father of the country, and a tour of George Washington Birthplace National Monument offers insight into his early days. This 550-acre park holds the foundation of the home in

Did You Know.....?

- Virginia was admitted into statehood on June 25, 1788.
- The state's nickname is "Old Dominion."
- Eight Presidents were born in the state.
- George Washington, Thomas Jefferson, James Madison, James Monroe, William Harrison, John Tyler, Zachary Taylor, and Woodrow Wilson.
- The wives of Washington, Jefferson, Madison, Monroe, Tyler, Taft and Kennedy were also born in Virginia.
- Virginia is often referred to as "the birthplace of a nation."
- The first Thanksgiving celebration was held in Virginia in 1619.
- The state motto is "Sic Semper Tyrannis", which translates as "Thus always to tyrants."
- The motto appears on the state flag.
- "Carry Me Back To Old Virginia" is the state song.
- The American fox hound is the official state dog.
- Virginia has had a total of three state capitals: Jamestown, Williamsburg and Richmond, which is the present day capital.
- During the Civil War Richmond was also the capital of the Confederate States.
- Jamestown is the site of the first English settlement in the United States.
- Virginia was named after Queen Elizabeth I of England, who was referred to as the "Virgin Queen."
- Virginia was one of the original 13 colonies.
- Cornwallis surrendered in Yorktown, Virginia, thus ending the American.

which Washington was born, the cemetery where many of his relatives are buried, and a Memorial House, which depicts life in Washington's time. For more information write to George Washington Birthplace National Memorial, 1732 Popes Creek Road, Washington's Birthplace, VA 22443-5115.

Mount Vernon was Washington's home for 45 years, and his influence can be felt within the impressive mansion's many rooms. Guests of national importance were entertained in the dining room, the largest room in the house. It is easy to imagine the ornate furniture being cleared to the side in preparation for a dance, which was a favorite activity of America's founding father. The dining room was also the place where Washington received news that he had been elected the first president. Visitors can move on to Washington's private study, a haven entered by no one without expressed invitation. Nelly Custis,

Martha's granddaughter who lived with the Washingtons, married at Mount Vernon and gave birth to her first child there—her bedroom is also on display, as is the master bedroom, a sanctuary for Martha Washington which is festooned with the portraits of her grandchildren.

Mount Vernon is open every day of the year. Admission $11 for adults, $5 for children 6-11 and children under 5 are admitted free. For more information write 3200 George Washington Memorial Parkway, Mount Vernon, VA 22121 or call *703/780-2000*.

Practical Information

Address: Shenandoah National Park, 3655 U.S. Hwy. 211 E, Luray, VA 22835-9036

Telephone: *540/999-3500*

Operating Season: year round

Hours: always open

Cost: $10 per vehicle for 7-day pass

Website: *www.nps.gov/shen/index.htm*

Learning About Shenandoah

Ransom, Candice and Kimberly Bulcken Root (Illustrator). *When the Whippoorwill Calls.* 1995.

Vicksburg National Military Park
Mississippi

The sadness of a country divided by war echoes over Vicksburg, now a quiet, thoughtful place for children to learn about the Civil War. The park is adjacent to the Vicksburg National Cemetery, which contains the graves of over 17,000 Union soldiers. Sadly, the names of over 12,000 are lost to the mist of time. Soldiers Rest, Cedar Hill Cemetery is the final resting place for 5,000 Confederate soldiers, of which 3,500 remain unknown.

Are We There Yet?

From I-20, take Vicksburg Exit 4B. Continue on Clay Street (US 80) west for a quarter mile to the park entrance.

What's There To Do Here?

Your first stop will be at the visitor center at Clay Street. Families can watch an 18-minute film about the battlefield where the fateful siege took place.

One of the most interesting stops in the park is the USS Cairo. This complex includes a museum and a restored Union ironclad gunboat which was sunk during the war. You can reach the Cairo by following a 16-mile driving trail that parallels the Union and Confederate battle lines (the museum is located at milepost 7.8). The museum has some interesting exhibits on daily life aboard the gunboat.

Guided tours are also available if your family would like more in-depth knowledge. The cost is $30 per car ($40 per van) and reservations are requested, *Tel. 601/636-3827* or *601/636-0583 ext. 8028.* You can also rent a self-guided driving tour cassette tape.

When Are We Going?

April through July mark the peak months at this park. If you visit during the summer, expect warm, sticky conditions, so dress cool.

How Long Are We Staying?

Most families will want two or three hours at the park but if you are visiting for more in-depth educational purposes (there are 661 monuments, 594 position markers, and 70 bronze castings on display), plan on an entire day.

What Should I Bring?

Good walking shoes are important and if you go in summer, cool, breathable cotton clothes.

What Are We Doing Next?

Vicksburg has a good selection of attractions for families including:

Biedenharn Museum of Coca Cola Memorabilia, 1107 Washington St., *Tel. 601/638-6514.* Coca-Cola buffs can view the first building in the world where Coca-Cola was first bottled in 1894. The museum includes everything from antique soda fountains to bottling works. After a tour, you can have a fountain Coke or an ice cream float; a gift store sells Coca-Cola items. The museum is open 9am-5pm Monday through Saturday and 1:30pm-4:30pm on Sunday. Admission is $2.25 for adults and $1.75 for kids under 12.

Yesterday's Children Antique Doll and Toy Museum, 1104 Washington St., *Tel. 601/638-0650.* This museum contains dolls and toys dating back to the 1880s. The museum is open 10 am-4 pm Monday through Saturday; admission is $2 for adults and $1 for kids under 12.

Glide down the Mighty Mississippi on **"Sweet Olive"**, an enclosed boat with large panoramic windows, as you learn the history of the area on a 1 1/2 hour narrated tour. Mississippi River Tours is located at 1010 Levee St. Admission $17 for adults, $10 for those 7-12, $5 for children age 3-6, and kids under 2 admitted free. Call *601/883-1083* or toll free at *866/807-BOAT (2628).*

Did You Know.....?

- In 1898 root beer was invented in Biloxi, Mississippi.
- The Mississippi River is often referred to as Old Man River.
- The state song is "Go Mis-sis-sip-pi."
- Magnolia is the state flower.
- Mississippi's nickname is Magnolia State.
- The first football player to be featured on the front of a Wheaties box was Walter Payton from Columbia, MS.
- The state motto is "virtute et armis", which means "by valor and arms."
- The mockingbird is the official state bird.
- The state capital is Jackson.
- Famous Mississippians (either born here or who lived here) include:

Lance Bass—member of NSYNC

Brandy—singer and actress

Jimmy Buffett—singer

Lacy Chabert—TV actress on Party of Five

Sam Cooke—singer

Bo Diddley—one of the founders of rock and roll music

John Dye—TV actor on Touched By An Angel

Brett Farve—football player

Morgan Freeman—movie star

Bobbie Gentry—singer

Jim Henson—creator of The Muppets

Faith Hill—country singer

James Earl Jones—famous actor

B.B. King—blues singer

Jerry Lee Lewis—rock and roll pioneer

Elvis Presley—known as The King of Rock and Roll

Le Ann Rimes—country singer

Jimmie Rodgers—singer

Marty Stuart—country singer

Conway Twitty—country singer

Oprah Winfrey —television personality

Tammy Wynette—country singer

Which One Is My Room?

There are no campgrounds and no accommodations in the park but you'll find a full range of facilities in Vicksburg. For more information, contact the **Vicksburg Convention and Visitors Bureau**, Clay Street and Old Highway 27, Vicksburg, MS 39181, *Tel. 601/636-9421 or toll free 800/221-3536.*

Practical Information

Address: Vicksburg National Military Park, P.O. Box 110, Vicksburg, MS 39183

Telephone: *601/636-0583*

Operating Season: year round; closed Dec. 25

Hours: Visitors Center open 8 am-5pm daily; Cairo Museum open 8:30 am-5pm daily from November to March, 9:30 am-6pm other times.

Cost: $5 per vehicle for 7 days

Website: *www.nps.gov/vick/index.htm*

Learning About Vicksburg

Clapp, Patricia C. *Tamarack Tree: A Novel of the Siege of Vicksburg.* William Morrow and Company, 1986. Young adult.

Wisler, G. Clifton. *The Drummer Boy of Vicksburg.* Lodestar Books, 1997. Young adult.

Chapter 6

THE MIDWEST

Agate Fossil Beds National Monument
Nebraska

For fossil lovers and those with an interest in Native American lore, this 2,270 acre park is the place to go. The home of the Lakota people, this land offers history of another culture as well as a glimpse into prehistoric times—fossils over twenty million years old have been discovered at this site in northwestern Nebraska.

Are We There Yet?

The park is located on Highway 29 about 35 miles north of Mitchell, Nebraska.

What's There To Do Here?

The visitors center, with three rooms of exhibits, the Hitchcock Theater and an extensive display of Native American artifacts, offers an education of both the landscape and its inhabitants. Step back in time with an interactive computer tour and life-sized fossil dioramas, while at the James H. Cook Collection, with over two hundred artifacts which help to paint a portrait of the Lakota way of life, you can imagine the smoke rising from the pipe used by Chief Red Cloud before the signing of the Ft. Laramie Treaty of 1868, and see a war club brandished by American Horse, a leader of the Oglala people.

Children can learn about the wildlife which inhabit this region with a display of deer antler, rattlesnake skin, and turtle shells which they can handle, and the Junior Ranger program lets kids play detective as they go on a search throughout the center for answers to questions on fossils and Native

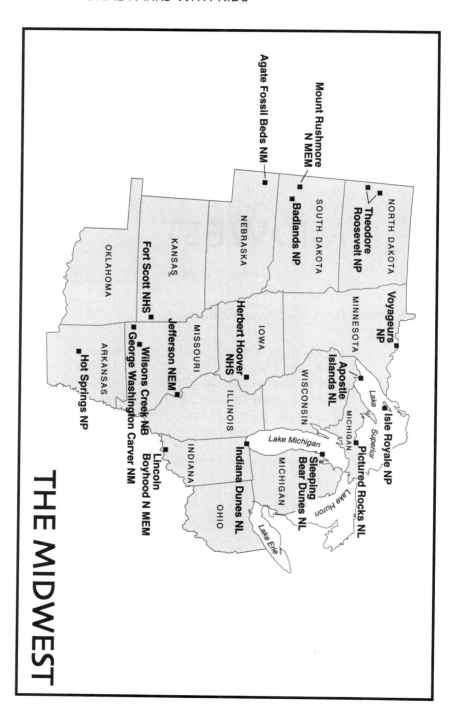

THE MIDWEST

Americans in an activity book. Once completed, the child will receive a Junior Ranger badge. The visitors center is open year round. For further information call *308/668-2211*.

When Are We Going?
Summer is the busiest time in the park, although crowds are rarely a problem.

How Long Are We Staying?
You'll just need an hour or two for a look around.

What Should I Bring?
Good walking shoes are recommended for the hike, and cool clothes for summer.

Which One Is My Room?
There are no accommodations or camping in the park but you'll find rooms in Harrison, Nebraska about 20 miles away.

Where Are We Going Next?
Piercing the prairie sky like a beacon is **Chimney Rock**, an American landmark which made such an impression upon the over half a million individuals brave enough to journey westward that many attempted to capture its beauty in both written word, through numerous journal and diary entries, as well as through drawings. A video presentation of America's westward expansion and exhibits offering a taste of pioneer life can be seen at The Ethel and J. Abbott Visitors Center.

Chimney Rock National Historical Site is located only 72 miles away from Agate Fossil Beds National Monument. For visitor information call *308/586-2581* or *email chimrock@scottsbluff.net.*

A journey of only 125 miles will take your family back to the Ice Age with a visit to **The Mammoth Site of Hot Springs**, South Dakota. A thirty-minute guided tour and ten-minute video provide an introduction into the time when mammoths ruled the land, and you have the opportunity to view their fossilized remains, as well as those of other prehistoric animals, such as camels and llamas.

At the Muller Exhibit Hall children are able to grasp the enormity of these extinct creatures up close as they stand by "Napoleon," a thirteen-foot mammoth replica, and children age four through thirteen can participate in a simulated dig with the Junior Paleontologist Excavation Program (held only during the summer months— reservations for this event is required). Open year round.

For further information contact mammoth@mammothsite.com or see *www.mammothsite.com.*

Practical Information

Address: Agate Fossil Beds National Monument, 301 River Rd., Harrison, NE 69346-2734

Telephone: *308/668-2211*

Operating Season: year round

Hours: 8am- 5pm; closed Thanksgiving, Christmas and New Year's Day

Cost: $5 per car

Email: *AGFO_RangerActivities@nps.gov*

Website: *www.nps.gov/agfo/index.htm*

Apostle Islands National Lakeshore
Wisconsin

A popular weekend getaway especially on summer days, this park offers lots of fun along Lake Superior.

Are We There Yet?

The park is located on the south side of Lake Superior off WI Route 13 in Bayfield, Wisconsin. The park is about 90 miles east of Duluth, Minnesota.

Once you are at the lakeshore park, you can take a cruise out to see one or more of the Apostle Islands. Transportation out to the islands is provided by **Apostle Islands Cruise Service,** PO Box 691, Bayfield, WI 54814; *Tel. 800/ 323-7619*. The service offers a three-hour "Grand tour" which takes a look at all the 22 Apostle Islands. The cost is $25.95 for adults; children 6-12 are charged $14.95. Reservations are strongly recommended. Other cruises include schooner cruises, evening cruise, inner island shuttle, and lighthouse cruise.

What's There To Do Here?

History and nature come together in this park so there's something for everyone. Some choices include:

Headquarters Visitor Center. You'll probably start your visit here for a look at the options in the park. There are also visitors centers at Little Sand Bay and Stockton Island.

Hokenson Brothers Fishery Museum. This fishery operated for over 30 years and today stands as a reminder of this local industry.

Manitou Island Fish Camp. Typical of the fish camps built in the 1930s and 1940s, you can visit this camp for a ranger-led tour during the summer months.

Raspberry Island Lighthouse. If you can just visit one of the lighthouses at the Apostle Island park, it probably should be Raspberry Island. During the summer months the lighthouse is manned by a ranger and you can tour the structure and learn more about this important building.

Other lighthouses you can visit are:
- **Sand Island Lighthouse.** This is a structure with a heroic past. In 1885 the lights of Sand Island Lighthouse shone for its keeper as valiant man helped to save the crew of a burning ship. Guided tours are given at this Gothic style sandstone lighthouse which is still used today.
- **Devils Island Lighthouse**
- **Michigan Island Lighthouse**
- **Outer Island Lighthouse**

Hiking Trails. You can choose from over 50 miles of hiking trails. Hikers will find nearly 15 miles on Stockton Island alone.

Kayaking. Several local operators offer sea kayak rentals. (Consider a wet suit if you want to participate.)

When Are We Going?

Summer months are the best time to visit this park. Summer temperatures hover around 70 degrees although lake temperatures are cooler. Bring along layers as well as rain gear in case of afternoon thunderstorms.

How Long Are We Staying?

Budget a whole day to see the main visitors center and at least do one of the island cruises. If you'd like to spend time on the islands, consider two or three days for your trip.

Origin of The Dream Catcher

Although used by several Indian nations today, dreamcatchers were introduced by the Ojibwe people. Consisting of a circular wooden hoop (willow is often the material of choice) with woven cords forming a web-like design, the dreamcatcher is made in honor of the Spider Woman (Asibikaashi) who, according to Native American lore, protects her people to this day by "catching" bad dreams in her snare, allowing only good thoughts to filter through the small hole in the center of the web. Dreamcatchers are often placed over a newborn's cradle, insuring that no evil will come to the child. In days gone by the Ojibwe dangled a feather from the dreamcatcher, which was for both the child's entertainment as well as educating the baby about the importance of air. An owl feather was employed for a girl, to symbolize wisdom, while a little boy received an eagle feather, to represent courage. Today gem stones have replaced feathers.

What Should I Bring?

Layered clothing is important any time of year as well as rain gear. Insect repellent is a must.

What Are We Doing Next?

Isle Royale National Park, which is covered in this book, is located 180 miles from Apostle Islands, and 232 miles away is scenic Saint Croix National Scenic River, where your family can enjoy the various hiking trails and canoe downstream just like the Dakota, Ojibwe and *voyageurs* of the past. This park is free to the public. For further information call *715/483-3284* for a recorded message, or write 401 Hamilton Street, P.O. Box 708, Saint Croix, WI 54024 or *email SACN_Interpretation@nps.gov.*

Which One Is My Room?

You won't find camping on the mainland, but you can camp on 18 of the 22 islands. Facilities vary from developed sites to wilderness camping, but you will need a permit for all camping. Permits can be obtained up to 30 days in advance; for reservations call *715/779-3398 ext. 6.*

Practical Information

Address: Apostle Islands National Lakeshore, Route 1 Box 4, Bayfield, WI 54814

Telephone: *715/779-3397* headquarters; for a recorded message *715/779-3398*

Operating Season: year around; closed Thanksgiving, Dec. 25, Jan. 1

Hours: Visitor center daily from May-October 8am-5pm (until 6 during summer); Monday-Friday 8am-4:30pm from November-April

Cost: free

Website: *www.nps.gov/apis/index.htm*

Learning About Wisconsin

Blashfield, Jean F. *Awesome Almanac: Wisconsin*. B&B Publications, 1994

Bratvold, Gretchen. *Wisconsin* (Hello USA). Lemer Publications Co., 1991. Ages 9-12.

Fradin, Dennis Brindell. *Wisconsin* (From Sea to Shining Sea). Children's Press, 1994. Ages 4-8.

Hillestad, Butler Dori and Eileen Dawson (Illustrator). *W Is for Wisconsin*. Wisconsin Trails, 1998. Ages 4-8.

Thompson, Kathleen. *Wisconsin*. Raintree/Steck Vaughn, 1996. Ages 9-12.

Wilder, Laura Ingalls. *Little House in the Big Woods*. Harpercrest, 1971. Ages 9-12.

Wilder, Laura Ingalls. *Winter Days in the Big Woods* (My First Little House Books). Demco Media, 1995.

Did You Know.....?

- America's first kindergarten was founded in Watertown in 1856.
- Wisconsin's nickname is The Badger State.
- The ice cream sundae was invented in Two Rivers, Wisconsin.
- Wisconsin is the dairy capital of the United States.
- The state bird is the robin.
- The first performance of Ringling Brothers Circus was held in Baraboo in 1884.
- The state capital is Madison.
- The state song is On Wisconsin.
- Wisconsin comes from the Cheppewa "Ouisconsin," which means "grassy place.
- The inner tubing capital of the world is Somerset.
- The state flower is the Wood Violet.
- Just a few of the famous people who have lived in Wisconsin are magician Harry Houdini, architect Frank Lloyd Wright, actor Don Ameche, and WW II General Douglas MacArthur.

Badlands National Park
South Dakota

The Sioux Indians named it *"mako sica"* or "land bad." The early French-Canadian trappers called it *"les mauvaises torres a traverser"* or "bad land to travel across."

Today travelers from around the world call the Badlands a great vacation destination.

This year-around park boasts some of the most spectacular geological formations outside the Grand Canyon. Purple, yellow, gray, tan, red, orange and white layers hint at the varied sedimentary layers that make up this quickly eroding land. (Its one inch annual erosion is one of the highest rates known.)

Prairie dogs, badgers, deer, fox, antelope, bighorn sheep and coyotes share the park with over 400 bison which graze among 50 kinds of grasses and 200 varieties of wildflowers that thrive here. Wildlife can usually be seen during the early morning and late evening hours, also the best times for photographing the brilliant hues.

Unlike many national parks, this one is generally not crowded, and visitors can drive the winding roads without traffic, imaging what the journey was like for the first settlers who crossed the area with no drinkable water and no firewood. Today's travelers have a much easier journey, with paved roads, full service campgrounds, and the Cedar Pass Lodge, with dining, air conditioned cabins, and a gift shop featuring locally made items. The lodge is located near the Cedar Pass Visitor Center, which features displays of prehistoric bones found in the park. Sabre-toothed cats, miniature camels and horses, and even a rhinoceros-like mammal called the titanotheres once roamed this land, and exhibits of many of these early residents are on display at the center.

Are We There Yet?

Although the Badlands geological region extends into North Dakota and even southern Canada, most visitors experience this rugged land in the Badlands National Park, located 51 miles east of Rapid City on I-90. From the Wall Drug Store exit, head south on SD 240 , the Badlands Loop Road. This 32-mile loop takes travelers on a scenic tour past rainbow colored ridges and steep canyons formed by centuries of erosion.

What's There To Do Here?

Badlands isn't the spectacular kind of Western park like Yellowstone or Grand Canyon, its beauty takes a more careful look and appreciation. The best way to get an appreciation for its delicate ecology is with a visit to one of the Visitors Centers. The largest is the **Ben Reifel Visitor Center at Cedar Pass**, *Tel. 605/433-5361,* where you'll find films on the park as well as exhibits. During the summer months, a second visitor's center, the **White River Visitor Center**, *Tel. 605/455-2878*, is open in the Stronghold District area of the park.

Powwows

Experience Nativeamerican culture first-hand by attending a pow-wow. These lively events, which are a showcase foramerican Indian dance, crafts, and cuisine, are held annually throughout the state of South Dakota. Call the numbers provided for further information:

Flandreau Santee Sioux Tribe Annual Wacipi, Flandreau, SD, held in mid-July, *Tel. 605/997/3844*

Oglala Nation Powwow and Rodeo, Pine Ridge, SD, held in early August, *Tel. 605/867-5821*

Lower Brule Sioux Tribe Annual Fair and Powwow, Lower Brule, SD, held in mid-August, *Tel. 605/473-5561*

Crow Creek Sioux Tribe Annual Powwow, Fort Thompson, SD, *Tel. 605/245-2221*

Cheyenne River Labor Day Fair and Rodeo, Eagle Butte, SD, held in early September, *Tel. 605/964-4155*

Northern Plains Tribal Arts Show and Powwow, Sioux Falls, SD, held in mid-September, *Tel. 605/334-4060*

Once you've learned more about the park, a good way to see it is on the **30-mile Loop Drive**. (There's also the 30-mile Sage Creek Road but it is gravel.) If the day's not too hot, you can take a hike on one of five trails.

An interesting stop is the **Prairie Homestead Historic Site**, *Tel. 605/433-5400; www.prairiehomestead.com,* located on the east entrance to the park (exit 131). This sod house was home to some of the area's early settlers and today it's the only sod house on public display in the state. Look for prairie dogs when you visit!

The best view of the park is from the air and **Badlands Helicopter Rides** makes it possible to see the whole park. You can pick from four tour lengths; prices start at $12.50. To reach the heliport, take Exit 131 off I-90 to the park; call *605/433-5322* for information.

When Are We Going?

The summer months are the park's busiest, but even then you won't find huge crowds. This park gets about 1.3 million visitors a year.

A summer visit here is generally hot. If you come in the winter, expect lots of snow and possibly wind.

How Long Are We Staying?

Most visitors stay about half a day, enough time to check out the visitors centers, explore some of the trails, and have a look at this unique geology.

What Should I Bring?

Sunscreen, sunglasses, hats, water, and cool clothes are requirements for summer visits, and warm clothes and windbreakers for late fall and winter.

What Are We Doing Next?

Mt. Rushmore National Monument and **Jewel Cave National Park** are top attractions in this area; see those chapters for more information.

The number one attraction near Badlands is **Wall Drug.** Wall Drug is to drug stores what Bloomingdale's is to department stores. Travelers from around the world come to this massive store on the edge of the Badlands National Park to shop, dine, and just soak up the off-beat Western atmosphere.

Grossing $10 million, things are busy today at Wall Drug, but business wasn't always so prosperous. In 1931, the Hustead family moved to Wall and soon found themselves living in the back of the drug store, whose only asset was a broken soda fountain. The country around Wall was rugged and arid; drinking water had to be hauled in over 12 miles. The nation was in the midst of the worst economic depression ever suffered. The Husteads gave themselves five years to make a go of it.

Even during the worst of the Great Depression, however, travelers continued to drive near Wall Drug on Route 16A towards Yellowstone. When the sound of passing cars kept Dorothy Hustead awake one hot afternoon as she tried to nap, she hit upon a plan to make those drivers stop.

Free ice water. Even though it meant cutting 150 pound blocks of ice during the long South Dakota winter and storing them to last throughout the summer, the Husteads figured their ice water giveaways would be a hit. And to make sure the travelers knew about the ice water, Mrs. Hustead put out a few signs.

"It was embarrassing, but it sure brought in business," recalls son Bill Hustead, now the pharmacist at Wall Drug. His mother put signs on the road from Denver, then branched out to other neighboring states. Before long, the highways were dotted with Wall Drug ads. Today, the operation has over 3,000 signs across the fifty states.

During World War II, Wall Drug went international. When the local bank cashier headed to duty in Europe, he decided to do some promotion. Soon

Learn A Few Words in Sioux

Animals
bear: ma to
cat: ig mu
coyote: 'sung ma he tu
crow: kan 'gi
deer: ta 'hca
dog: 'sun ka
eagle: wam bli
horse: 'sun ka wa kan
wolf: 'sung manitu tan ka

Numbers
one: wan ji
two: nu pa
three: ya mni
four: to pa
five: zap tan
six: 'sa kpe
seven: 'sa ko win
eight: 'sa glo 'han
nine: ne p'cun ka
ten: wi k'ce mna

Hello friend!: How kola!

signs such as "81 kilometers to Frankfurt, 17 kilometers to Mannheim, 4321 miles to Wall Drug Store" began appearing on U.S. military bases.

At the end of the war, ex-G.I.'s who had seen those signs brought their families through the area on vacation. Word of Wall Drug spread. Today the drug store dominates the tiny town of Wall (population 800), and employs over 200 workers in retail and food service.

What began as a store carrying a few extra items for the tourist trade has now turned into a virtual mall of Western goods. Inside the doors of Wall Drug, visitors find themselves on a recreated Western street, with stores featuring cowboy boots, western hats, western artwork, and books. Popular Black Gold jewelry, produced in South Dakota, is sold at the store as well, featuring tri-color gold designs of grapes and leaves. A restaurant seats 500 and offers local specialties like buffalo burgers.

In case you find that traveling hasn't agreed with you, there's still a pharmacy at Wall Drug. The apothecary downstairs is museum replica of the early drug store but upstairs Bill Hustead dispenses drugs as three generations of his family have done since 1890.

"I feel that Wall Drug keeps alive one of the most wholesome institutions in America today – the small Western drug store," says Hustead. And to bring tourists in to prove it, he's still following mom's advice: give 'em free ice water. Be sure to pick up your free cup of ice water when you visit as well as one other freebie: your own Wall Drug sign to take home and post like the millions of others before you.

For more information on **Wall Drug Store**, write Wall Drug, 510 Main Street, Wall, SD 57790, *Tel. 605/279-2175*. Wall Drug is open 7 days a week from 6:30am-6pm except Thanksgiving, Christmas and New Year's Day.

Which One Is My Room?

Most visitors at Badlands come as day trippers, arriving from the Black Hills area. If you want to extend your stay, however, you will find nearby lodging.

In the park, lodging is available at **Cedar Pass Lodge**, *Tel. 605/433-5460*, from mid-May through mid-October. The lodge offers 24 individual cabins with air conditioning, showers, linens, (but no cooking facilities. A cottage home with two bedrooms, kitchen, dining and living room and a fenced yard is available. You might also want to add that the restaurant offers Native American food such as Indian fry bread and buffalo tacos.

Cedar Pass is also home to a campground, available for $10 per night in the summer, $8 in winter. Available on a first come, first served basis. Accommodations are also available in nearby **Wall**, *Tel. 888/852-9255*.

Practical Information

Address: Badlands National Park, PO Box 6, Interior, SD 57750
Telephone: *605/433-5361*

Operating Season: year round
Hours: open 24 hours day
Cost: $10 per car
Website: *www.nps.gov/badl/index.htm*

Learning About the Badlands

Marsh, Carole. *South Dakota: Indians.* Gallopade Publishing Group, 1995. Ages 9-12.

Marsh, Carole. *South Dakota Facts and Factivities.* Gallopade Publishing Group, 1996. Ages 9-12.

Marsh, Carole. *South Dakota History!: Surprising Secrets About Our State's Founding Mothers, Fathers & Kids!* Gallopade Publishing Group, 1996. Ages 9-12.

Fort Scott National Historical Site
Kansas

The distant echo of a bugle playing reveille still lingers in the air around this army post, which was built in the 1840's to maintain peace during the westward expansion movement, and a thirty- star American flag still watches over the twenty historic buildings and five acres of restored tall grass.

Are We There Yet?

The park is located 90 miles south of Kansas City at the intersection of US 69 and US 54.

What's There To Do Here?

A short audiovisual presentation will give you an overview of the fort's history, and exhibits ranging from items used in a soldier's daily life to the simple childhood toys used by the boys and girls from a bygone era help bring into focus the lives of these frontier people. Special events are held throughout the year, including a Fourth of July Weekend, when families can participate in tug of war and sack races together, and in September children can watch and possible even participate in an authentic Native American dance during the American Indian Heritage Weekend.

The park contains 20 historic buildings and five acres of restored tall grass prairie. You can enjoy self-guided tours of the historic buildings and have a look at interpretive exhibits. There's a short AV program that will give you the history of the fort as well.

When you're ready for a walk, you'll find a short trail that winds through the prairie.

When Are We Going?
Summer is the busiest time at the park, but you'll find spring and fall months very pleasant.

How Long Are We Staying?
The park is small so just budget about an hour for an overview of the facilities.

Which One Is My Room?
There are no accommodations in the park. For local lodging, call the city of **Fort Scott,** *Tel. 800/245-FORT* or see *www.fortscott.com.*

Where Are We Going Next?
Let Dolley The Trolley be your hostess as Historic Trolley Tours introduces your family to all the sites the town of Fort Scott has to offer. An hour long narrated tour passes by not only Fort Scott National Historic Site, but also takes you back to a gentler time with a display of Victorian architecture found in both the scenic downtown area and on the facades of the mansions which grace the town. For further information contact Historic Trolley Tours, 231 E. Wall Street, Fort Scott, KS 66701 or call *800/245-3678.*

Only 100 miles away is the Harry S. Truman National Historic Site, where items ranging from political memorabilia to sentimental objects such as daughter Margaret's dolls and the wicker rocking chair used by Truman's grandmother draw an intimate portrait of the nation's thirty-third president. Tours of both the Truman home in Independence MO, a majestic Victorian structure referred to as the "summer White House" during Truman's years in office, and the farm home in Grandview, a place where Truman's ideals were sculpted as he labored there as a young man, are available. For visitor information, contact *816/254-9929* or write Harry S. Truman National Historic Site, 223 North Main Street, Independence, MO 64050-2804, *email HSTR_Superintendent@nps.gov* or see *www.nps.gov/hstr/index.htm.*

Practical Information
  Address: Fort Scott National Historic Site, PO Box 918, Fort Scott, KS 66701-0918
  Telephone: *620/223-0310*
  Operating Season: year round
  Hours: Daily 8am-5pm April through October and daily 9am-5pm rest of year. Closed Thanksgiving, Christmas, and New Year's Day.
  Cost: $3.00 per adult 17 and over
  Website: *www.nps.gov/fosc/index.htm*

George Washington Carver National Monument
Missouri

The life of George Washington Carver can be an inspiration to all young children, so this site is highly recommended. Carver was born on this farm as a slave, orphaned and often ill as a child, yet he went on to become a great scientist, inventor, and educator.

Are We There Yet?

From Neosho or Carthage, take US 71 alternate to Diamond. Take State Highway V for two miles west to County Road 16Q. Go south for one mile.

What's There To Do Here?

Start your visit with a tour of the visitors center for an overview of the life of George Washington Carver. From there, enjoy a stroll along the Carver Trail, which winds for three-fourths of a mile through undeveloped land that's changed little since the days when Carver roamed this area as a child. The trail goes by the site of his birthplace, and although the cabin no longer exists you can still see the remnants of the cramped fourteen by fourteen foot quarters that was once his home.

Take a moment to commune with nature at a statue of the inventor as a boy, then visit the spring where he retrieved water for the Carver family. Williams Spring is home to a variety of wildlife, and Paris remembers seeing a beaver along this trail when she visited here as a child. A stop by the Moses Carver house is next— George Washington Carver stayed in this tiny structure several times when he returned to visit the place of his birth. Moses and Susan Carver are buried in the family cemetery, which is also on the trail.

When Are We Going?

The peak months for visitation are May through July. During the summer months, expect temperatures to be hot so bring hats and sunscreen, especially if you'll be taking the walking trail.

How Long Are We Staying?

You'll want to budget about two hours to tour the house and take the walking trail.

What Should I Bring?

Don't forget good walking shoes for the trail.

Which One Is My Room?

There is no camping in the park but you'll find accommodations in nearby **Diamond**, *Tel. 417/325-4220*; **Neosho**, *Tel. 417/451-1925;* and **Carthage**, *Tel. 417/358-2373.*

Where Are We Going Next?

The battlefield at **Pea Ridge National Military Park**, located 105 miles from the George Washington Carver National Monument, is a virtual time capsule of the Civil War era. You can almost hear the echo of the cannons which are still sprinkled throughout the land, and reenactors in military uniform add to this portrait of life during a time of war. A 28-minute film, "Thunder In The Ozarks" and museum at the **Visitor Center** explains the significant struggle which occurred in this area in 1862, and a drive through the battlefield takes you past ten spots of interest, including the **Elkhorn Tavern** historic structure, which was once used as a field hospital. For nature lovers, a hiking trail lets you soak in the scenic enchantment of this area. For further information, call *501/451-8122* or write Pea Ridge National Military Park, P.O. Box 700, Pea Ridge, AR 72751-0700 or *email PERI_Interpretation@nps.gov*.

Less than two hours away from Diamond, Missouri is the city of **Branson**, recognized as "the live music show capital of the world." Branson offers several large family-oriented attractions, such as **Silver Dollar City** and **The Shepherd of The Hills**, but there is also a variety of entertainment at smaller venues guaranteed to entertain adults and children.

Take a nostalgic trip back to the days when the good guys wore white hats at **The Roy Rogers- Dale Evans Museum**. A vast array of memorabilia ranging from Roy Rogers comic books and toy guitars to the fanciful costumes worn by this beloved western star is on display. Children under the age of six

George Washington Carver Quotations

"How far you go in life depends on you being tender with the young, compassionate with the aged, sympathetic with the striving and tolerant of the weak and the strong. Because someday in life you will have been all of these."

"Ninety-nine percent of the failures come from people who have the habit of making excuses."

"Anything will give up its secrets if you love it enough. Not only have I found that when I talk to the little flower or to the little peanut they will give up their secrets, but I have found that when I silently commune with people they give up their secrets also—if you love them enough."

"I love to think of nature as an unlimited broadcasting station, through which God speaks to us every hour, if we will only tune in."

"Reading about nature is fine, but if a person walks in the woods and listens carefully, he can learn more than what is in books, for they speak with the voice of God."

"When you do the common things in life in an uncommon way, you will command the attention of the world."

are admitted free, $8.90 for children ages six through twelve and $14.40 for those thirteen and up. Open 9am- 6pm. Closed Easter Sunday, Thanksgiving, and December 22-25 and December 29-January 1. For a recorded message call *417/339-1900* or see *www.royrogers.com,* or write Roy Rogers-Dale Evans Museum, 3950 Green Mountain Dr., Branson, MO 65616.

Children of all ages will love **The World's Largest Toy Museum**, where thousands of playthings from the 1800's to present day are on display. Share your memories of your favorite cuddly teddy bear or toy train with your children as you stroll through the displays on your own or take a guided tour. Open Mondays through Saturdays. For further information call *417/332-1499* or write 3609 West Hwy 76, Branson, MO 65616.

Two thousand butterflies greet you at **The Butterfly Place**, a 9,000-square-foot. glass building where butterflies from around the globe flutter past in a rainbow of color. Children learn about the life cycle of these beautiful insects in a continuously running video presentation and witness the "birth" of a butterfly in the emergence room, where they break free from their chrysalids. The Butterfly Place is located at 2400 State Highway 165 in Branson; for more information, call *417/332-2231.*

Special Events at G.W. Carver National Monument

Ranger programs are operated in the summer months, usually twice a day, and cover both the environment and Carver's life. Throughout the year, the park also celebrates many holidays and special dates with programs ranging from Black History Month in February to Carver Day in July to Holiday Open House in December.

Practical Information
Address: *George Washington Carver National Monument, 5646 Carver Rd., Diamond, MO 64840*
Telephone: *417/325-4151*
Operating Season: *Year round; closed Thanksgiving, Christmas, New Year's Day*
Hours: *9am-5pm daily*
Cost: *free*
Website: *www.nps.gov/gwca/index.htm*

Learning about George Washington Carver
The Story of George Washington Carver. Scholastic Trade, 1991. Baby-preschool.

Benitez, Miena and Meryl Henderson (Illustrator). *George Washington Carver: Plant Doctor.* Raintree/Steck-Vaughn, 1989. Ages 4-8.

George Washington Carver. Chelsea House Publishers, 1998. Ages 9-12.
Moore, Eva and Alexander Anderson (Illustrator). *The Story of George Washington Carver.* Scholastic Paperbacks, 1995. Ages 4-8.

Herbert Hoover National Historic Site
Iowa
The 31st president of the United States is remembered at this park which includes his birthplace. Several historic buildings are also found in the park.

Are We There Yet?
From Iowa City, head east on I-80 to West Branch and take exit 254. The park is 4/10 of a mile away.

What's There To Do Here
Hoover's life and times are well represented on this 186 acre site. Begin at the visitor center, which offers exhibits on the region as well as a twelve minute orientation film, then move on to the Birthplace Cottage, a cozy two room structure built by Hoover's father and grandfather. Sadly, Hoover's father died at a young age, leaving his son with few memories. One of his recollections was of playing outside his father's blacksmith shop, and a recreation of Mr. Hoover's establishment is on display.

Two important elements in the lives of those of the Quaker faith were the practice of their religion and education, and you can tour a one room schoolhouse and Quaker meeting house. You may be surprised to find a large bronze statue of Isis on the grounds— this was a gift from the people of Belgium in recognition of Hoover's aid during WWI.

The highlight of the park is the Presidential Library-Museum. Begin at the rotunda and see the map of the world made of red granite. Exhibits at the

Herbert Hoover Facts
- Hoover was the youngest graduate in Stanford University's first graduating class.
- His family and friends called him "Bert". His brother Theodore was known as "Tad" and his sister Mary was called "May."
- Hoover received a total of 84 honorary degrees in his lifetime.
- He was the first president to donate his salary to charity.
- Herbert Hoover was of the Quaker faith.
- He was the first president to have an asteroid named in his honor.
- Herbert Hooker spoke Chinese.

museum trace Hoover's life through his presidential years. Before you go, stop by the final resting place of Herbert Hoover and his wife.

When Are We Going?
Summer is the peak time for a visit to this park, although conditions are pleasant in spring and fall as well.

How Long Are We Staying?
The park doesn't take long to see. Budget one or two hours for a look at the cottage and the library.

Where Are We Going From Here?
The community of West Branch, located nearby has many historic buildings and nice country restaurants. West Branch Chamber of Commerce, City of West Branch, P.O. Box 218, 304 East Main Street, West Branch, Iowa 52358 or call *319/643-5888*.

Winterset, only 2 1/2 hours away, is the home town of Hollywood royalty, and any wild west lover in your family will enjoy **John Wayne's Birthplace**. See the four-room childhood home of The Duke as well as such tinsel town memorabilia as the famous eyepatch from True Grit, the cowboy hat worn in Rio Lobo and a suitcase used in the classic western Stagecoach. Open seven days a week from 10am-4:30pm. Adults $2.50 children 12 and under $1. 216 S. 2nd Street, *Tel. 515/462-1044*.

Dyersville, about two hours away, can also boast of a Hollywood connection. Just like the characters in the movie, your family can play ball at the Field of Dreams Movie Site. Open from April through November from 9am-6pm, no admission charge. Located at 28963 Lansing Rd. Call toll free *888/875-8404*.

While in Dyersville you should also visit the **National Farm Toy Museum**, with over 30,000 farming-related toys on display. Open 7 days a week from 8am-7pm. Admission: $4 adults, $1 for children 6-11, children 5 and under admitted free. 1110 16th Ave. Ct. SE. Call *563/875-2727*.

Any doll enthusiast will love **Dyer-Botsford Doll Museum**, a Victorian home which houses over 1,000 dolls, a replica of a 1850 castle, and a revolving German Christmas tree. Open May through November 10am-4pm weekdays,

Happy Hooverfest!
One of the busiest times at the park is Hooverfest, held the first weekend in August. The event celebrates President Hoover's birthday and includes crafts demonstrations and fireworks.

and 1pm-4pm Saturday and Sunday. Located at 331 1st Ave. East. Call *563/ 875-2414*.

Which One Is My Room?

There is no lodging at the park but you will find some accommodations nearby, including:

The Presidential Motor Inn, West Branch, *Tel. 319/643-2526*
The Inn Nearby the Wapsinonoc, West Branch, *Tel. 319/643-7484*
Highlander Inn & Convention Center, Iowa City, *Tel. 319/354-2000*
Econolodge, West Liberty, *Tel. 319/627-2171*

Practical Information

Address: Herbert Hoover National Historic Site, PO Box 607, West Branch, IA 52358
Telephone: *319/643-2541*

Did You Know.....?

The capital of Iowa is Des Moines.
The state bird is the Eastern Goldfinch.
Iowa is the only state with a name that starts with two vowels.
The official state flower is the Wild Prairie Rose.
Iowa's motto is "Our liberties we prize and our rights we will maintain."
Iowa's nickname is the Hawkeye State.
The official state tree is the oak.
The state song is The Song of Iowa.
Many famous people were born in Iowa including:
Johnny Carson— TV personality (born in Corning)
William "Buffalo Bill" Cody— Pony Express rider and showman (born in Le Claire)
Mamie Dowd Eisenhower— former first lady (born in Boone)
Bob Feller— member of the Baseball Hall of Fame (born in Van Meter)
Fred Grandy— TV star ("The Love Boat") and politician (born in Sioux City)
Ann Landers— advice columnist (born in Sioux City)
Glenn Miller— big band leader (born in Clarinda)
Donna Reed— TV and movie star (born Donnabelle Mullenger in Denison)
Abigail Van Buren— advice columnist (born in Sioux City)
John Wayne— legendary movie cowboy (born Marion Robert Morrison in Winterset)
Elijah Wood— actor who starred in "The Lord of The Rings" (born in Cedar Rapids)
Grant Wood— artist who painted "American Gothic" (born in Anamoso)

Operating Season: year around; closed Thanksgiving, Dec. 25, Jan. 1
Hours: 9am- 5pm daily
Cost: $4 per adult age 17 and over (free for kids)
Website: *www.nps.gov/heho/index.htm*

Hot Springs National Park
Arkansas

The city of Hot Springs is named for the centerpiece of this park— you guessed it, hot springs. There are nearly 50 hot springs at "The American Spa", a nickname for this region. The oldest park in the National Park system (Yellowstone comes in second) has long lured travelers for treatment of arthritis.

Are We There Yet?

Hot Springs National Park is easy to find–it's located downtown in the city of Hot Springs. The park is located on Bathhouse Row on Central Avenue; national park signs lead the way from throughout the city.

What's There To Do Here?

The visitors center is housed in the former **Fordyce Bathhouse**, a Spanish Renaissance Revival style structure which is one of eight bathhouses that once filled Bathhouse Row. In its time, the Fordyce boasted elegant mosaic floors and stained glass windows.

Approximately 26 miles of hiking trails wind through the park. At only half a mile in length, the **Grand Promenade**, a pathway of red and yellow bricks which makes its way behind Bathhouse Row, is an easy stroll. For a more vigorous excursion try the Peak Trail, which takes you to the top of Hot Springs Mountain and Mountain Tower. Kids can take part in a Junior Ranger Program at the visitor's center as well.

When Are We Going?

The summer months are the peak time for a visit to this park. Dress coolly during these months; temperatures can be hot and humid.

How Long Are We Staying?

You'll want about half a day for a look around the park.

What Should I Bring?

Bring comfortable walking shoes for strolling along Bathhouse Row and sunglasses and a hat during summer months.

Did You Know.....?

- Alma, Arkansas is considered the Spinach Capital of The World.
- The first Wal-Mart opened its doors in Bentonville.
- The state bird is the mockingbird.
- The official state instrument is the fiddle.
- Arkansas is the only Northamerican state where diamonds are found and mined.
- The diamond shape on the state flag symbolizes this fact.
- The state motto is "regnat populus", which translates as "the people rule."
- The Natural State is the nickname for Arkansas.
- Milk is the state beverage.
- The name Arkansas derived from the Sioux word "acansa," which means "downstream place."
- Stuttgart, Arkansas is home to the yearly World's Championship Duck Calling Contest.
- The apple blossom is the state flower.
- The Loblolly Pine is the state tree.
- Little Rock is the state capital.
- Many famous people were either born or raised here, including:

Bill Clinton— 42nd president
Johnny Cash— singer/songwriter
Patsy Montana— country singer
General Douglas MacArthur
Barry Switzer— football coach
John Grisham— author
K.T.Oslin— country singer
Glen Campbell— country singer
Al Green— singer
Scott Joplin— ragtime musician
Billy Bob Thornton— actor
Paul "Bear" Bryant— football coach
Maya Angelou— author of "I Know Why The Caged Bird Sings"
Dee Alexander Brown— author of "Bury My Heart At Wounded Knee"
Charlie Rich— country singer
Conway Twitty— country singer
Scottie Pippin— basketball player

Which One Is My Room?

Camping is available at Gulpha Gorge Campground. Hot Springs offers plenty of hotel and motel options, call *800/SPA-CITY* for information. No showers or hookups, however modern restrooms are available. No reservations are allowed. Fee is $10 per night.

What Are We Doing Next?

Magic Springs Theme Park and **Crystal Falls Water Park** provides two attractions for the price of one! The brave at heart can ride the Arkansas Twister roller coaster and Rum Runner Pirate Ship while youngsters will enjoy the Kit 'N Kaboodle train ride, Fearless Flyers and the carousel. Crystal Falls offers a respite from the heat of an Arkansas summer with a wave pool and splash zone. Located in the Ouachita Mountains in Hot Springs National Park. Admission $31.99 plus tax for adults, $19.99 plus tax for children and toddlers under 2 admitted free. Open weekends only in April and May and May through September, open daily during the summer months.

Practical Information

Address: Hot Springs National Park, PO Box 1860, Hot Springs, AR 71902-1860

Telephone: *501/624-2701*

Operating Season: year round; closed Thanksgiving, Christmas, New Year's Day

Hours: 9am-5pm daily; occasionally hours are extended during summer months

Cost: Free

Website: *www.nps.gov/hosp/index.htm*

Indiana Dunes National Lakeshore
Indiana

The lakeshore, located on the southern shore of Lake Michigan, offers both historic and natural attractions ranging from a working 1900-type farm to pristine dunes.

Are We There Yet?

Located 50 miles southeast of Chicago, the park is accessible from I-94 or Indiana Toll Road I-80/90. Take the exit for US 49 North and continue to US 12. Continue and follow the signs to the park.

What's There To Do Here?

You'll find plenty of activity options in this busy park including:

• **Hiking**—There are over forty-five miles of trails to choose from with views of the dunes and forest. Two of the easiest to maneuver are the Heron Rookery Trail, a two mile walk through farmland which will be of particular interest to bird watchers, and the Pinhook Bog Trail, a 0.75 mile ranger-guided hike.

- **Fishing**—You can fish along the shores of Lake Michigan or in the Little Calumet River but you will need an Indiana State fishing license.
- **Swimming**—There are three beaches manned by lifeguards from mid-May through Labor Day, a great option for families. **West Beach** offers the most facilities including concessions, showers and a picnic area.
- **Dune Climbing**—Kids can climb along the marked dune trails in West Beach and Mt. Baldy.
- **Chellberg Farm**—This inviting 1900's brick farmhouse was home to three generations of the Chellberg family, and it is an opportunity for children to learn about life at the turn of the century.

When Are We Going?

Summer is the best time to visit the park, although late spring and fall months can be pleasant as well.

How Long Are We Staying?

You can see the highlights of the park in just a couple of hours or, to really get a feel for the park, you can make it a longer stay.

Which One Is My Room?

If you get lucky, you just might get a campsite at the **Dunewood Campground**, the only one at the lakeshore park. You can't make reservations but you can get there early for your best chance at one of the 79 sites. The campground includes hot water showers.

You'll also find accommodations at the state park and in nearby Beverly Shores, Chesterton, Michigan City and Portage, Indiana.

Where Are We Going Next?

Indianapolis is less than three hours away from Porter, IN and there you will find **The Children's Museum of Indianapolis**, a treasure trove of over 100,000 artifacts depicting the beauty of diverse cultures . Broaden your child's horizons with displays of toys and festive costumes from around the globe. Exhibits, many of which are hands-on, are constantly changing. The museum is open seven days a week from March 1 to Labor Day and six days a week (Tuesday through Sunday) from Labor Day through February. Hours are 10am-5pm. Closed Easter, Thanksgiving, and Christmas Day. Admission is $9.50 for adults and $4 for children. *Tel. 317/334-3322*, Address: 3000 N. Meridian St., Indianapolis, IN 46208-4716, *www.childrensmuseum.org/catalog/home.asp*.

Ride The Raven, considered the number one wooden roller coaster in the world, at **Holiday World** in Santa Claus, IN, less that six hours from Porter.

This theme park, which is open in the summer months, has been entertaining children for over half a century, and offers such rides as the Raging Rapids and Rough Riders bumper cars.

Let the kids take the wheel as they drive through the **Doggone Trail** on track-guided jeeps. Younger visitors will be enchanted by the Freedom Train as it chugs through Mother Goose Land, and tots will love the merry-go-round at **Rudolph's Reindeer Ranch** and Holidog's Treehouse in **Holidog's Fun Town**. For further information call toll free *877/Go-Family (877/463-2645)* or write Holiday World and Splashin' Safari P.O. Box 179, Santa Claus, IN 47579, *email: fun@holidayworld.com; www.holidayworld.com.*

Practical Information

Address: Indiana Dunes National Lakeshore, 1100 North Mineral Springs Rd., Porter, IN 46304

Telephone: *219/926-7561 ext 225*

Operating Season: year around; closed Thanksgiving, Dec. 25, Jan. 1

Hours: Visitors center open 8am-4:30pm (until 6pm in summer)

Cost: free; fees for beaches

Website: *www.nps.gov/indu/index.htm*

Did You Know.....?

• The creator of the comic strip Garfield, Jim Davis, hails from Indiana?

• Many famous people were born in this state, including movie star James Dean, basketball player Larry Bird and late night talk show host David Letterman.

• Indiana's motto is "The crossroads of America."

• The state song is "On The Banks of The Wabash."

• Indiana's state flower is the peony.

• The official state tree is the yellow poplar, and sitting upon a branch of a poplar you might see a cardinal, which is the state bird.

• The origin of Indiana's name is "Land of The Indians."

• The state capital is Indianapolis.

• Indiana's nickname is the Hoosier State.

Learning About Indiana

Fradin, Dennis Brindell and Judith Bloom Fradin. *Indiana* (From Sea to Shining Sea). Children's Press, 1997. Ages 9-12.

Major, Charles. *The Bears of Blue River*. Indiana University Press, 1984. Ages 9-12.

Swain, Gwenyth. *Indiana* (Hello U.S.A). Lerner Publications Co., 1997. Ages 9-12.

Wyman, Andrea. *Red Sky at Morning*. Holiday House, 1991. Ages 9-12.

Isle Royale National Park
Michigan

For those who dream of a forested land tucked in amid an enormous lake, this is it. Isle Royale is as wild as this country gets: search for a moose, take out a canoe, listen for birds in the forest, climb a lighthouse for a view of this massive lake, fish for your own dinner. This beautiful park is a great summer destination for families eager to enjoy nature.

Are We There Yet?

The park is located in Lake Superior 17 miles southeast of Grand Portage, Minnesota or 45 miles north of Copper Harbor, Michigan.

What's There To Do Here?

Walkers and hikers will be especially happy here thanks to the park's 165 miles of trails around the island. Also, canoeing is a very popular activity here.

Don't miss the visitor centers at **Rock Harbor** and **Windigo** for more information about the natural history of the region.

A sightseeing cruise on the lake is a wonderful activity for everyone. Operated by National Parks Concessions Inc., these sightseeing boats offer a peek at many sights you can only see from the water. Call **National Parks Concessions Inc.**, *906/337-4993* in the summer, or *502/773-2191* in the winter.

When Are We Going?

The peak time for visitors is July and August, the warmest season. The park, in fact, closes during the winter months. Fall and spring are quiet times with limited transportation services.

How Long Are We Staying?

You'll want to budget several days to enjoy this park. The natural attractions here have to be taken at a leisurely pace.

What Should I Bring?

Everyone should bring along layers, even during the summer months. At this latitude, summer evenings can be chilly, especially if there's a breeze on the lake. Rain gear is a good idea as well to protect against summer downpours. Insect repellent is also important in the summer months.

Did You Know.....?

• The name Michigan originated from the Chippewa Indian word "meicigama", which means "great water."

• Michigan has two nicknames— The Wolverine State and The Great Lakes State.

• The state motto is "Si quaeris peninsulamamoenam, circumspice", which translates as "If you seek a pleasant peninsula, look about you."

• The state flower is the apple blossom.

• The robin is the state bird.

• The state reptile is the painted turtle.

• Detroit is considered to be The Car Capital of The World.

• "Michigan, My Michigan" is the state song.

• The official state tree is the Eastern White Pine.

• Isle Royale Park is home to one of the largest moose herds in the United States.

• The state capital is Lansing.

• Many famous people have either been born or raised in Michigan including:

Ellen Burstyn— actress
Francis Ford Coppola— director
Edna Ferber— author
Henry Ford— industrialist
Charles A. Lindbergh— aviator
Madonna— singer
Gilda Radner— comedian
Della Reese— singer/actress
Diana Ross— singer
Steven Seagal— actor
Bob Seger— singer
Lily Tomlin— comedian
Danny Thomas— entertainer
Stevie Wonder— singer

Which One Is My Room?

You'll find tent camping on a first come, first serve basis. Lodging is also available at **Rock Harbor Lodge**, managed by the National Parks Concessions, Inc. *Call 906/337-4993* for information (May through September) and *270/773-2191* from October through April.

Where Are We Going Next?

Referred to as "Kitchi Onigaming," or "the Great Carrying Place" by the

Chippewa Indians, Grand Portage National Monument is a time capsule of the days of the voyageurs. Canoes of birchbark and cedar still sit on the banks near the remains of historic fur trade buildings. During the second weekend in August, reenactors bring these times back to life at the Grand Rendezvous, a celebration filled with period music, games and crafts which is held in conjunction with the Rendezvous Days Pow Wow. Grand Portage National Monument is only 14 miles away from Isle Royale. For further information call *218/387-2788*.

Practical Information
Address: Isle Royale National Park, 800 East Lakeshore Drive, Houghton, MI 49931

Telephone: *906/482-0984*

Operating Season: Open mid-April through the end of October

Hours: daily mid-April through Oct. 31 but full transportation services don't begin until mid-June and end after Labor Day

Cost: $4 per person; children 11 and under are free

Website: *www.nps.gov/isro/index.htm*

Learning About Lake Superior
Armbruster, Ann. *Lake Superior* (True Book). Children's Press, 1996. Ages. 9-12.

Curtis, Rebecca S. and Catherine Baer (Illustrator). *Charlotte Avery on Isle Royale*. Midwest Traditions, Inc., 1997. Ages 9-12.

Donohoe, Kitty et al. Bunyan and Banjoes: *Michigan Songs & Stories*. Thunder Bay Press, 1997.

Field, Ellyce. *Kids Catalog of Michigan Adventures* (Great Lakes Books). Wayne State University, 1995. Ages 4-8.

Hyde, Dayton O. and Emma Witmer (Illustrator). *The Bells of Lake Superior*. Boyds Mills Press, 1995. Ages 9-12.

Kalbacken, Joan . *Isle Royale National Park* (True Book). Children's Press, 1997. Ages 9-12.

Kantar, Andrew. *29 Missing: The True and Tragic Story of the Disappearance of the SS Edmund Fitzgerald*. Michigan State University Press, 1998. Young Adult.

Seymour, Tres. *The Gulls of the Edmund Fitzgerald*. Orchard Books, 1996. Ages 4-8.

Sivertson, Howard. *Once upon an Isle: The Story of Fishing Families on Isle Royale*. Silvertson Gallery, 1992. Young Adult.

Jefferson National Expansion Memorial
Missouri

When you fly into St. Louis, there's no missing it – the gleaming arch which looms over this Midwest city and the winding Mississippi River. Some said it could not be built.

The idea for a monument to commemorate the pioneers of the Westward Expansion movement began before World War II. The war brought the project to a halt until 1948, when Eero Saarinen was judged the winner of a $225,000 competition for the best memorial design. His inverted catenary curve design, in principle the strongest curve known, was the same shape which a heavy chain would take when suspended freely by two points.

But the choice of the memorial design was just the first step, because the **Gateway Arch** was truly a unique undertaking. The only other monument which would surpass it was the Eiffel Tower, and although about a dozen were longer, no bridge in the world was as tall as the proposed arch. A look at the measurements is astonishing. The sides of each of its triangular legs are 54 feet wide at the ground, tapering to 17 feet at the pinnacle. This gives the arch, which is 630 tall and 630 feet wide, the appearance of being much taller than it is wide.

Construction began in February 1961. From the outset, incredible exactness was required because the legs were built simultaneously. Even an error of a fraction of an inch at the base would have meant that the two sections could not have been joined when workers reached the top. Margin for error was a scant 1/64 of an inch.

To assure accuracy, nightly measurements were taken. Like the western explorers over a hundred years before, the workers took their readings by starlight. It was too risky for the measurement to be taken during the day, when shadows could have caused a miscalculation.

On Oct. 28, 1965, the last piece was lowered into place, and steamboats blew their whistles up and down the Mississippi. It was the completion of a 30 year project, and a 2-1/2 year construction job. Despite a grim prediction of the loss of 13 men, not a single life had been lost on the project.

Today, you'll find several hours worth of activities at the Gateway Arch. Underground, beneath the arch, lies the visitor center, the **Museum of Westward Expansion**, and tram rides to the top of the Arch. After spending a few moments contemplating this incredible structure, visit the visitor center for a look at how this memorial was built and, even more importantly, why it was built.

Are We There Yet?

You can't miss this park–just look for the silver arch. The park is located downtown right on the Mississippi River; parking is available at the **Arch Parking Garage** on Washington Street.

What's There To Do Here?

The Visitors Center shows Charles Guggenheim's film, *Monument to the Dream*, throughout the day to show visitors the often hair-raising work of the construction crews who put the arch into place. There's no better way to appreciate the precision and hard work the project required than to view the 35-minute documentary. Don't be surprised to hear more than one gasp during the film from your fellow movie-goers – some of the high-rise scenes are enough to make your palms sweat.

Nearby you can experience big-screen fun at the **Odyssey Theater**. This wide screen theater boasts a screen over four stories tall and features various specially produced films.

The **visitor center** welcomes three million visitors a year, and is just one part of a number of underground attractions. Unless you are claustrophobic, head for the tram rides, located beneath the north and south legs.

The trip up the arch is unlike any other tram ride you've ever taken. From the moment you enter one of the eight cars (which look like giant clothes dryer drums!), you know you're in for something different. Together with four other passengers, you'll make the four-minute journey up the Arch in a series of moves which prevent the cars from arriving at the observation area on their sides!

The ride up the arch may be somewhat cramped and stuffy, but step out on the observation area and you'll know it was all worthwhile. The totally enclosed area is eight feet wide and 64 feet long, with windows lining both sides for views eastward across the Mississippi into Illinois and westward across the sprawling city of St. Louis.

When you look west, you'll see all of downtown. **St. Louis–Busch Stadium**, the home of the Cardinals, Union Station, once the busiest railroad station in the country, and Forrest Park, location of the zoo.

But it's also possible to look out and imagine a much smaller St. Louis. This was once a city of steamboats, fur trappers, and explorers. The Gateway Arch is built on the very site of the original village of St. Louis, founded as a trading center in 1764 by Pierre LaClede. The frontier settlement outfitted Lewis and Clark for their three year exploration of the Louisiana Purchase, and later it was the last look of "civilization" the settlers had as they began their long journey west.

The history of these explorations is traced in the Museum of Westward Expansion, located near the Visitors Center. Thomas Jefferson stands at the entrance to the museum, looking out at the exhibits which trace the exploration of the West. Jefferson's foresight is responsible for the Louisiana Purchase, and he sent explorers Lewis and Clark on their famous journey to chronicle life in the West.

When you leave the underground museum and return to the sunshine reflecting off the 165,000 square feet of shining stainless steel, you may look to the West and remember Lewis and Clark and the hardy pioneers who braved the unknown wilderness. Or you may think of Eero Saarinen and the daredevil construction workers who completed a project that had never before been tried. The silver arch stands glimmering against the St. Louis sky as a tribute to all of these brave pioneers.

When Are We Going?

Peak season is during the summer months, although you can also expect to see school groups at the park during late spring. This is a busy park with over 4 million visitors last year, so come early in the day to avoid crowds.

How Long Are We Staying?

You'll want at least half a day to enjoy the **Museum of Westward Expansion**, watch the films, and ride to the top (allow time for long lines during the peak season). Allow extra time if you'll be touring the Old Courthouse.

What Should I Bring?

Most of the park is indoors, so just be comfortable. Binoculars are fun for viewing from the arch.

What Are We Doing Next?

Grants Farm, South St. Louis County, *Tel. 314/843-1700, www.grantsfarm.com*. Ulysses S. Grant once farmed on this land, and the log cabin he and his bride called home is on display today. A covered wagon is parked outside, as is a civil war cannon. This farm is now owned an operated by the Anheuser-Busch Company, and the emphasis here is on animals. Children can hand-feed camels and other exotic mammals at Tier Garten, watch wild deer grazing freely in Deer Park, and see an elephant and bird show.

Magic House, St. Louis Children's Museum, 516 S. Kirkwood, one mile north of 1-44 on Lindbergh, *Tel. 314/822-8900, www.magichouse.com*. This children's museum is a hands-on learning center.

St. Louis Carousel, Faust Park 15185 Olive Blvd. Chesterfield MO, *Tel. 636/537-0222*. We loved our ride on this 1920s carousel that has been lovingly restored. Don't fight over which horse you ride! The carousel is operational Wednesday through Sunday noon to 5pm and is located indoors, so weather is no problem. Carousel rides are $1, and the carousel is operational Tuesday through Sunday 10am-4pm.

St. Louis Science Center, 5050 Oakland Ave., *Tel. 314/289-4444, 800/ 456-SLSC x 4444, www.slsc.org*. This science center has several hours of activities, from an Omnimax Theater to a planetarium with laser shows.

Six Flags Over Mid-America, 30 minutes from the city on I-44, Allenton Exit, *Tel. 636/938-4800*. This theme park has lots of rides and activities for kids of all ages; open April through October.

St. Louis Zoological Park, Forest Park, *Tel. 314/781-0900, www.stlzoo.org*. This zoo is one of our favorites. It's large and, no matter what your child's favorite animal is, you'll probably find it here. Admission is free although there's a small charge for the children's zoo and the zoo train. Open daily 9am -5pm closed Thanksgiving, Christmas, and New Year's Day. Fee for children's zoo ($4), insectarium ($2), and carousel ($2).

Union Station, Market Street between 18th and 20th Sts., *Tel. 314/421-6655, www.stlouisunionstation.com*. This restored railroad station, which is an elegant reminder of yesterday's rail travel, has been restored to its full glory, with a 2,000 piece, Tiffany stained glass window representing the three main railroad areas of the country at that time: San Francisco, New York, and St. Louis.

In its heyday, the station saw over 100,000 travelers a day, but as rail travel diminished so did use of the station. In 1978, the last train pulled out and the station remained unused for several years, until a massive restoration project turned the station and the adjoining train shed (the largest single span shed in the world) into a festival marketplace with shops, restaurants, and even children's entertainment under the train shed.

Which One Is My Room?

The park is located right in the heart of downtown, where you'll find many good hotels. St. Louis is home to many excellent hotels within walking distance of the arch. The **Adam's Mark**, *Tel. 800/444-ADAM*, offers a club for children five through twelve. Adam's Marks Kids is free to the children of guests, and the club offers complimentary ice cream sundaes, cooking classes, and discounts on area attractions. For more information call *Tel. 314/342-4688*.

For more information, call the **St. Louis Convention and Visitors Commission,** *Tel. 800/916-8938, www.explorestlouis.com*.

Practical Information

Address: Jefferson National Expansion Memorial, 11 North 4th St., St. Louis, MO 63102

Telephone: *314/655-1700*

Operating Season: year around; closed Thanksgiving, Christmas and New Year's Day

Hours: Gateway Arch 8am to 10pm daily Memorial Day through Labor Day; 9am- 6pm the rest of the year. The Old Courthouse open daily from 8am- 4:30pm except Thanksgiving Christmas and New Year's Day.

Cost: The tram tickets are $8 for adults age 17 and over ($5 with a National Park Passport), $3 for children age 3-12, and $5 for youth ages 12-16. Tickets may be purchased online at *www.gatewayarch.com*.

Website: *www.nps.gov/jeff/index.htm, www.gatewayarch.com*

Did You Know.....?

• Many famous people have called Missouri home including author Mark Twain, former president Harry S. Truman, actress and dancer Ginger Rogers, and author Laura Ingalls Wilder, who penned the series of "Little House" books.

• In 1899 Congressman Willard Duncan Vandiver uttered the line "I'm from Missouri and you've got to show me." This phrase was the origin of Missouri's nickname, the "Show me state."

• Iced tea was invented at the St. Louis World's Fair of 1904.

• The bluebird is the official state bird.

• The official state flower is the hawthorn.

• Standing eight feet eleven inches in height, the tallest man in recorded history, Robert Pershing Wadlow, hailed from St. Louis.

• The capital of Missouri is Jefferson City.

• Missouri's motto is "the welfare of the people shall be the supreme law."

• The state animal is the mule.

• The state horse is the Missouri Fox Trotting Horse.

• The fiddle, which was used to entertain Missouri's earliest settlers, is the state musical instrument, and it is played today while people square dance, which is the official state folk dance,

Learning About the Arch & the Westward Expansion Movement

Doherty, Craig A. and Katherine M. Doherty. *The Gateway Arch* (Building America). Blackbirch Marketing, 1995. Ages 9-12.

Herb, Angela M. *Beyond the Mississippi: Early Westward Expansion of the United States* (Young Readers' History of the West). Lodestar Books, 1996. Ages 9-12.

Silverman, Jerry. *Singing Our Way West: Songs and Stories from America's Westward Expansion*. Millbrook Press, 1998. Ages 9-12.

Lincoln Boyhood National Memorial
Indiana

The boyhood of Abraham Lincoln is always fascinating to children. They can learn more about his childhood years in the farm town at this site. Lincoln's mother died when he was nine and is buried here at the farm.

Are We There Yet?

The park is located two miles east of Gentryville in the far southern reaches of the state. To reach Gentryville from I-64, take exit 57 for US 231. Continue south through Dale on US 231 to Gentryville, where you'll head east on Indiana Highway 162 for two miles.

What's There To Do Here?

There are several visitor sites at this park:

Memorial Visitor Center. This center includes a museum and two memorial halls for Abraham Lincoln and his mother, Nancy Hanks Lincoln. Children can explore exhibits about Lincoln's boyhood and the life the Lincoln family led as Indiana pioneers at a time when this part of the country was wilderness. There's a film about Lincoln's childhood days here as well.

Lincoln Living Historical Farm. This pioneer farm recreates the days of the 1820s with costumed rangers, cabins, farm animals, and gardens. It's a favorite stop with children. The farm is open daily from mid-April through September and weekends only in October.

Trails. There are three walking trails in the park. Of special interest is the Lincoln Boyhood Nature Trail.

When Are We Going?

Summer is the busiest time at this park.

How Long Are We Staying?

The National Park Service recommends about a two hour visit at this site.

What Should I Bring?

Good walking shoes and insect repellent are helpful if you're taking the trail.

Which One Is My Room?

You won't find any lodging or camping in the park, but overnight accommodations are available in the communities of **Dale**, *Tel. 812/937-4445,* and **Santa Claus**, *Tel. 812/937-2848.* **Lincoln State Park**, adjacent, offers campground facilities, *Tel. 812/937-4541.*

Practical Information

Address: Lincoln Boyhood National Memorial, PO Box 1816, Lincoln City, IN 47552

Telephone: *812/937-4541*

Operating Season: Year around, closed Thanksgiving, December 25, and January 1

Hours: 8am-6pm daily in summer, 8am-5pm in winter; closed Thanksgiving, Dec. 25, Jan. 1

Cost: $2.00 per person ages 17 and older or $4.00 per family.
Website: /www.nps.gov/libo/index.htm

Learning About Abraham Lincoln's Early Years

Brandt, Keith and John Lawn (Illustrator). *Abe Lincoln: The Young Years.* Troll Communications, 1989. Ages 9-12.

Brenner, Martha and Donald Cook (Illustrator). *Abe Lincoln's Hat* (Step into Reading : Step 2 Book, Grades 1-3) .Demco Media, 1994.

Harness, Cheryl. *Abe Lincoln Goes to Washington, 1837-1865.* National Geographic Society, 1997. Ages 9-12.

North, Sterling. *Abe Lincoln: Log Cabin to White House* (Landmark Books). Random House, 1987. Ages 9-12.

Schaefer, Lola M. *Abraham Lincoln.* Capstone Press, 1998. Ages 4-8.

Usel, T. M. *Abraham Lincoln.* Capstone Press, 1998. Ages 4-8.

Wellman, Sam. *Abraham Lincoln.* Barbour and Co., 1998. Young Adult.

Mount Rushmore National Memorial
South Dakota

The most recognized site in South Dakota, and one of the most in the entire West, is Mt. Rushmore National Memorial. No matter how many times you've seen those famous busts in films and photos, nothing can prepare you for the enormous scale of this project. Although visitors view the mountain from a distance, the busts of Washington, Jefferson, Lincoln and Roosevelt still seem to loom over the Visitors Center. A look at the dimensions and it's no wonder: the height of the figures from chin to forehead is 60 feet. The length of a nose is 20 feet; an eye is 11 feet across. And the mouths of these great giants? 18 feet wide each.

Admission to Mount Rushmore is free, and the park is open year around. You'll find the best viewing (and the smallest crowds) in the morning. Save time during your visit for a look through the Visitor's Center, with its continuous film on the project, and a visit to the sculptor's studio where you can learn more about **John Gutzon de la Mothe Borglum**. The son of Danish immigrants, Borglum started the project in 1927 – when he was 60 years old.

Are We There Yet?

You can't miss this park–just look for the carved mountain. It's located 24 miles from Rapid City (which is located off I-90). From Rapid City, take Highway 16 southwest to Keystone then Highway 244 to the park.

What's There To Do Here?

No, you can't climb the mountain. You can take a hike to the base of the mountain, though, called the **Presidential Trail**, a half-mile walk to the base of the mountain for a different perspective on the giant statues. The best view is from the Grandview Terrace. It's easy to find – just follow the Avenue of Flags, flags from each of the states and territories.

Be sure to save some time for the visitors center. The center, like the other facilities in the park, has recently been redeveloped and has new, expanded displays. Over 20 exhibits explain the monument, how it was made, and more about the workers and the sculptor.

When Are We Going?

The park is open year round but crowds peak in July and August. Avoid weekends if you can (especially the 4th of July weekend) and go early in the summer if possible.

The best time of day for viewing the mountain is usually morning, both to avoid crowds and to miss possible afternoon showers that sometimes develop during the summer months.

How Long Are We Staying?

You'll want at least two hours to view the visitors center, view the mountain, take a hike to the base of the mountain, and just experience the park.

What Should I Bring?

Sunscreen, sunglasses, hats, and good walking shoes are must-haves for summer visitors. Binoculars are a good items, too, for having a closer view of the mountain.

What Are We Doing Next?

Mt. Rushmore is tucked in the heart of the **Black Hills**, an area that's rich in visitor attractions.

Today the "capital" of the Black Hills region is Rapid City, the second largest community in South Dakota. It's a town filled with motels to accommodate the many family vacationers who head to these hills every year. The town is also dotted with shops selling "Black Hills jewelry" made from tri-color gold, alloys that produce gold, pink and green hues.

Just at the edge of Rapid City lies an unusual attraction that, while it may not be as well known as other Black Hills sites, should not be missed. **Reptile Gardens**, six miles south of Rapid City, *Tel. 800/335-0275, www.reptilegardens.com,* may sound like just another collection of lizards and snakes, but for over 50 years this family-owned attraction has delighted visitors with its huge collection of poisonous snakes and lizards from around the world, including king cobras, rattlesnakes, mambas, and bushmasters. You'll probably want to stop to have a look at the two story Sky Dome, home to free flying parrots and finches. Among the orchids and tropical greenery there are also a few harmless reptiles as well. Children enjoy riding on miniature horses and giant tortoises (and visiting Methuselah, a tortoise that had a role in the Disney movie, *Swiss Family Robinson*), watching alligator wrestling or a birds of prey exhibition, spying curious prairie dogs in their enclosed "town," and cuddling small creatures in the petting zoo.

To get an idea of what Mount Rushmore was like while under construction, make a stop at **Crazy Horse**, *Tel. 605/673-4681, www.crazyhorse.org,* a mountain sculpture in progress. Crazy Horse Memorial is located 15 minutes away from Mt. Rushmore. Like the well-known national landmark, the Crazy Horse sculpture is also a mountain carving, but it is being done in the round. When completed, it will be larger than its presidential neighbor. Currently this is the only mountain carving in the world in progress, and it is the only one to have ever been led by a woman. Ruth Ziolkowski, whose husband Korczak began the project over 50 years ago, now directs the work along with her children.

The memorial honors the Sioux leader Crazy Horse who defeated General Custer in the Battle of Little Big Horn. For generations, the Black Hills have been sacred to these Indians, so they felt this was an appropriate place to honor their leader.

Both Mount Rushmore and Crazy Horse are just minutes from another Black Hills attraction: **Custer State Park**, five miles east of Custer on US16A, *Tel. 605/255-44605, www.custerstatepark.info.* Although you may have never visited this 71,000-acre park, chances are you'll recognize some of its rolling hills and open prairies. The nation's largest state park has been used in movies including *How the West Was Won* and *Stagecoach*.

Today the park is a popular stop for the two million travelers who view Mount Rushmore every year. It is a welcome retreat for vacationers looking for quiet campsites, miles of hiking and walking trails, scenic vistas, bountiful wildlife, and a chance to see the beauty of the Black Hills. The park is so large that you'll feel like you're returning to the wild west and can imagine how the pioneers saw the land over a century ago.

For a view of the largest public buffalo herd in the western hemisphere, take a guided jeep tour. The herd was started here in the 1920's and has expanded to over 1400 head. The jeep tour follows the Wildlife Loop and onto some smaller park roads. You can drive the loop in your car as well (although you'll find some sections rough, and some park roads are not recommended for RVs and passenger cars). If you travel in your own vehicle, do not step out to approach buffalo. Bulls can weigh over 2000 pounds, jump a six foot fence, and run for 30-35 miles per hour for short distances. Although the buffalo are accustomed to vehicular traffic, they consider people on foot to be a threat and may charge unexpectedly.

If you're at the park in the evening hours, don't miss the **Evening Lighting Ceremony**. This 30-minute event is held at 9pm.

Mount Rushmore Quiz

How well do you know the president's on Mount Rushmore? Take this quiz to find out!

1. Which president had a pet mockingbird named Dick who lived in the White House?

2. Who was the first president to ride in an airplane?

3. Who was the only president who never lived in Washington DC ?

4. _____ was the first president to be born outside of the original thirteen colonies.

5. This president was blind in his left eye due to a boxing accident. Who was he?

6. Who was the first president to be honored with a postage stamp bearing his likeness?

7. President_____ loved to play the violin.

8. This president's favorite saying was "Bully!", which means "great!"

9. Edgar Allan Poe was one of the favorite authors of this president.

10. President _____ wore a ring to his inauguration which held a lock of Abraham Lincoln's hair.

11. He was the first president who was photographed at his inauguration. Who was he?

12. Seventeenamerican cities are named in honor of this president.

13. Over the course of his life, President _____ wrote over 20,000 letters.

14. The teddy bear was named after this president.

15. Who holds the record as the youngest president?

16. _____ was the first president who insisted on shaking hands instead of bowing.

17. This president's favorite sport was wrestling.

18. This president's inaugural speech was only ninety seconds long.

19. _____ had to borrow money in order to attend his own inauguration.

20. Who was the first president to win the Nobel Peace Prize?

ANSWERS

1. Thomas Jefferson
2. Theodore Roosevelt
3. George Washington
4. Abraham Lincoln
5. Theodore Roosevelt
6. George Washington
7. Thomas Jefferson
8. Theodore Roosevelt
9. Abraham Lincoln
10. Theodore Roosevelt

11. Abraham Lincoln
12. George Washington
13. Thomas Jefferson
14. Theodore Roosevelt
15. Theodore Roosevelt
16. Thomas Jefferson
17. Abraham Lincoln
18. George Washington
19. George Washington
20. Theodore Roosevelt

Which One Is My Room?

There are no accommodations or campsites in the park but you'll find plenty nearby. The Black Hills claim to have enough sites to bed 25,000 campers nightly and there's no shortage of motel rooms either. You'll find beautiful historic lodges in Custer State Park as well, so whatever your interest or budget, you can find a good home away from home.

Keystone is the community closest to Rushmore; for accommodation information call *800/456-3345, www.keystonechamber.com.* **Rapid City** is home to over 4,000 motel rooms; call the **Convention and Visitors Bureau,** *Tel. 800/487-3223 www.rapidcitycvb.com,* for information. **Custer**, *Tel. 800/ 992-9818,* has many campgrounds as well as motels. **Custer State Park**, *Tel. 605/255-4460,* has several lodges as well as B&Bs.

An excellent source of information on attractions, lodging and dining is the free "South Dakota Vacation Guide," available from **South Dakota Department of Tourism**, *Tel. 800/S-DAKOTA (800/732-5682).*

Practical Information

Address: Mount Rushmore National Memorial, 13000 Highway 244 Building 31, Suite 1 Keystone, SD 57751-0268

Telephone: *605/574-2523* headquarters; for visitor information recorded message *605/574-3171*

Operating Season: year round; closed Dec. 25

Hours: Summer 8am-10pm; winter 8am-5pm

Cost: free; $8 fee for parking

Website: *www.nps.gov/moru/index.htm*

Learning About Mt. Rushmore

Doherty, Craig A. and Katherine M. Doherty. *Mount Rushmore* (Building America). Blackbirch Marketing, 1995. Ages 9-12.

Rey, Margaret and H.A. Rey. *Curious George and the Hot Air Balloon.* Houghton Mifflin, 1998. Ages 4-8.

Sleeping Bear Dunes National Lakeshore Michigan

Tucked on the shore of Lake Michigan lies this hidden gem of a park. The park stretches not only along 35 miles of lakeshore, but it also takes in two islands: North and South Manitou Islands. There's a little bit of everything here, from beaches to forests to museums.

Are We There Yet?

The park is located west of Traverse City on M-72 or north from Frankfort on M-22. The visitors center is located on M-72 at the east end of Empire.

What's There To Do Here?

Make your first stop at the visitor's center in Empire (there's another small visitor's center out on South Manitou Island) for an overview of the park's many features. From there you can plan your course of action which might include:

Canoeing. Several operators rent equipment so you can paddle down the Crystal or Platte rivers.

Island hopping. Ferry service links the lakeshore to the islands.

Touring the historic farming district. You can also take a tour out on South Manitou Island of an historic farming area.

Hiking. There are over 55 miles of trails wind through the park.

Cross country skiing. Winter visitors can take advantage of those hiking trails, too - just strap on the skis.

Maritime Museum. Open Memorial Day through Labor Day from 10am-5pm. Exhibits on ships and shipwrecks. Children can "save" Raggedy Ann and Andy when they take part in a buoy rescue drill.

Pierce Stocking Scenic Drive. Pierce Stocking Scenic Drive is a 7 mile stretch offering views of Lake Michigan, The Sleeping Bear Dunes plateau and Manitou Islands

When Are We Going?

The months of July and August are the peak times for this park, but even then you won't find big crowds. The summer weather here is nice and comfortable. During the winter months, however, you'll find this an extreme place to visit; watch for snowstorms and below freezing temperatures.

How Long Are We Staying?

You'll want to budget most of a day for a complete look at the park, the visitor's center, and the museum.

The Tale of Sleeping Bear

According to Ojibway lore, long ago a Mother bear and her two cubs tried to swim to Michigan in an attempt to escape a forest fire. Although Mother Bear was able to reach their destination, her two little ones were not strong enough for the journey. The Great Spirit felt pity for the mother as she looked out on the waters of Lake Michigan, and he fashioned two islands where the cubs disappeared to honor her children, and a lone dune on the shore to represent the mother bear. This moving story is brought to life in the children's book The Legend of Sleeping Bear by Kathy-Jo Wargin, published by Sleeping Bear Press.

What Should I Bring?

Insect repellent, sunscreen, sunglasses, and good walking shoes are at the top of the list during the summer months. Bring along some layers, too, for chilly evenings.

Which One Is My Room?

The Platte River Campground, 179 sites available year round, has all the comforts of home: rest rooms, electric hookups, hot water showers, and more. $16 per night. For reservations, call *800/365-CAMP* or *231/325-5881* for more information. If you don't need all that, the D.H. Day Campground has outhouse-type toilets. Open from April through November on a first come, first served basis. 88 sites available, $12 per night. For further details call *231/334-4634*. Primitive camping is also available on the two islands.

Practical Information

Address: Sleeping Bear Dunes National Lakeshore, 9922 Front St., Empire, MI 49630

Telephone: *231/326-5134*

Operating Season: year round; closed Thanksgiving, Christmas, New Year's Day

Hours: Summer hours are 9am-6pm; other hours are 9:30am-4:00pm. Philip A. Hart Visitor Center hours are 9am-6pm in summer, 9am-4pm rest of year

Cost: $10 per week

Restrictions: dogs must be on a leash no longer than six feet and are not permitted on the Dune Climb or ski trails

Website: *www.nps.gov/slbe/index.htm*

Theodore Roosevelt National Park
North Dakota

Why is there a park in North Dakota for a New Yorker who served in Washington, DC? Because of his contributions to the conservation of North Dakota's resources. Theodore Roosevelt, who came to the region to hunt buffalo, later came back and started some cattle ranches. He began to notice that the number of wildlife was diminishing along with the grasslands and started conservation efforts for the new state.

Are We There Yet?

There are two units to the park, both in western North Dakota. To reach the South Unit Visitors Center, take I-94 for 135 miles west from Bismark. The North Unit Visitors Center is 16 miles south of Watford on US 85.

The North and South units are about 70 miles apart.

What's There To Do Here?

Loop drives and hikes are the top activities at both units. There's a 36-mile loop drive in the south unit which you can see after a tour of the **Medora Visitor's Center**. The north unit also has a visitors center plus some self-guided walks.

Behind the Medora Visitor's Center stands Theodore **Roosevelt's Maltese Cross Cabin**, a cozy house where the 26th president would wile away the hours in his favorite rocking chair or sitting at his desk, feverishly writing his book, "Hunting Trips of A Ranchman." These and other of Roosevelt's personal effects can be seen on a self-guided tour of the log cabin from September through May. During the summer months ranger-guided tours are available.

Theodore Roosevelt National Park is the perfect place to commune with nature, and you have the option of viewing the area in the manner favored by the former president— on horseback. Contact Peaceful Valley Ranch/Shadow Country Outfitters, *Tel. 701/623-4568*. Any way you choose to traverse the land you may find yourself lucky enough to come across a pack of wild horses or herd of bison running across the prairie. Although beautiful, these animals can be dangerous if provoked, so keep a respectful distance.

Young travelers between the ages of 6 and 12 can become a junior ranger while at the park. Stop by the visitors center for a booklet which includes activities for you to complete. You'll also attend a ranger-led program and hike a trail. Once you're done, return to the visitors center with the completed book to pick up your badge and certificate.

When Are We Going?

Summer months are the peak time for a visit. Winters can be extremely cold.

How Long Are We Staying?

You'll want at least a full day if you are going to stop by both units; plan on about half a day to visit a single unit.

What Should I Bring?

Bring a pair of binoculars for spotting wildlife.

Which One Is My Room?

Cottonwood Campground in the south unit is available for tent camping as well as trailers and RVs. There are water, sewer and electrical hook-ups available. No reservations are accepted for these 70 sites. The cost is $10 a night. Call *701/623-4466*.

Juniper Campground in the North Unit offers campsites for tents, trailers and RVs but does not have hook-ups. This campground is also on a first-come, first-served basis. Campgrounds are $10 a night from May through September, $5 a night October- April. Call *701/842-2333*.

Where Are We Going Next?
   Knife River Indian Villages is a 1,758-acre park which preserves the heritage of the Northern Plains Indians. Take a self-guided tour of three village sites and view a fifteen minute film which explores the lifestyle of the Hidatsa tribe.
   Located roughly 100 miles from Theodore Roosevelt State Park in Stanton, ND. Call *701/745-3300* for visitor information.
   Another nearby excursion is **Fort Union Trading Post National Historic Site**, a time capsule of the days of a bustling fur trade with numerous Native American tribes. Explore tipis, the Indian Trade House, and admire the view of the tranquil Missouri River. Many special events are held here each year, including the Labor Day Living History Weekend and the Indian Arts Showcase, a celebration of Native American culture complete with storytelling, traditional music, arts and crafts from the people from both North Dakota and Montana reservations. This event is held each August. For more information on Fort Union Trading Post contact *701/572-9083*.

Practical Information
   Address: Theodore Roosevelt National Park, Box 7, Medora, ND 58645
   Telephone: South Unit, *701/623-4466*; North Unit *701/842-2333*

Did You Know.....?
   • The Western Meadowlark is the state bird.
   • The state capital is Bismarck.
   • North Dakota has three nicknames: The Roughrider State, Flickertail State, and Peace Garden State.
   • "Liberty and Union, now and forever, one and inseparable" is the state motto.
   • Milk is the official state beverage.
   • North Dakota was named after the Dakota tribe.
   • The word Dakota translates as "friends."
   • North Dakota grows more sunflowers than any other state.
   • The state flower is the wild prairie rose.
   • The American Elm is the state tree.
   • Actress Angie Dickinson, singer Peggy Lee, author Louis L'Amour and band leader Lawrence Welk are only a few of the famous personalities from North Dakota.

Operating Season: year round; some areas may close due to weather
Hours: 24 hours daily. Visitor's center hours change seasonally. Contact Park for information
  Cost: $5 per person, maximum $10 per vehicle for 7-day pass
  Website: *www.nps.gov/thro/index.htm*

Voyageurs National Park
Minnesota

A great way to introduce your kids to this park is to ask "What's a *voyageur*?" Just so you know before you ask, a *voyageur* is a French-Canadian canoeist. These hearty explorers plied these waters in birch bark canoes, trading and exploring and opening up this region for later settlement.

Today this park is a favorite for water buffs. Canoeists can enjoy many different trips based on skill level, from short day trips to week-long excursions. This park is great for those who want to combine a love of nature with the thrill of canoeing, kayaking, boating, and fishing.

Are We There Yet?

Voyageurs is located on the US-Canada border. From Minneapolis-St. Paul, the park is a five hour drive; from Duluth the drive is three hours. If you are traveling from Winnipeg, the park is a three-hour drive.

To reach the park, travel to US 53 between Duluth and International Falls. There is an airport in International Falls.

What's There To Do Here?

Fishing. Fishing is one of the top activities at this park. Anglers are in search of walleye and these lakes are rated as some of the nation's best. You'll need a Minnesota fishing license.

Canoeing. Canoeing is a great way to see this region, slipping silently through the waters for a chance to spot wildlife and enjoy the solitude found in many reaches of this park.

Kayaking. You'll find many kayak excursions available; concessions rent equipment.

Boating. In Crane Lake you'll find several concessions offering boat rental; houseboat rentals are available in Crane Lake, Ash River, and International Falls.

Boat touring. Let someone else man the helm and enjoy a lake cruise on Rainy Lake or Lake Kabetogama. Several different cruises are offered including sunset cruises, naturalist cruises, and more.

Hiking. Miles of hiking trails wind through the forest and along the lakes.

Cross Country Skiing. Winter visitors can use 10 miles of groomed trails near the Rainy Lake Visitor Center. Seven miles of trails are available near the Kabetogama Lake Visitor Center.

Snowmobiling. This park is a favorite with snowmobilers thanks to the 110 miles of trails on the frozen lakes.

When Are We Going?

The summer months are the peak time to visit this park. Summers here are very temperate with highs ranging from 60 to 80 degrees. The summer evenings may find you plagued with mosquitoes, however.

Winter months definitely mean winter conditions here–this is a park only for true cold weather lovers and snowmobilers during the off peak season. Expect highs of only 10 to 30 degrees on many days. The lakes freeze during November.

How Long Are We Staying?

Because this isn't a park you just swing by on the way somewhere else, you'll want at least two or three days to enjoy the facilities.

What Should I Bring?

Don't forget the insect repellent! During the summer months we've found these pesky to be enough to drive you crazy. One summer while fishing in Minnesota we could literally see a cloud of mosquitoes hanging just inches from our repellent-smeared faces. Don't forget! If you're camping, you may want to bring citronella candles as well, the scent of which also repels mosquitoes.

Did You Know.....?

• Many famous people come from Minnesota, including Peanuts creator Charles Schulz, Walter Mondale, who was the 42nd vice-president, author F. Scott Fitzgerald, singer/songwriter Bob Dylan, actress Winona Ryder, and Judy Garland, who will be forever remembered as Dorothy in The Wizard of Oz.

• The state capital of Minnesota is Saint Paul.

• The state motto is "L'etoile du nord", which means "the star of the north."

• The monarch is the state butterfly.

• The name Minnesota comes from a Dakota Sioux word meaning "sky-tinted water."

• Scotch tape was invented in Minnesota, as was Wheaties cereal.

• The state song is *Hail! Minnesota*.

• The state flower is the pink and white lady's- slipper.

You'll also want to bring along layered clothing, even during the summer months when evenings can be downright chilly. Quick- drying shoes are helpful for boaters and canoeists.

What Are We Doing Next?

The **Boundary Waters Canoe Area Wilderness** is a good destination for those who just can't get enough canoeing. For more information, call the permit office, *Tel. 877/550-6777.*

Children will be over the rainbow when they tour the home of Dorothy herself, **Judy Garland**, who spent her early years in Grand Rapids, less than a three hours drive from International Falls. Open seven days a week from 10am-5pm, you can take a nostalgic look at the home where Judy first sang alongside her sisters and visit the Judy Garland museum adjacent to the house, where the carriage which bore Dorothy and her companions through Emerald City is on display along with other Wizard of Oz memorabilia, including Dorothy's pinafore dress. Admission is $5. For further information call *800-664-JUDY (5839)* or visit *www.judygarlandmuseum.com.*

Which One Is My Room?

The park offers 400 traditional campsites plus 150 boat-in sites. The sites are on a first-come, first-served basis and no reservations are taken. The good news? There's no fee for camping at the present time.

You'll find bear-proof containers at the campsites–*use them*. Black bears are found throughout the park and have a way of tracking down even small bits of food.

Another option is the **Kettle Falls Hotel**, 10502 Gamma Road, Lake Kabetogama, MN 56669, *Tel. 888/534-6835,* which is accessible by boat, ski plane, float plane or snowmobile.

Practical Information

Address: Voyageurs National Park, 3131 Highway 53 South, International Falls, MN 56649-8904

Telephone: *218/283-9821*

Operating Season:

Hours: Rainy Lake Visitor Center is open daily from 9am - 5pm from May - September, and from 9am-5pm Wednesdays-Sundays from October through mid-May; Kabetogama Lake Visitor center open 9am-5pm, closed October - mid-May; Ash River Visitor Center open 9am-5pm, closed October - mid-May

Cost: Admission is free.

Website: *www.nps.gov/voya/index.htm*

Learning About Minnesota

Blair, Al. *Moosewhopper: A Juicy, Moosey Min-Min-Minnesota Burger Tale*. Northcountry Publishing Co., 1983. Ages 4-8.

Marsh, Carole. *Minnesota Facts and Factivities*. Gallopade Publishing Group, 1996. Ages 9-12.

Marsh, Carole. *Minnesota History!: Surprising Secrets About Our State's Founding Mothers, Fathers & Kids!* Gallopade Publishing Group, 1996. Young Adult.

Marsh, Carole. *Minnesota: Indian Dictionary for Kids*. Gallopade Publishing Group, 1995. Ages 9-12.

Marsh, Carole. *Minnesota Indians!* Gallopade Publishing Group, 1995. Ages 9-12.

Marsh, Carole. *The Minnesota Mystery Van Takes Off!* Gallopade Publishing Group, 1992. Ages 9-12.

Marsh, Carole. *My First Book About Minnesota*. Gallopade Publishing Group, 1992. Ages 9-12.

Wilson's Creek National Battlefield
Missouri

"Where are you from?" The uniformed Union soldier shined a lantern in our faces.

"Texas."

The soldier nodded. He had found what he was looking for. "We heard there were Confederate spies in these ranks. You're going to have to come with me."

And so we marched through the Missouri night, the sounds of battle played out nearby. In the far corner of the field, we could see the lights of a battlefield hospital beneath a white tent, "wounded" soldiers laid out on white cots.

This was the anniversary of the Wilson Creek Battle, a reenactment played out every August 10th. The event recalls the battle fought here August 10, 1861, the first major Civil War battle west of the Mississippi River.

Today visitors can learn more about the battle and the war with a visit to the park and visitor's center.

Are We There Yet?

(OK, follow these directions carefully. We went to Wilson's Creek on a chartered bus and the driver got lost on the way and had to stop for directions.)

If you're traveling east-west on I-44, take exit 70. Head south on Rt. MM to Rt. ZZ. Continue south to the intersection of Farm Road 182. The park is at the intersection of Rt. ZZ and Farm Road 182.

What's There To Do Here?

Make your first stop at the visitor's center, where you can watch a video telling more about the battle. You can then go on to see exhibits relating to this period.

From there, you can head off on a self-guided auto tour with eight stops. From the driving tour, several trails lead off to explore on foot. There's also a trail for horseback or bike riding.

An interesting stop is the **Ray House**, which served as a field hospital during the battle. The house is open weekends from Memorial Day through Labor Day.

When Are We Going?

The peak times for visits are June through September, although April and May can be busy with school groups.

How Long Are We Staying?

You'll want to budget about half a day for seeing the visitors center and driving the auto tour.

What Should I Bring?

There are no grocery stores, food stops, or concessions in the park so bring along some snacks for the auto drive and some water.

What Are We Doing Next?

There are several good attractions in nearby Springfield, the largest city in the area and rich with a variety of attractions. Take a 50-minute tour of **Fantastic Caverns**, about 30 minutes North of Springfield off I-44 and Highway 13, *Tel. 417/833-2010, www.fantasticcaverns.com*, aboard a motorized tram (the only such tour in the country).

One of the premier attractions in Springfield is actually a store. **Outdoor World**, intersection of Highway 60 and Highway 160 at 1935 S. Campbell, Springfield, *Tel. 417/887-7334, www.outdoorworld.com*, the showroom for Bass Pro Shops, is a sure stop for camping families. The largest outdoor retail store in the country, it contains a three-story waterfall, flowing streams, a two story cabin with a working waterwheel, and aquariums so large that the fish are fed by scuba divers!

It's a 40-minute drive down Highway 65 to **Branson**, the hub of Ozark tourism, a town always filled with vacationers. The main route through Branson is Highway 76, often called "The Strip" because of its glittery light displays. Mile after mile, you'll see motels and miniature golf courses, shops and shows, so many attractions, in fact, that traffic jams are not uncommon.

Branson is a vacation wonderland, with attractions of just about every description. Many rely on a "hillbilly" theme, and most of the attractions cater to families. There are no high-priced restaurants or hotels here, and, in spite of their glitter, the evening shows are very reasonably priced, children are welcome, and dress is casual.

Probably the best way to get an overview of the Branson area is to take a tour aboard The Ducks, amphibious vehicles that were designed for troop transport in World War II. Board The Ducks at, where else, the **Duck Dock** on Highway 76 *2320 West Highway 76, Tel. 417/334-3825, www.ridetheducks.com,* for an open-air driving tour of Branson then a close-up look at the nearby lakes. Be prepared for squeals from your fellow travelers when The Duck drives right into Table Rock Lake, splashing the passengers at the very back of the boat.

Branson may now be a tourist hot-spot, but it started out as a river stop in an isolated part of the country. Cut off by the Ozark Mountains, the people of this area were fiercely self-sufficient. Many only heard tales of "city life" that existed beyond the barriers of the endless rolling hills.

In order to explore these hills, you'll want to spend at least three days exploring the many attractions which lie within 15 miles of Branson. First, head for the **Shepherd of the Hills Homestead**, Highway 76, *Tel. 417/334-4191 or 800/OLD-MATT,* for a look at the Ozarks of an earlier time, before roads and railroads allowed easy access. This park is built on the very birthplace of Ozark tourism, the spot where, in 1907, Harold Bell Wright wrote a book called *The Shepherd of the Hills*. Today, you can enjoy a tram tour of the hills and valleys which Harold Bell Wright once maneuvered on horseback. At night, be sure to return to the park for the outdoor dramatization of *The Shepherd of the Hills*, the most attended outdoor drama in the U.S.

Just down the road from Shepherd of the Hills lies **Silver Dollar City**, Highway 76, *Tel. 417/338-2611 or 800/475-9370 www.silverdollarcity.com,* probably the most successful operation in the Ozarks. Plan to spend all day here. Silver Dollar City is the only crafts park in the country. Your admission to Silver Dollar City includes a guided tour of Marvel Cave, and on hot summer days there's no better way to beat the heat than some natural Ozark air-conditioning! Along with the crafts, you can enjoy fast rides, wandering musicians and storytellers, and a nightly show at the **Echo Hollow Amphitheater**, much like the family music shows in Branson.

As the sun starts to set, head back for Branson, where several hours of entertainment still lie ahead. Take your pick from numerous music shows featuring Country, Big Band, Gospel, and even Tex-Mex music. Most of the shows are variety acts, with a little bit of everything including comedy acts, to delight the visitors who jam Branson's music theaters every night.

Two of the most beloved author's of children's literature called Missouri home, and in nearby Mansfield you can turn back the clock to the days of the pioneers at the **Laura Ingalls Wilder Home**. Laura's husband Almanzo built the Rocky Ridge farmhouse, and items such as the clock he bought for the

Special Events at Wilson Creek Battlefield
• **Anniversary of the Battle**, August 10
• **Living History Programs**. These weekend programs are scheduled from Memorial Day through Labor Day and demonstrate life during the Civil War period with special attention to battle skills. For specific dates and times, check with the park.

family, which was immortalized in one of Laura's books, and the writing desk where she penned her novels are on display.

An English-style rock house, a gift from their daughter Rose, stands nearby. The author and her husband lived there for several years, and it is here that Mrs. Wilder wrote the first in her series of Little House books. A museum offers exhibits on pioneer life in general, and includes an item familiar to Little House readers—Pa's fiddle. Open to the public from March 1-November 15 Monday - Saturday 9am-5pm and Sundays 12:30pm-5:30pm. Open daily from June through August to 5:30pm. Admission is $8 for adults, $4 for children 6-18 and those under 6 are admitted free.

A trip to **Hannibal**, a few hours away from Wilson Creek's Battlefield, is like walking through a Mark Twain novel. The man born Samuel Clemens drew from his early days to create such American classics as Tom Sawyer and The Adventures of Huckleberry Finn, and at The Mark Twain Museum you can view Twain's boyhood home, the house where the real Becky Thatcher lived, the Justice of The Peace office which was the inspiration behind the courtroom in Tom Sawyer, as well as view a ten minute video on the author's life and see one of his legendary white suit jackets at the Museum annex and see memorabilia from the many movie versions of his works at the museum. The admission, $6 for adults and $3 for children ages 6 - 12 covers all the buildings. Mark Twain Museum, 208 Hill Street, Hannibal, MO 63401-3316 For more information, call *573/221-9010*.

Which One Is My Room?
There are no accommodations in the park but many accommodations are found in Springfield. For more information, call the **Springfield Area Chamber of Commerce**, *Tel. 800/678-8767 or 417/862-5567*. For accommodations in Branson, call the **Branson Chamber of Commerce**, *Tel. 417/334-4136 or 800/214-3661*.

Practical Information
Address: Wilson's Creek National Battlefield, 6424 W. Farm Road 182, Republic, MO 65738

Telephone: *417/732-2662*
Operating Season: Year round, closed Christmas and New Year's Day
Hours: Visitors Center is open 8am-5pm daily. The park is open April 1 - October 31, 8am-7pm, November 1 - March 31, 8am - 5pm
Cost: $3 admission per person, $5 per vehicle. Children 16 and younger are free
Website: *www.nps.gov/wicr/index.htm*

Learning About Missouri

Marsh, Carole. *Missouri: Indian Dictionary for Kids.* Gallopade Publishing Group, 1995. Ages 9-12.

Marsh, Carole. *Missouri Dingbats! Book 1: A Fun Book of Games, Stories, Activities & More About Our State That's All in Code for You to Decipher.* Gallopade Publishing Group, 1991. Ages 9-12.

Marsh, Carole. *Missouri Facts and Factivities.* Gallopade Publishing Group, 1996. Ages 9-12.

Marsh, Carole. *Missouri History!: Surprising Secrets About Our State's Founding Mothers, Fathers & Kids!* Gallopade Publishing Group, 1996. Ages 9-12.

Chapter 7

THE SOUTHWEST

Amistad National Recreation Area
Texas

When travelers are looking for nature, shopping, history, movie excitement, camping and fishing rolled into one, there's only one Texas border town that fills the bill: Del Rio. Perched on the Rio Grande almost directly west of San Antonio, this town calls itself "The Best of the Border," and works to fulfill that promise with attractions that draw visitors with all types of interest.

Just outside Del Rio lies Lake Amistad and Amistad National Recreational Area. Tucked right on the U.S.-Mexico border, this lake is formed by three rivers including the Rio Grande. Amistad, derived from the Spanish word for friendship, was a joint project between Mexico and the U.S. The lake offers 1000 miles of shoreline, tempting fishermen with bass, crappie, catfish, and striper.

This park is especially popular with families looking for a quiet lake getaway. Houseboat rentals are a popular way to see the lake and enjoying some relaxing down time filled with fishing, slowly motoring alongside the lake cliffs, and just taking it easy.

Are We There Yet?

The park is located west of Del Rio on US 90. To reach Del Rio from San Antonio, follow US 90 west for about 150 miles.

What's There To Do Here?

Amistad is a favorite with those looking for good swimming, fishing, and archaeological sites.

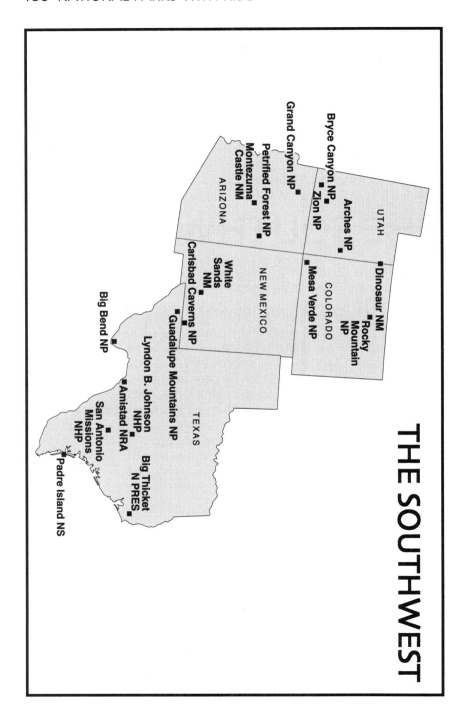

THE SOUTHWEST

Grand Canyon NP

Bryce Canyon NP

Petrified Forest NP

Montezuma
Castle NM

ARIZONA

Zion NP

Arches NP

UTAH

Carlsbad Caverns NP

White
Sands
NM

NEW MEXICO

Dinosaur NM

Mesa Verde NP

COLORADO

Rocky
Mountain
NP

Big Bend NP

Guadalupe Mountains NP

Lyndon B. Johnson
NHP

Amistad NRA

San Antonio
Missions
NHP

Padre Island NS

Big Thicket
N PRES

TEXAS

The best way to see the lake is aboard a boat, and the most luxurious ride is aboard a houseboat. With innumerable coves tucked inside sheer canyon walls, houseboaters can find seclusion as well as some beautiful, spring-fed swimming holes. Houseboats sleeping 4-12 people are rented by Lake Amistad Resort and Marina, a short drive from Del Rio.

How Long Are We Staying?

The length of your visit depends on the number and types of activities you choose. For a houseboat trip, two nights is a good length we think. If you just want to come down to the park, do a little fishing or swimming, and then go back to Del Rio that night, that's an easy order to fill.

What Should I Bring?

Bring cool clothes, a hat, sunglasses and sunscreen. Don't forget fishing gear if you want to go.

Summer Heat

Many of the national parks are located in areas where you'll find the mercury regularly rising to the three-digit level on summer days. In these conditions, you'll need to take extra precautions to make sure the kids – and you – don't fall ill.

The first concern is heat cramps, muscle cramps caused because of lost water and salt in the body. From there, it's not far to heat exhaustion, in which the body is trying to cool itself off while the victim feels, well, exhausted and nauseated. Finally, heat stroke can set in, a life-threatening condition.

What can you do to avoid these conditions?

• First, drink water–lots of water. Everyone should drink plenty of water and don't wait until you're thirsty to reach for the water jug. Thirst is an early sign of heat stress so start drinking before it reaches that point. Everyone should have their own water bottle.

• Slow down. Curtail your activities whenever possible and do like the animals do in the high heat–move slowly.

• Take lots of breaks.

• Stay out of the direct sun.

• Make sure everyone is protected from the sun. Put wide brimmed hats and caps on the kids as well as sunglasses.

• Wear sunscreen. Sunburned skin is a definite no-no.

• Avoid the hours between 10 a.m. and 2 p.m., when the sun's rays are the strongest. Enjoy an early morning hike, then kick back and take a swimming break that afternoon.

What Are We Doing Next?

From the moment you see Del Rio, you'll realize that this city is different. Unlike other border cities, Del Rio is blessed with abundant water. Perched at the edge of the Chihuahuan desert, the city is an oasis lush with vegetation thanks to the San Felipe Springs, artesian wells gushing over 90 million gallons of water through the town daily.

For a look at the founding residents of Del Rio, visit the **Whitehead Memorial Museum**, 1308 South Main Street, *Tel. 830/774-7568*. This collection of early area buildings includes a replica of the Jersey Lilly, the infamous saloon where Judge Roy Bean dispensed his frontier justice. (The original Jersey Lilly is located northwest of Del Rio in Langtry.) Behind the saloon replica lie the graves of Judge Bean and his son, Sam. Admission: adults-$5, ages 13-18 - $3, ages 6-12 -$2

Almost every Del Rio visitor takes at least a short trip to **Ciudad Acuña, Mexico**, located directly across the border. "Mexico is nicer than it has ever been," says Susan Leonard, Tourism and Convention Director for the Del Rio Chamber of Commerce. "We hear comments all the time that Acuña is the nicest area to visit across the border."

In Ciudad Acuña you'll find English-speaking shopkeepers selling a profusion of Mexican goods. Some of the best buys are silver jewelry, blankets, leather goods, Mexican liquor and beautifully embroidered Mexican dresses.

Northwest of Del Rio about nine miles past the town of Comstock lies **Seminole Canyon**, *Tel. 432/292-4464* or *800/792-1112*. Here delicate pictographs, drawn on canyon walls by ancient Indians about 8,500 years ago, represent animals, Indians, and supernatural shamans, but their meaning is still unknown. Archaeologists believe the early residents of Seminole Canyon were hunter-gatherers, living on plants and small animals. Hunting was limited to deer and rabbits, and instead the Indians survived as foragers, living on sotol, prickly pear, and lechugilla. The culture that made its home in this canyon produced the artwork now seen on guided tours. Sign up at the visitor's center for the ranger led walk to the Fate Bell Shelter. This rock overhang boasts the oldest rock art in North America, ochre, black and white paintings. One painting, known as the three shamans, portrays three figures, one with antlers atop his head.

Seminole Canyon State Historical Park is open daily; tours of the Fate Bell Shelter are given Wednesday through Sunday. Seminole Canyon is located west of Del Rio on US 90. Travel west of Del Rio on US 90 to the town of Comstock and continue nine miles to the park entrance. Twenty three park campsites have water and electricity as well as a dump station. Reservations are needed at least four weeks in advance during busy season (March through June), and can be made up to 90 days in advance. For camping information, write Box 820, Comstock, TX 78837, *Tel. 915/292-4464.*

East of Del Rio lies Brackettville, the home of the **Alamo Village Family Amusement Park,** *Tel. 830/563-2580*, located seven miles North Highway 647 and open daily. Remember John Wayne's version of *The Alamo?* It was filmed here in a replica of the Texas shrine that you can still tour today. Alamo Village is sometimes called the movie capital of Texas, and for good reason. Walk among its streets and you'll recognize buildings used in commercials, television shows, and many movies, as well as the popular TV mini-series *Lonesome Dove.*

The village also includes a Wild West town, used frequently as a movie and TV set. Don't be surprised to see familiar faces here; the park remains open even when movies are being shot.

Take a tour of the buildings, some featuring movable walls to facilitate the work of film crews. You'll see a bank that has been the scene of numerous movie holdups, a working carriage shop, the John Wayne museum, and a church that even "explodes" on cue! And even if you miss the explosion, you'll have the chance to witness a "shootout" several times daily right in front of the saloon. Enjoy a root beer and a plate of Texas barbecue at the saloon, entertained by talented "showgirls" who perform Old West shows daily.

For more information on Del Rio area attractions, write the **Del Rio Chamber of Commerce**, 1915 Veterans Blvd., Del Rio, Texas 78840, *Tel. 830/775-3551* and *800/889-8149.*

Which One Is My Room?

You'll find accommodations both in the park and in nearby Del Rio so take your pick of everything from an air-conditioned motel room to a floating houseboat that sleeps even the biggest family to a primitive campsite.

Primitive Camping. You'll find four primitive campgrounds in the park; three of these have no water or electricity (the exception being Governor's Landing Campground, which has water. This campground is available at a higher cost— $8 per night or $4 per night with a Golden Age/Access Passport) The other sites cost $4 per night or $2 a night with a Golden Age of Golden Access Passport. Improved Campsites and RV Parks

Improved Campsites and RV Parks. Del Rio is home to eight full service campgrounds. The **American Campground Mobile Home Park**, *Tel. 800/LAKE-FUN,* is located on US 90 West, offering boat rentals, Del Rio and Mexico tours, fishing guide service, miniature golf, horse stables, recreation room, and swimming pool. The **Amistad R.V. Park**, *Tel. 830/774-6578*, also on US 90 West, offers fishing guide service and recreation room. For a complete listing of all local campgrounds with prices, contact the Del Rio Chamber of Commerce for a free copy of the "Motel Campground Guide."

Houseboat Rentals. For information on houseboat rentals, contact **Lake Amistad**, PO Box 420635, Del Rio, TX 78842, *Tel. 830/774-4157*. The Lake

Amistad Resort and Marina is located on US 90. Both 36' and 50' boats are available, sleeping six and 10 persons respectively.

Practical Information
Address: Amistad National Recreation Area, HCR 3,Box 5-J, Hwy 90 West, Del Rio, TX 78840-9350
Telephone: *830/775-7491*
Operating Season: year around. Closed Thanksgiving, Dec. 25, Jan. 1
Hours: 8am-5pm weekdays, 9am-5pm weekends and holidays
Cost: No admission fee. Three-day lake permit is available for $10 or $5 with a Golden Age or Golden Access passport.
Restrictions: Pets must be on a leash
Website: *www.nps.gov/amis/index.htm*

Did You Know.....?

• The name Texas came from the Caddo Indian word for "friends", and "friendship" is the official motto of Texas.
• The Texas state flag is red, white and blue. Red represents bravery, white is for strength, and blue stands for loyalty.
• Texas's nickname is the "Lone Star State."
• The official state bird is the mockingbird.
• Bluebonnets are the state flower, and each spring a virtual sea of bluebonnets bloom alongside the roadways.
• "Texas, Our Texas" is the state song.
• The state capital is Austin.

Learning about Life the US-Mexico Border
A good book to gain insight into life on the US-Mexico border can be found in the book *In My Family/En Mi Familia* (Children's Book Press, 1996), by Carmen Lomas Garza and Harriet Rohmer. The book is aimed at ages 4-8 but all members of the family will find it informative.

Big Thicket National Preserve
Texas
Big Thicket is one of Texas' most unusual parks, a place where time seems to have stood still.

Are We There Yet?
The park has several entrance points but most visitors stop by the Turkey

Creek Unit for the Visitors Information Station. This unit is located on FM 420 seven mile north of the town of Kountze.

What's There To Do Here?

Hiking is the number one activity in Big Thicket. You'll find eight trails from which to choose and they offer a excursion for everyone, from that toddling young one to a bustling teen.

Before you head off on the trails, make a stop at the Big Thicket Information Center, located north of Kountze off Highway 69/287. Watch for the signs then turn off on FM420 east for 2-1/2 miles to the station, a small building on the left. Here you'll find a helpful ranger, displays on Big Thicket wildlife and plants, information on upcoming programs, videotapes and books, and, always important before hitting the trail, restrooms.

Just outside the visitors center lies the Kirby Nature Trail, a good choice for families and those visiting the park for the first time. This is a double loop trail. The inside loop is 1.7 miles long and you can pick up a booklet for a self-guided tour of the cypress-shaded region.

Feral Hogs & Mountain Lions

No matter what trail you and your family select, it's important to make clear some very important safety rules before heading out. Big Thicket is a huge area and still very wild. It's the home of many feral hogs as well as mountain lions.

Feral hogs generally run from people but if they have young, these creatures will defend and become aggressive. It is very important to tell children never to approach a piglet.

Mountain lions are increasing in number in the park, perhaps because of the growing number of feral hogs. Never let children go first on the trail. The park keeps track of hog and lion sightings so report your experiences at the Information Station or at trail registers found on the trailheads.

What do you do if you see a mountain lion? The National Park Service recommends:

• Looking dominant. Wave your arms, talk very loudly, throw whatever you can find, do whatever you need to do to look like you're in charge. If you've got kids with you, put them up on your shoulders so you look even taller and more domineering (and the kids don't bolt).

• Never turning your back on the lion. Walk backwards away from the lion but don't turn around.

• If the mountain lion is feeding, leave it alone. Back out quietly.

Big Thicket is a paradise for bird watchers— the park has been deemed " a globally important bird area" by the prestigious American Bird Conservancy. Peak migrations are in late March and early May. There are several trails to choose from, and along the Birdwatchers Trail (travel 3.1 miles North of Romayor on FM 2601 to Oak Hill Drive) you will have the opportunity to view shorebirds, raptors, and a variety of migrating songbirds, while at Collin's Pond (FM 1276 3.3 miles South of US Hwy 190) you will spot herons and egrets.

IMPORTANT NOTE: This area, and all of Big Thicket, can flood in a heavy rain. Never cross a trail that's underwater.

Some other trail choices include the Pitcher Plant Trail, a half-mile walk through the forest for a look at some of the region's most interesting residents: carnivorous plants! The first half of this trail is also wheelchair accessible.

When Are We Going?

Anytime of year is a good time for Big Thicket, but realize that during the summer months you'll be battling high heat, high humidity, and some mean mosquitoes.

How Long Are We Going to Stay?

Big Thicket is an enormous area and you could easily spend two weeks here if you're really into camping and hiking. If you just want to have a look at the visitors center and do the nearest trail, budget a half day at the park.

What Should I Bring?

Mosquito repellent is a must-have on your packing list. Beyond that, be sure to bring good walking shoes, cool clothing during the summer months, water containers for hikes, and sunscreen.

What Are We Doing Next?

One of the top stops in the Big Thicket area is the **Alabama-Coushatta Reservation** near Livingston, *Tel. 800/444-3507*. A museum contains dioramas about the history of these Native Americans and during peak season your family can take a train ride through the woodlands and watch traditional dances. The reservation is open to visitors March through November.

If the Beaumont area is your home base, you'll find several attractions:

Spindletop/Gladys City Boomtown, University Dr. at US 69, Beaumont, *Tel. 409/835-0823*. This is a recreation of the world's first oil boomtown. Kids can check out the blacksmith shop, the old post office, and even the wooden oil derricks. Admission is charged; the park is open Tuesday through Sunday afternoons only.

Babe Didrikson Zaharias Museum and Visitors Center, I-10 and MLK Parkway, Exit 854, *Tel. 409/833-4622*. Beaumont's most famous resident was

"Babe" Didrikson Zaharias, an athlete who won three Olympic gold medals, was a three-time basketball All-American, and was one of the first women golfers. Her life is remembered in displays at the center which also serves as an information office for the region and a good place to pick up maps and brochures. The center is open daily 9am - 5pm

If you're venturing as far as Houston, you'll find many excellent attractions of interest to kids:

Battleship Texas, 3523 Battleground Rd., La Porte, *Tel. 281/479-2431*, is one of the state's top historic attractions. The USS Texas fought in both World Wars and was renovated by money raised by the schoolchildren of Texas. The ship is open daily from 10am to 5pm; admission.

Houston Museum of Natural Science, *1 Hermann Circle Dr., Tel.* 713/ 639-4629, is the most highly visited science center in the nation and is home to a planetarium, an IMAX Theater, a butterfly house and tropical rainforest, and lots more. The center is open year around; admission.

Houston Zoological Gardens, 1513 N. MacGregor, *Tel. 713/533-6500,* is a great family stop that includes primate exhibits, a giraffe exhibit, a pygmy hippo exhibit, sea lion training exhibitions, and even vampire bat feedings. Open daily 10 AM - 6 PM March - September, 9 AM - 5 PM October - February.

Space Center Houston, 1601 NASA, *Tel. 281/244-2100,* is actually located near the community of Clear Lake about 20 minutes south of Houston. The interactive $70 million complex created by Disney brings the technology of space travel to a level that any visitors can enjoy. Starting with a mock-up of the space shuttle, the center is filled with hands-on displays. **Kids Space Place** offers 17 interactive areas where children can ride across the moon's surface in a Lunar Rover or command a space shuttle. At Mission Status Center, guests can eavesdrop on conversations with the crew of the space shuttle. "The Feel of Space" hands-on area offers computer simulators that permit guests to land the space shuttle or retrieve a satellite. After a view of flying at the IMAX theater, participants can take a NASA tram tour for a behind-the-scenes look at the Johnson Space Center to view the weightless environment training facility, the control center complex, and an outdoor park with retired flight hardware. Open daily except Christmas Day; admission.

Six Flags Houston AstroWorld/WaterWorld, South Loop 610 at Fannin, *Tel. 713/799-1234,* is the amusement park center for this part of Texas. AstroWorld is open daily in summer and weekends in May and September; call for opening hours at WaterWorld. Admission.

Children's Museum of Houston, 1500 Binz, *Tel. 713/522-1138,* has 14 galleries for children to explore everything from the environment to art to science. Open Tuesday through Sunday (Sunday afternoons only) year around; admission.

Which One Is My Room?

You'll find a wide assortment of campgrounds and hotel/motel accommodations near the park, although there are no developed campgrounds in the national preserve itself. Families who want a backcountry experience can do so with a backcountry permit; to obtain one call the **Visitor Information Station**, *Tel. 409/246-2337*.

If you're not ready to rough it to that extent, here are some other options:

Corps of Engineers Federal Campground. This campground is located on B.A. Steinhagen Lake at US190 from Woodville or Jasper or Highway 92 from Beaumont. Here you'll have four options. Sandy Creek and Magnolia Ridge are available for a fee; these camps offer water and electricity. Campers Cove and East End are free campgrounds and offer water only. The camps are open year around and include boat ramps, fishing pier, volleyball courts, and trails. For information, call *409/429-3491*.

Alabama Coushatta Indian Reservation. This is a unique campground where you can hike, fish or swim in the day and enjoy demonstrations of traditional Native American dances during your stay as well. The campground is located between Livingston and Woodville on US 190. The park includes tent and trailer sites (with utilities) and facilities for swimming, fishing, hiking, and shopping at a convenience store. During the peak summer months, train rides, a restaurant, and a gift shop are also available. For information and directions, call *936/563-1221* or *800/926-9038*.

Nearby State Parks. Big Thicket is located close to four Texas state parks, all open year around. **Lake Livingston State Recreation Area**, FM 3126 6 miles southwest of Livingston, *Tel. 409/365-2201*, offers campsites with water and electricity as well as screened shelters; facilities include showers, a boat ramp, hiking, and a store. On the B.A. Steinhagen Lake, **Martin Dies Jr. State Park**, 17 miles east of Woodville on US 190 and Park Rd. 48, *Tel. 409/ 384-5231*, has campsites with water and electricity as well as screen shelters with water and electricity. Campers can hike, boat, and swim. **Sea Rim State Park**, 10 miles west of Sabine Pass, *Tel. 409/971-2559*, has fun along miles of coastline as well as acres of marshland that include a boardwalk nature trail, boat trails into the marsh, and more. Campers can select from many sites includes beach camping and trailer sites. **Village Creek State Park**, 10 miles north of Beaumont on US96 in Lumberton, *Tel. 409/755-7322*, is known for its birding and canoeing; camping includes tent sites and RV hookups.

For reservations at any of the Texas state parks, call the **reservation center**, *Tel. 512/389-8900*, Monday through Friday 9am-6pm. To cancel reservations call *512/389-8900* Monday-Friday 9am - 8pm and Saturday 9am-noon.

Private Campgrounds. The region is home to several private campgrounds including **Oak Leaf Park KOA**, east of Beaumont on I-10, *Tel. 409/886-4082*; **Mill Creek RV Park**, west of Silsbee, *Tel. 409/385-3053*; and **Chain-O-Lakes Campground**, southwest of Romayor, *Tel. 832/397-4000*.

Hotels and Motels. You'll find a large selection of hotels and motels in nearby Beaumont. We highly recommend **Holiday Inn Beaumont Plaza**, *Tel. 409/842-5995*, a reasonably-priced facility that includes an on-site restaurant, gift shop, and, oh so important with those vacationing kids, an indoor swimming pool.

For more information on Beaumont's hotels and motels, contact the **Beaumont Convention and Visitors Bureau**, *Tel. 800/392-4401*.

Special Events at Big Thicket

You'll find plenty of activities that center around the ecology of this interesting region. The park has operated several programs for children including:

• **Wildflower Walk**. This two-hour hike teaches kids eight and up about the park's spring wildflowers.

• **Insects for Lunch**. Children five and over can enjoy this one- to two-hour stroll through the forest to see what sounds like the stuff of movies: insect-eating plants!

• **Night Prowl**. Hoo-hoo...bring along the flashlight and try your luck and locating and identifying the night creatures of the Big Thicket. This program is available for kids eight and over and last two to three hours.

• **Through the Looking Glass**. What's down there? Some of the tiniest creatures of the forest are revealed with magnifying lenses in this event available for kids five to 12 years.

For more information on naturalist programs, contact the **Information Station**, *Tel. 409/246-2337*, or drop by while you're touring.

ও

Practical Information

Address: Big Thicket National Preserve, 3785 Milam Street, Beaumont, TX 77701-4724

Telephone: *409/246-2337*

Operating Season: year round; closed Dec. 25

Hours: 9am-5pm daily; headquarters 8am-4:30pm

Cost: free

Website: *www.nps.gov/bith/index.htm*

Learning About Big Thicket

A good introduction to this area is found in *East Texas Memories: Growing Up in the Big Thicket* (Larksdale Press, 1995) by Arley Walters, aimed at teen readers and adults. Young readers will enjoy *Lost in the Big Thicket:*

A Mystery and Adventure in the Big Thicket of Texas (Eakin Publications, 1997) by Wanda A. Landrey and A. Ann Wilson (Illustrator).

Big Bend National Park
Texas

Does your family have a "been there, done that" attitude when it comes to many national parks? Then Big Bend may just be the answer. This remote park is a real place to get away from it all and enjoy nature along the banks of the Rio Grande.

That massive river, the border between Texas and Mexico, marks the location of Big Bend. Picture a map of Texas and where the river (and thus the boundary) makes a big bend, well, you guessed it. This remote region is home of this little-visited park where you can truly get away from the crowds. With truly Texas-size proportions, the park spans over 800,000 acres—plenty of space for even those families looking for lots of elbow room.

Are We There Yet?

Big Bend National Park is located in far west Texas. To get here, travel from Marathon (70 miles) on US 385 to the north entrance of the park or on TX 118 from Alpine (108 miles) to the west entrance. The west entrance can be reached by taking RR 170 from Presidio to Study Butte then TX 118 to the west entrance. Want to fly in? The closest air service is Midland (235 miles) or El Paso (330 miles).

What's There To Do Here?

This isn't a park for families looking for a lot of organized fun but if you are ready to make your own adventure it can be a great getaway. Enjoy a scenic drive through the huge park for an overall look at the park; the best vistas are found on the Ross Maxwell Scenic Drive and the road to the Chisos Mountain Basin. (Don't try these two while towing a trailer, though.) You'll also see plenty of dirt roads crisscrossing the park, but these are only recommended for those with high-clearance vehicles.

Hiking is definitely the number one activity; hikers can choose all grades of trails that span over 150 miles of the park. Guided nature walks led by naturalists are offered year around (several a day in the peak months from November through April). Check with the visitors centers for current offerings. The park also offers wildlife viewing and birdwatching trips.

Several outfitters located just outside the park can offer one of the most exciting ways to view this region aboard a float trip.

This remote landscape is home to an abundance of wildlife. Big Bend attracts over 450 types of birds, more than any other park in the United States, so have your binoculars ready— you may spot a hawk flying overhead or a roadrunner darting between clumps of cacti. Rock crevices are good hiding places for a variety of lizards as well as snakes, so use caution on your sightseeing ventures.

When Are We Going?

Remember, this park is perched in the southernmost area of the US and parts of the park are right on the desert floor. Here temperatures can be griddle-like in the summer months, but in the mountains you'll find more temperate conditions. The hottest months here are May and June, with cooling rains starting in July and continuing through October. Winter temperatures are usually pretty comfortable but light snow can occur.

The best packing tips for this park are to come prepared (you're not going to run out to the Wal-Mart and grab and extra layer if it does turn chilly). Be sure to bring a hat for everyone in the family, plenty of sunscreen, at least a gallon of water per person for every day you'll be in the park, comfortable walking shoes, and any must-have items.

How Long Are We Staying?

This isn't a park you just swing by on the way to somewhere else–you've got to be going here to wind up here. With its remote location, you'll want to stay at least a couple of nights to get a feel for the park.

What Should I Bring?

Come prepared with layers of clothing, even during summer months when evening temperatures can be cool. Rain gear is also important in case of afternoon thunderstorms. Insect repellent is a must during summer months.

What Are We Doing Next?

Visiting the border towns near the park are an excellent way to experience another culture. The closest border towns are Coahuila and Santa Elena, both in the state of Chihuahua. You do need to cross at an approved border crossing (illegal boat crossings are operated up and down the Rio Grande) so check with the visitors center for directions.

Twenty four structures as well as the ghostly remains of over 100 ruins still stand guard over Fort Davis, which is only 135 miles from Big Bend. Begin your tour at the visitors center, housed in what was once the barracks for the enlisted men. There you can watch a 15 minute orientation film and view exhibits to learn about life on this 1800's military post. From there visit the post hospital, commissary, lieutenant's quarters and officer's kitchen. During spring break and summer months volunteers turn back the clock as they perform reenactments in period costume. Children can earn a patch by signing up for the Mystery of The Talking Walls, where they round up clues found on the site to decode a hidden message. Admission is $3 for 7 days for adults, no admission charge for those 16 and under. For further information call *532/ 426-3224 ext.20.*

Which One Is My Room?

You've got several choices when it comes to accommodations in the park. Lodging is limited, though, so at peak times (Easter weekend, spring break, Thanksgiving weekend, Christmas week) be sure to book early if you are planning to stay at the lodge (and come early if you're hoping to get a campsite). The months of August and September are usually the quietest as kids head back to school and vacationers avoid the end of summer heat.

Hotel. The park is home to the **Chisos Mountain Lodge**, which is operated by the **National Park Concessions, Inc**. For information, call *432/ 477-2291* or see *www.chisosmountainlodge.com.*

Developed Camping. Campers have several options. Developed campsites are found at Rio Grande Village (100 sites), Chisos Basin (65 sites), and Cottonwood (31 sites). Each of these sites have water. Only Rio Grande and Chisos Basin provide flushing toilets; Cottonwood only has a "pit toilet" only. No hookups are available. Cost is $10 per night per site and each campsite is limited to eight campers and two vehicles. Reservations can bee made from November 15-April 15. Go to www.reserveusa.com for more details

RV Park. At **Rio Grande Village**, you'll find a full service RV park with hookups. For information, call *432/477-2251.*

Primitive camping. Families who are ready to do some backcountry hiking will find primitive camping opportunities. You'll need a backcountry permit.

International Good Neighbor Day

A special time in the park is the annual **International Good Neighbor Day Fiesta**, scheduled for the third Saturday in October. Celebrating the bond between the US and Mexico, this special event is filled with local foods and music.

Practical Information

Address: Big Bend National Park, PO Box 129, Big Bend National Park, TX 79834

Telephone: *432/477-2251*

Operating Season: Year round

Hours: 24 hours a day, every day. The Panther Junction Visitors Center is open 8am-6pm daily but closes for Christmas and New Year's Day. The other visitors center have varying hours

Cost: $15 per car for a one week pass. Golden Access, Golden Age, and Golden Eagle passes are honored

Restrictions: Pets are only allowed on roads and in the drive-in campground and must be on a leash. Pets cannot be carried into the backpacking and hiking areas of the park.

Website: *www.nps.gov/bibe/index.htm*

Learning about Big Bend

A good introduction to Big Bend is found in *Tales of the Big Bend by Elton Miles* (Texas A&M University Press, 1995).

Guadalupe Mountains National Park
Texas

Picture Texas and you probably think of flat plains, perhaps broken up by the rolling hills of central Texas or the forests of East Texas.

Well, you haven't seen West Texas, particularly the Guadalupe Mountains. The only true mountains in Texas, these peaks rise up out of the desert to a height of 8,749 feet, nosebleed territory in Texas. The pinnacle of the park is found at Guadalupe Peak, Texas' highest point, but other notable formations include El Capitan limestone formation and McKittrick Canyon, home of some of the best fall color in the Lone Star State thanks to bigtooth maple, walnut, ash, oak, and the Texas madrone.

Several hikes offer varying degrees of difficulty but are rewarded with plenty of color, serenity, and the chance to enjoy natural beauty. Fall color here isn't accompanied by fall festivals or lines of cars, just peace and quiet and the opportunity to reflect on the changing seasons.

Are We There Yet?

Guadalupe Mountains National Park is located about 100 miles east of El Paso. This is one of those parks you have to be going to in order to reach–you don't just pass through here on the way somewhere else.

To reach the park, travel 110 miles east of El Paso on US 62/180 or 55 miles southwest of Carlsbad, New Mexico on US 62/180. If you are in the Big Bend region, travel 65 miles north of Van Horn, Texas on TX 54.

Once you're in the park, head to the Visitor Center at Pine Spring on US 62/180.

What's There To Do Here?

Most of the fun at this park comes in the form of hiking. You'll find numerous hikes of varying difficulty throughout the park. Some other attractions include the visitors center with natural history exhibits and the Frijole Ranch Museum, a historic site with exhibits on local history.

Be sure to bring in whatever you might need during your stay. There are no facilities in the park–no gas, no food, no ice, nothing. It's a long 35-mile drive to White's City, New Mexico if you find you need picnic supplies.

El Paso and the surrounding area offers a variety of attractions from which to choose. For those on an educational odyssey, tour the **War Eagles Air Museum,** filled with the flying machines that patrolled the air during World War II and the Korean Conflict. Open Tuesday through Sunday from 10am to 4pm. Located at 8012 Airport Road in Santa Teresa, NM. Call *505/589-2000* for more information.

Only 15 minutes from El Paso is **The Mission Trail**, where three of the oldest missions in the United States are still used as houses of worship. Mission Ysleta is a structure rebuilt numerous times after flooding tore down the earlier establishments. The most recent, completed in 1851, stands proudly today, its famed silver dome catching the sunlight like a beacon to the faithful. Originally a military garrison, work on the adobe-style Presidio Chapel San Elceario was completed in 1877. Socorro Mission was destroyed by floods twice. The version standing today was completed in 1843. Take special notice of the support beams overhead, which were hand-carved and decorated by Native Americans. To reach The Mission Trail take I-10 East to the Zaragosa exit, turn South then follow the historical markers. Call *Tel. 915/534-0630* for further details.

If your family is on a quest for fun, try **Western Playland Amusement Park** at 6900 Delta, El Paso. For the little ones there are kiddie rides like The Red Baron, while thrill seekers will want a turn on Pharaoh's Fury , the El Bandido roller coaster or the Tsunami water ride. Open late March through mid October. Admission. Call *915/772-3953*

Cool down during the summer months at **Wet 'N' Wild Waterworld**, a 37-acre water park with 22 rides from the Toddler's Cove for the youngest to Alien Vortex and Raging Rapids for the brave at heart. Open every day from May 31- August 17 and weekends until September 7. Admission. Take I-10 West for 17 miles to Anthony exit.

How Long Are We Staying?

With the distance that this park is from other sites, you'll want to stay at least one or two nights to get a feel for the place.

What Should I Bring?

Sunscreen, hats and glasses as well as good walking or hiking shoes are essential. Be sure to bring in plenty of water with you as well as food supplies.

What Are We Doing Next?

One of the nearest attractions is Carlsbad Caverns National Park (see **Carlsbad Caverns** entry for additional attractions in that region). Big Bend

National Park (see **Big Bend National Park** entry for more attractions) is another option in this part of the state.

Which One Is My Room?

Dog Canyon Campground offers 9 tent sites as well as four RV sites, although there are no hookups or dump station. Flush toilets are available, but not showers. The cost is $8 per night, $4 with a Golden Age and Golden Access Passport. Pine Springs Campground is located 1/3 mile from the headquarters visitor center, and offers 20 tent sites and 19 RV sites. Water, restroom and pay telephone are available. No dump station or hookups. The cost is $8 a night or $4 with a Golden Age and Golden Access Passport.

The nearest motel accommodations are in White's City, New Mexico, near Carlsbad Caverns. For a complete rundown of accommodations in that area, see the Carlsbad Caverns National Park entry.

Special Events at Guadalupe Mountains National Park

During the summer months, park naturalists offer programs at the amphitheater. Check with the visitors center for program times and topics.

Practical Information

Address: Guadalupe Mountains National Park, HC 60, Box 400, Salt Flat, TX 79847

Telephone: *915/828-3251*

Operating Season: Open year round. Closed Christmas Day

Hours: Visitor Center 8am-4:30pm (extended hours in the summer months). Gate to McKittrick Canyon day-use area is locked at night.

Cost: $3 for seven days. Campsites in the park are $7 a night

Restrictions: Pets must remain on a leash and are not allowed on the trails. No fires (or even barbecues with charcoal) are permitted anywhere in the park.

Website: *www.nps.gov/gumo/index.htm*

Lyndon B. Johnson National Historic Park
Texas

If you're looking for a day of history and heritage that won't include museum admission costs and tour fees, then head to Johnson City. This is the land that President Lyndon Baines Johnson called home, just as his ancestors had years before when Texas was first being settled. Today it's one of the best bargains in Central Texas for families looking for an inexpensive excursion, an easy trip from either San Antonio or Austin.

Are We There Yet?

The Lyndon B. Johnson National Historic Park takes in two areas: Johnson City and the LBJ Ranch. To reach Johnson City from San Antonio, follow US 281 north through Blanco and then on to Johnson City where US 281 joins US 290. Turn left on US 290 toward Fredericksburg.

From Austin, follow US 290 west for 42 miles to the intersection of US 281. Turn north and continue for six miles to Johnson City. The LBJ Ranch is located about 15 miles west of Johnson City on US 290.

To reach the visitor's center and Johnson Settlement while in Johnson City, go left three blocks on US290 at the intersection of US281 and follow the signs.

To reach the LBJ Ranch, travel west on US 290 from Johnson City for 16 miles (toward Fredericksburg).

What's There To Do Here?

Start your visit in downtown Johnson City at the LBJ National Historic Park (US 290 and 9th St.). Stop by the new Visitors Center for brochures and a look at some exhibits on the late president's family, then walk to two historic areas. Don't miss the kids' room, complete with a television camera where children can see for themselves what it would be like to give a presidential address to the nation.

From 1913 to 1934 Lyndon Johnson lived in a simple white frame house. Johnson's father, Sam Ealy Johnson, Jr., was a state representative, the home often echoed with political debate. At the same time, a future statesman was being tutored on the front porch at the knee of his mother, Rebekah Baines Johnson.

The home is still furnished with the Johnsons' belongings. Guided tours run every half hour.

After your tour, head toward the Johnson Settlement, a restoration of the cabin and buildings which belonged to Sam Ealy Johnson, Sr., LBJ's grandfather. The Settlement can be reached on a path from the boyhood home, a walk through pastures which were once the Johnson's livelihood.

Photos, farm implements and clothing from the 1800's are displayed in the visitor's center. An old cypress cistern serves as a mini-auditorium in which you may hear recorded readings of letters the original settlers wrote about this rugged land.

Past the center is the Sam Johnson cabin, which also served as headquarters for his longhorn drives up the Chisholm Trail. Several head of longhorn graze in the pasture, just as they have for generations. At one point, this cabin also served as aid station for the wounded following the Deer Creek Indian Battle.

Don't be surprised to smell something cooking from the black pot hanging over the fireplace. If the house still looks lived-in, it's because of the efforts of the costumed guides who stay at the Settlement, carrying on with chores just as Sam and Eliza Johnson did over 100 years ago. A spinning wheel stands on the front porch, and inside are all the implements needed to run the typical household of the 1800's.

Once you've seen Johnson Settlement, it's just a short drive to the **LBJ State Historical Park**. Leave Johnson City on US 290 to Stonewall, then turn on Ranch Road 1 to the park entrance. When LBJ was alive, much of this area comprised his private ranch. Security was tight, and Secret Service men guarded the grounds.

Today, however, the National Park Service conducts tours of the LBJ ranch. Your visit to the park begins at the visitor's center, a building of native rock constructed in a typical Texas style. Displays of LBJ's family, the ranch, and the Hill Country can show you what life was like during the pioneer times, as well as the hectic days when LBJ was president. A short walk away from the building are pens of huge buffalo, native white-tailed deer and wild turkeys.

While you're in the visitor's center, sign up for a guided tour of the ranch. An air-conditioned bus, with a guide, will take you on a drive around the ranch and the back pastures. The drive takes you across the mighty **Pedernales River**, through a countryside dotted with cattle, live oaks and the beauty of the hill country at its best. This is the land that LBJ loved, and returned to as

German Spoken Here!

The community of Fredericksburg takes pride in their German heritage and it is not unusual to hear German spoken among local residents.

Here are a few German phrases you can learn:

Good morning— Guten Morgen
Good day— Guten Tag
Good evening— Guten Abend
Good night— Gute Nacht
Good-bye— Auf Wiedersehen
Thank you— Danke
Thanks for everything— Vielen Dank für alles
How do you do? Wie geht es Ihnen?
Pleased to meet you— Sehr erfreut
I'm traveling with my family— Ich reise mit der Familie
What do you call this in German?— Wie heisst das auf deutsch?
I like it a lot here— Mir gefällt es hier sehr

often as possible. Often during the tour, the words of LBJ and Lady Bird are broadcast over the bus' loudspeaker, as they describe their feelings for the area.

Immediately after crossing the Pedernales River, your tour bus will slow down for photographs of the one-room schoolhouse where LBJ began his education at the age of four. A few minutes later, you'll stop at a re-creation of the home where LBJ was born. Built in a breezy style typical of Texas homes of the period, the house is filled with furnishings of the Johnsons. Before heading back to the bus, stop by the family cemetery nearby. It lies under the shade of huge oak trees and overlooks the Pedernales River. LBJ and many members of his family are buried here.

Your tour continues with a drive past the **Texas White House**, a large white home sprawled under shady oaks. Many national and international names visited this Texas White House during LBJ's lifetime. Nearby, a carport is filled with a fleet of cars which served the President on his rounds of the ranch. One ordinary-looking car is actually an amphibious vehicle, used by LBJ to surprise unknowing passengers, who found themselves suddenly driving into the river or a nearby pond!

For the remainder of the tour, you'll see just what ranch life is like in central Texas. Cattle graze lazily over the many pastures; ranch hands cut hay; workers clean the stockbarn used for cattle sales. This is still very much a working ranch.

Shortly before returning to the visitor's center, your bus will stop at the **Sauer-Beckmann Farm.** Watch park employees in authentic dress carrying out farm chores as you wander among the two farmhouses, a smokehouse, garden, and barn. Young visitors will be delighted with the farm animals who freely roam the grounds. Everything from chickens to horses to baby sheep and goats transform the barnyard into a petting zoo.

When Are We Going?

Summer months are the most popular time for a visit, but expect hot and humid temperatures. Dress cool and drink plenty of water. Spring and summer months are the best times for a visit; if you plan your excursion in late March or early April it will coincide with the Texas wildflower season. President Johnson's wife, Lady Bird Johnson, is responsible for many of the state's wildflowers that line its roadways.

How Long Are We Staying?

If you are just doing the Johnson City site, budget about two and a half hours for a look at the boyhood home, museum, and the Johnson Settlement. If you extend the visit with a trip to the LBJ Ranch (and we highly recommend it) set aside the whole day, grab a picnic lunch to enjoy in the park, and make a day of it.

What Should I Bring?

Good walking shoes, sunscreen, and cool clothes are important for summer visitors. Bring along a picnic lunch to enjoy at the Stonewall park.

What Are We Doing Next?

Although the LBJ sites can easily fill a day, you'll find plenty of other diversions in Johnson City and nearby Fredericksburg. For a look at early Fredericksburg, visit the **Pioneer Museum Complex** at 309 West Main Street, *Tel. 830/997-2835*. This collection of historic old homes includes a 1849 pioneer log home and store, the old First Methodist Church, and a smokehouse and log cabin. Also on the premises you'll see a typical 19th-century "Sunday house." Built in Fredericksburg, Sunday houses catered to farmers and their families who would travel long distances to do business in town, often staying the weekend. The museum is open Monday- Saturday 10am - 5pm, Sunday 1pm - 5pm Admission is $4 for ages 11 and up.

Have another look at Fredericksburg's rich history at the **Vereins Kirche Museum** at Market Square on Main Street. You can't miss this attraction: It's housed in an exact replica of an octagonal structure erected in 1847. The museum is sometimes called the Coffee Mill (or Die Kaffe-Muehle) Church because of its unusual shape. Exhibits here display Fredericksburg's German heritage, plus Indian artifacts from archaeological digs. Admission is $1; the museum is open Monday- Saturday 10am-4pm and Sunday 1pm-4pm.

More about that early history can be learned with a visit to **Fort Martin Scott Historic Site**, located two miles east of town on US 290, *Tel. 830/997-9895*. Established in 1848, this was the first frontier military fort in Texas. Today the original stockade, a guardhouse, and a visitors center with displays on local Indians are open to tour, and historic reenactments keep the history lesson lively. The Museum is open Tuesday - Sunday 10am - 5pm

More recent military history is explored at the **Museum of the Pacific War**, formerly the Admiral Nimitz State Historical Park at 340 East Main Street, *Tel. 830/997-4379*. Admiral Chester Nimitz, World War II Commander-in-Chief of the Pacific (CincPac), was Fredericksburg's most famous resident. He commanded 2.5 million troops from the time he assumed command 18 days after the attack on Pearl Harbor until the Japanese surrendered. Kids especially enjoy the Gallery of the Pacific War, an outdoor collection of planes, submarines, and vessels from World War II.

Fall and spring are the best time to have a look at the biggest attraction in the Fredericksburg area: **Enchanted Rock State Natural Area**. Looming over the Texas hillside like a massive bald mountain, this enormous dome of pink granite rises 325 feet above the small stream flowing at its base. Covering over a square mile, the formation is second in size only to Georgia's Stone Mountain. The park is a favorite playground for rock climbers, backpackers, and even sedentary tourists who don't mind a lung-expanding walk up the dome for a look at mile after mile of rural Texas.

If you want to explore the life and times of the 36th president further, take a day trip to the state capital of Austin for a visit to **the Lyndon Baines Johnson Library and Museum**. The 1968 Presidential limousine and gifts from heads of state, such as a painting by famed artist Diego Rivera, which was presented by then President of the United Mexican States and a ceremonial headdress offered by then President of the Republic of Senegal, are just a few of the displays representing his years in office. Johnson's personal life is documented as well with home movies and even love letters to his sweetheart, Lady Bird. The museum is located at 2313 Red River St., Austin, TX 78705, *Tel. 512/721-0200.* Open every day but Christmas from 9am-5pm Admission: free.

Strolling through the First Lady's Gallery at the Lyndon Baines Johnson Library and Museum will peak your interest about this unique Texas native. While visiting Austin, be sure to stop by the **Lady Bird Johnson Wildflower Center**, which was established in 1982 by the former first lady and actress Helen Hayes in order to educate the public about the environment and beautify the area. Open Tuesday - Sunday from 9am- 5:30pm, a walk through the many nature trails and various gardens promises an afternoon's respite from a sometimes hectic vacation schedule. Located at 4801 La Crosse Avenue, call *512/292-4100* for further information.

Which One Is My Room?

There are no accommodations in the park but you will find many accommodations in both Johnson City and nearby Fredericksburg. For more information on Johnson City including local bed and breakfast inns, write the **Johnson City Chamber of Commerce**, PO Box 485, Johnson City, TX 78636, *Tel. 830/868-7684.* For more information on Fredericksburg, give the **Fredericksburg Convention and Visitors Bureau** a call at *830/997-6523.*

Practical Information

Address: Lyndon B. Johnson National Historical Park, PO Box 329, Johnson City, TX 78636

Telephone: *830/868-7128 ext. 244*

Operating season: Open year round except Christmas and New Year's Day

Hours: Visitors Center open 8:45am-5pm Johnson Settlement available for tour from 9am-dusk daily. Bus tours of LBJ Ranch available from 10a.m.-4p.m. daily. LBJ self-guided portions open until dusk daily

Cost: Free to enter the parks; $3 fee for bus tour for vacationers seven years or older (children under seven are free)

Website: *www.nps.gov/lyjo/ndex.htm*

Learning About President Lyndon B. Johnson

Eskow, Dennis. *Lyndon Baines Johnson* (An Impact Biography). Franklin Watts, 1993. For teen readers.

Hargrove, Jim. *Lyndon B. Johnson: Thirty Sixth President of the United States.* Children's Press, 1987.

Lindop, Edmund. *Dwight D. Eisenhower, John F. Kennedy, Lyndon B. Johnson.* Twenty First Century Books, 1996. For ages 9-12.

Padre Island National Seashore
Texas

Padre Island National Seashore is known for its miles of unspoiled beach and a favorite with serious birders, surfers, beach campers, and anyone looking for a dune-filled beach. This 110-mile-long barrier island protects much of the Texas coast from hurricanes and tropical storms. Generally, the northern stretch of island paralleling the area from Corpus Christi to Port Mansfield is called Padre Island; from that point to the tip of Texas, the land mass is named South Padre Island.

Padre Island features beaches dotted with rolling dunes, clean sand, and flocks of gulls. The surf is usually gentle and shallow enough to walk for hundreds of yards before reaching chest-deep water. Occasionally, the undertow is a problem, but on most summer days the waves are gentle and rolling, and the water is warm.

Are We There Yet?

To reach Padre Island, head out on South Padre Island Drive, also called TX 358, from Corpus Christi. The road is lined with shell shops, windsurfing rentals, bait stands, and car washes. In the shallow waters along the drive, many fishermen stand waist deep in salt water alongside tall herons and pelicans looking for a meal.

When you cross the Intracoastal Waterway via the enormous J.F.K. Causeway Bridge, you leave the mainland for Padre Island. To reach the Padre Island beaches, continue straight on South Padre Island Drive (Park Road 22). Visitors find several parks here from which to choose, each with its own special charm.

What's There To Do Here?

One of the most popular beaches is the **Padre Balli Park**, which is named for the priest who managed a ranch on the island in the early 19th century. It offers a 1,200-foot fishing pier. The Padre Island National Seashore has a snack bar, and showers are available at **Malaquite Beach**. Although vehicles are allowed on most Padre beaches, Malaquite is one where vehicles are not permitted.

Beach Safety

Follow a few rules of safety. Portuguese Man-Of-War jellyfish are commonly seen on the beaches. Resist the urge to touch these iridescent purple creatures — their tentacles produce a nasty sting. If you are stung, locals claim the best relief is a paste of meat tenderizer and water applied to the bite.

A far less dangerous, but very annoying, aspect of the Gulf beaches are tar balls. These black clumps, formed by natural seepage and offshore oil spills, wash up on the beach and stick to your skin and your shoes. Many hotels have a tar removal station near the door to help you remove the sticky substance.

Beyond Malaquite lies 66 miles of protected beach in Padre Island National Seashore accessible only by four-wheel drive vehicles. **Little Shell** and **Big Shell** beaches are located in this area, both named because of the wealth of seashells found on their pristine sands.

Out on the island, the **Grassland Nature Trail**, a two-mile asphalt walk, is a favorite with hikers.

Here is a list of just some of the birds that call Padre Island home. See how many you can spot on your trip:
• American Oystercatcher
• American White Pelican
• Black Skimmer
• Brown Pelican
• Common Loon
• Great Blue Heron
• Horned Lark
• Inca Dove
• Killdeer
• Kiskadee
• Long-biller Curlew
• Mourning Dove
• Osprey
• Pied-billed Grebe
• Rock Dove
• Roseate Spoonbill
• Royal Tern
• Sandhill Crane
• Snowy Egret
• Snowy Plover

- Solitary Sandpiper
- White Ibis
- Willet

When Are We Going?

Summer is the peak time to visit this park and you can expect crowds on weekends and especially over Memorial Day, July 4th, and Labor Day weekends. The portions of the beach open only to four wheel drive vehicles don't get as crowded, however.

Spring break season is also a busy time at this park.

Fall and spring months can be very pleasant here. Winter months often bring nice days as well, although the waters are too cold for all but the most dedicated swimmers.

How Long Are We Staying?

The park can easily be enjoyed as a day trip from Corpus Christi.

What Should I Bring?

Bring all the beach gear: sunscreen, hats, swimsuits, beach toys, the works. Pack some picnic supplies and water as well.

What Are We Doing Next?

Save a day or two to explore the attractions of Corpus Christi. The marine life of the Gulf of Mexico are the featured residents at the **Texas State Aquarium**, 2710 N. Shoreline Blvd., *Tel. 361/881-1200, www.texasstateaquarium.org*. This must-see attraction showcases the aquatic animals and habitats indigenous to the Gulf of Mexico. You'll enter the interpretive center beneath a cascading waterfall, symbolic of the dive into coastal waters. It's a self-guided discovery through exhibits such as the Islands of Steel, a look at a replica of an offshore oil platform surrounded by nurse sharks, amberjack, and other marine creatures commonly found around these man-made reefs. Nearby, the Flower Gardens Coral Reef exhibit looks at the beautiful coral gardens found 115 miles off the coast, blooming with aquatic life and marine animals such as moray eels, tarpon, and rays. Outdoors, young visitors enjoy touch tanks filled with small sharks and rays; at the Otter Space playful river otters amuse visitors with their antics. Admission for ages 13 and older is $11.95, ages 4-12 $6.95, three and under get in free.

Travelers can learn more about local ecosystems at the **Corpus Christi Museum of Science and History**, 1900 N. Chaparral, *Tel. 361/826-4650*. This downtown museum is also home to the World of Discovery and The Ships of Columbus. The museum offers displays to fascinate all ages, covering everything from dinosaurs to Spanish shipwrecks. Don't miss the "Seeds of Change" exhibit, designed by the Smithsonian's National Museum of Natural

History for the 500th anniversary of the European discovery of America. After a look at exhibits that tell the story of these explorers and the impact they had on the New World, see what it was like to make the Atlantic crossing aboard the Niña, Pinta, and Santa Maria. Life-size replicas of these Spanish ships are located in a shipyard repair facility adjacent to the museum. A special treat is held each year during "Columbus Days", held the first two weeks of October. You will be whisked back in time as tour guides dressed to depict actual crew members of the Pinta and Santa Maria take you on a guided tour of the ships. Contact the museum for more information and to make reservations.

More recent maritime history can be explored at the **U.S.S. Lexington Museum on the Bay**, 2914 N. Shoreline Blvd., *Tel. 361/888-4873, www.usslexington.com,* housed in the most decorated aircraft carrier in U.S. Naval history. Five self-guided tour routes give visitors a close look at the ship termed "The Blue Ghost."

For more information, on area activities, contact the **Corpus Christi Convention and Visitors Department**, *Tel. 800/678-6232.*

Which One Is My Room?

Near Padre Island National Seashore, you'll find several hotels and condominiums including:

Holiday Inn North Padre Island, 15202 Windward Dr., *Tel. 800/HOLIDAY, 361-949-8041.* Here you can walk from the hotel directly to the beach. When you've had enough salt water, have a dip in the hotel swimming pool.

Island House, 15340 Leeward Dr., *Tel. 800/333-8806.* This beachfront condominium resort has well-furnished units, many with beautiful views of the Gulf. Each includes a furnished kitchen, a dining/living room, and two bedrooms. Spend the extra money for an oceanfront condo, with sliding glass doors in the living room and the master bedroom, and fall asleep to the sound of waves.

In nearby Corpus Christi, you'll find a wide range of family accommodations (check with the Convention and Visitors Bureau, above, for a complete list). Some of our favorites include:

Corpus Christi Omni Bayfront, 900 N. Shoreline Blvd., *Tel. 800/THE-OMNI.* This elegant 474-room hotel overlooks the bay and includes a health

Padre Island Hatchling Releases

Each year sea turtle eggs are collected and incubated in order to insure a thriving sea turtle population. Watch as baby sea turtles make their way to the Gulf of Mexico when they are released during the summer months. For further information on these releases, which are held at dawn, call the hatchling hotline, *Tel. 361/949-7163.*

≈

club, swimming pool, and rooftop dining room. Many of Corpus Christi's main attractions lie within walking distance.

Practical Information
Address: Padre Island National Seashore, Superintendent, P.O. Box 181300, Corpus Christi, TX 78480-1300
Telephone: *361/949-8068*

Operating Season: Open year round except Christmas and New Years Day
Hours: 24 hours daily
Cost: $10 for a seven day pass
Website: *www.nps.gov/pais/index.htm*

San Antonio Missions National Historic Park
Texas

Mention the missions, and most people think you're referring to the Alamo, the building that's called the "cradle of Texas liberty." But San Antonio is home to four other Spanish missions from the same period, each giving visitors a sense of both the Franciscan missionaries and the Indians who made the missions their home.

Texas at one time hosted 38 missions, all built by the Spanish, to convert the Indians to Catholicism and to stake a claim on the lands to which Spain's rival, France, was showing little interest. The San Antonio missions all sprang up near the river, which supplied water for drinking and crop irrigation. The water was channeled to the missions by means of an *acequia* or aqueduct.

The missions operated as independent communities led by Franciscan friars. When visiting the four structures along the Mission Trail you'll see the size and scope of these communities, which usually included a chapel, Indian living quarters, a blacksmith, a granary to store crops, and farmland.

The first San Antonio mission, the Alamo, was built to serve as a way-station between missions in East Texas and those in Mexico City. The East Texas establishment proved unsuccessful, however, due to the French influence in Louisiana and the widespread malaria that resulted from settling in the swampy woodlands. In 1731, three missions were relocated to San Antonio, forming the densest concentration of Spanish missions in the New World.

The Indians who lived in the missions were Coahuiltecans, hunter-gatherers from South Texas and northeastern Mexico. Because European diseases had taken their toll on the native population and nomadic tribes were moving in on their lands, the Indians allowed themselves to be recruited by the friars. By the late 1700s, however, the missions had become secularized, and the Indians moved to neighboring land. Many of the mission buildings began to fall to ruin.

In the 1920s the citizens of San Antonio began to preserve the deteriorating structures. Then, in 1978, the San Antonio Missions National Historic Park was established, protecting and operating the four sites. The cooperative effort between the Park Service, the San Antonio Conservation Society, the State of Texas, the City of San Antonio, and Bexar County was expanded by a cooperative agreement with the Archdiocese of San Antonio to keep the mission churches open for regular services.

Are We There Yet?

The park is located right in downtown San Antonio. The drive along the mission trail is somewhat hard to follow (even the National Park Service brochure warns that "the route that connects the four missions can be confusing for visitors"). The way is marked with brown park signs, but it twists and turns between residential neighborhoods and parks. Further, during heavy rains, two low-water crossings are closed, necessitating an alternate route. The free brochure from the National Park Service outlines both the traditional Mission Trail as well as alternate routes to take during inclement weather.

The easiest way to do the trail is to start at **Mission Concepcion,** and have park rangers give you directions to the next mission from there. To reach Mission Concepcion from I-10, take the Probandt exit and follow the National Park Service signs to the mission. See below for more details.

If you're on I-37, take the West Southcross exit and travel west on Southcross to Roosevelt Avenue. Turn left on Roosevelt Avenue and then take a left on Napier Avenue to reach the visitors center.

What's There To Do Here?

Today the missions are each open to the public. When planning your visit, remember that these are active parish churches (unlike the Alamo). Services are conducted every Sunday, and respectful visitors are welcome. Mission San Juan has a Mariachi Mass every Sunday at noon; it is very popular with visitors.

Most tours of the Mission Trail start at **Mission Concepcion,** 807 Mission Rd. at Felisa St., *Tel. 210/534-1540.* This site is tucked into a residential neighborhood, a quiet place far different from the bustling Alamo area.

Special Events at the San Antonio Missions

The weekly Mariachi Mass, every Sunday at noon, is held at Mission San Juan Capistrano and is one of the top events in the city, filled with the joy of mariachi music. All denominations are welcome.

～

Concepcion (pronounced "con-cep-see-OWN") was moved here in 1730. Its full name is a mouthful: *Mission of Nuestra Senora de la Purisma Concepcion de Acuna.*

Begin your visit with a stop at the modern visitors center to pick up a free Park Service brochure (a necessity for driving the Mission Trail), then start your self-guided tour of the chapel. The flagstone floor has borne thousands of worshippers, from barefooted Indians two centuries ago to tennis-shoed tourists today. Indeed, be sure that you do wear tennis shoes, or some type of sturdy walking shoes, for the mission tours. All the sites have irregular staircases and stone walkways that are especially slippery on rainy days.

Mission Concepcion is especially notable for its wall paintings. Geometric and religious symbols in ochre, blue, and brown decorate the ceilings and walls of several rooms. The most striking is the **Eye of the God**, a face emanating rays of light. Displays at each of the four missions illustrate different aspects of mission life. At Concepcion, the theme is *The Mission as a Religious Center*, appropriate for a place known as one of the oldest unrestored stone churches as well as the oldest unrestored Catholic church in the nation.

Like the Alamo just over two miles to the north, Mission Concepcion saw its own share of bloodshed. On October 28, 1835, Colonel James Bowie and 20 Texans were surprised by a detachment of the Mexican army. They fought well and forced the Mexicans, with 60 dead and 40 wounded, to retreat. The Texans only suffered one loss, further bolstering their spirits. Less than five months later, however, Bowie and his men would again fight the Mexican army, with far less success.

The second mission stop on the trail is the grandest in terms of size and architectural detail, so much so, in fact, that 200 years ago it was termed "Queen of the Missions." In its heyday **Mission San Jose**, 6701 San Jose Dr., *Tel. 210/932-1001*, boasted 300 residents, a granary that held 5,000 bushels of corn, and elaborate ornamentation. Its full name is *San Jose y Miguel de Aguayo*, named for the Governor of Texas at that time.

You may find yourself humming the tune *Do You Know the Way to San Jose?* when traveling the mission route to this second site. The route mapped by the Park Service is the most scenic but not the most direct. Just follow the signs, and be patient; when you do reach San Jose, the drive will have been worth the effort. Thanks to an extensive renovation in 1936 for the Texas Centennial, this mission is in spectacular condition. The elegant structure echoes with reminders of an earlier time, when Texas was a frontier and this mission was a haven in an unsettled land. The most famous detail here is **Rosa's Window**. Legend has it that an architect named Pedro Huizar created the window for his lost love, Rosa. (When you're downtown, look at the Dillard's exterior window displays at the Rivercenter Mall. These are copies of Rosa's Window, built by the former Joske's store.)

Walk around the grounds to get an idea of the size of this former community. Indians lived in rooms along the outside wall, and the priests lived in the two-story *convento*. The land in the quadrangle was used for crops. The theme of San Jose is *The Mission as Social Center and a Center for Defense*. Displays show that Indian residents were taught the use of guns and lances to help defend against raiding Apache and Comanche Indians.

Continue south along mission trail and you'll soon pass Espada Park and Acequia Parks. (Skip this route on rainy days.) Picnic tables afford a good place to take a scenic break halfway through the trail. The San Antonio River winds between these parks. At one time, *acequias* wound along both sides of the river; today only the one in Espada Park is active. The latter flows south to one of the most rural sites on the trail — **Mission San Juan**, 9101 Graff Rd., *Tel. 210/534-0749*. This mission, fully named *San Juan Capistrano*, was once completely self-sustaining, supplying all its own needs from cloth to crops. San Juan provided not only for its own agricultural needs, but it also supplied other communities in the area. Skilled artisans made ironwork and leather goods and wove cloth in the workshops.

To appreciate the natural richness of this area, take a hike on the **San Juan Woodlands Trail**. In about one-third of a mile, the trail winds along the low river bottom land and gives you a look at many of the indigenous plants used by the mission.

The chapel, with its bell tower and elaborate alter, was destroyed by a storm in 1886. In 1909 the building was repaired and in the 1960s it underwent an extensive renovation. Today it is an active parish church and a good example of how San Antonio continues to use its historic structures both for tourists and for the local community. San Juan also has a small museum featuring items found at the site and artifacts typically used by missionaries in Texas. The theme of San Juan is *The Mission as an Economic Center,* and displays show how this self-sufficient mission worked with others to provide food and goods.

From Mission San Jose, head west on Mission Road to Ashley, turn left, then right on Espada Road. This will take you to the most remote spot on the trail: **Mission Espada**, 10040 Espada, *Tel. 210/627-2021*. Located about nine miles from the downtown area, this mission was named for St. Francis of Assisi, founder of the Monastic order of Franciscans. The mission's full name is *Mission San Francisco de la Espada* (*de la Espada* means "of the sword," referring to a decision by St. Francis as to whether he should be a soldier of God or of Spain).

This mission's theme is *The Mission as a Vocational Education Center*, carried out through displays on the education of the Indians in blacksmithing, woodworking, and other vocational areas.

When Are We Going?

Any time of year is a good time to visit the Mission Trail thanks to San Antonio's semi-tropical weather. If you plan a visit during the summer months, however, be prepared to deal with Texas heat, humidity, and summer crowds. The months of April and May are also especially busy as school groups check out the historic sites.

Our tip: start early in the morning with Mission Concepcion and be on down the trail by the time mid-day crowds come out. Most visitors never make it all the way to stops three and four. If you're staying more than one day in San Antonio, save a second day for a visit to the Alamo.

How Long Are We Staying?

A minimum of three hours should be set aside for visiting the missions but allow longer if you plan to read many exhibits or visit each of the missions. Also, allow extra driving time on weekends.

What Should I Bring?

Summer visitors will want to stay cool–wear cool clothing, carry a hat, wear sunscreen, and carry water in your car.

What Are We Doing Next?

There's one thing you won't have to worry about in San Antonio: running out of things to do. The Alamo City is filled with year-around fun for all members of the family. Some of our top picks include:

The Alamo, 300 Alamo Plaza between Houston and Crockett Streets, *Tel. 210/225-1391, www.thealamo.org,* is called the "Cradle of Texas Liberty" and is probably the most famous spot in Texas. Established in 1718 as the Mission San Antonio de Valero, it plunged into history on March 6, 1836, when 188 men died after being attacked by the Mexican forces of General Santa Anna. Among the most famous defenders were Jim Bowie, William B. Travis, and Davy Crockett.

Symbol of the state's independence and courage, the Alamo draws continuous crowds throughout the year. Visitors entering the main building, the Shrine, can see exhibits such as Bowie's famous knife and Davy Crockett's rifle, "Old Betsy." Those interested also can take a self-guided tour of the museum, the Long Barracks, and the beautiful courtyard. The Alamo is open daily; admission is free.

River Walk or Paseo Del Rio, *Tel. 210/227-4262, http://thesanantonioriverwalk.com,* is one of the most pleasurable and least expensive attractions in town. This arm of the San Antonio River winds through downtown below street level and is a shady place to stroll, enjoy a riverside dinner, and do a little shopping. The kids love the open barge tours, 35-minute narrated cruises. The River Walk is open daily; there is a charge for barge tours. Tours are priced at $6 adults $1.25 for children 1-5.

Tower of the Americas, HemisFair Park, *Tel. 210/207-8615, http:// toweroftheamericas.com,* is a 750-foot tower topped by a rotating restaurant that serves lunch and dinner. An observation deck offers an unbeatable view of the city. The tower is open daily; there is an admission fee.

Institute of Texan Cultures, HemisFair Park, *Tel. 210/458-2300, www.texancultures.utsa.edu/public,* is a fascinating museum which features exhibits and a multimedia presentation showcasing the 26 different ethnic groups who came here from around the world to settle the new frontier called Texas. Kids enjoy the costumed docents who explain what life was like for a cowboy or a frontier woman. The museum is open Tuesday through Sunday; admission is $6.50 children 3-12 $3 2 and under free.

IMAX Theater, Rivercenter Mall, *Tel. 210/247-4629 or 800-354-4629, www.imax-sa.com,* features The Price of Freedom, a 45-minute movie about the battle of the Alamo. The six-story screen and six-channel sound immerses you in the glory of the struggle, and it's a good thing to see before visiting the historic site. The theater alternates this movie with other IMAX features, so call for show times. The theater is open daily; there is an admission fee per show.

Plaza Wax Museum, 301 Alamo Plaza, *Tel. 210/224-9299, www.plazawaxmuseum.com,* is cheap and touristy but hey, the kids like it. 225 figures allow you to get up close to your favorite movie and TV personalities. Fairy tale characters such as Sleeping Beauty and Peter Pan are also on hand, as well as a theater of horrors (young children should skip this one). The "Heroes of The Lone Star" section is interesting, with realistic scenes depicting the fall of the Alamo. Ripley's Believe It or Not, with over five hundred exhibits, is located in the same building. You can buy separate or combination tickets to the two attractions. Both collections are open daily; there is an admission fee.

At **The San Antonio Children's Museum**, 305 East Houston Street, San Antonio, TX 78205, *Tel. 210/212-4453,* there are over eighty interactive exhibits designed to entertain as well as educate. Kids get the chance to play grown-up as they "fly" a child-sized airplane, and for those under five there is the Tot Spot, filled with oversized building blocks and an aquarium. Open seven days a week, varying hours.

The Texas Adventure, 307 Alamo Plaza, *Tel. 210/227-8224, www.texas-adventure.com* , is a state-of-the-art attraction that calls itself the world's first Encountarium F-X Theater. The six-minute pre-show does a good job of telling the story of the events that led up to the battle of the Alamo, then guests are ushered into a bench-lined room where holographic versions of Davy Crockett, William Travis, and Jim Bowie tell their story. It's interesting for all but the youngest of children, who may be frightened by "figures" materializing and disappearing throughout the presentation. The show is presented daily 8:30am- 8pm; there is an admission fee.

El Mercado, Market Square, *Tel. 210/207-8600, http://tavernini.com/ mercado*, is the largest Mexican market in the US. Styled after a typical Mexican market, El Mercado's dozens of shops sell a rich profusion of goods, from silver jewelry, Mexican dresses, and piñatas to onyx chess sets, leather goods, and much more. Prices are slightly higher than in the Mexican markets, and you can't bargain with the vendors like you can south of the border. This is a great place to take kids shopping for inexpensive gifts like piñatas. Open 10 AM- 8 PM during the summer months 10 AM- 6 PM in the winter closed Thanksgiving, Christmas, New Year's Day and Easter; admission is free.

San Antonio Zoo, 3903 N. St. Mary's St., *Tel. 210/734-7183, www.sazoo-aq.org*, features barless "habitat cages" for many of its animals. The cliffs of an abandoned quarry house over 3,500 birds, fish, mammals, and other fauna, making the zoo the third largest animal collection in North America. There's a children's petting area, a reptile house, and an aquarium. The zoo is open daily. Admission: adults $8, children 3-11, $6 2 and under free.

Sea World of Texas, Ellison Dr. and Westover Hills Blvd., off TX 151, 17 miles northwest of downtown, between Loop 410 and Loop 1604, *Tel. 210/523-3611*, is the largest marine-life park in the world. It's the home of Shamu the killer whale, plus dolphins, penguins, sea otters, and more. Visitors can enjoy two fast-moving water rides as well as acres of quiet gardens dotted with statues of famous Texans. Entertainment includes 25 shows, featuring a water-skiing extravaganza and breathtaking cycling performances. The park is open daily March through November; weekends only during cooler months. Call for hours; there is a (hefty) admission fee.

Six Flags Fiesta Texas, I-10 and Loop 1604, 15 miles northwest of downtown, *Tel. 210/697-5050 www.sixflags.com/parks/fiestatexas/index.asp*. This $100-plus million theme park focuses on the history, culture, and music of San Antonio and the Southwest. Seven theaters delight visitors with over 60 performances daily, including the award-winning and always packed "Rockin' at Rockville High" Grease-style musical production. For thrill seekers, rides range from white-water rafting to The Rattler, one of the tallest wooden roller coasters in the world and a real white knuckle ride. The park is open seasonally March through November; call for seasonal hours. There is a (hefty) admission fee.

Which One Is My Room?

There are no accommodations in the park but downtown you'll find plenty of hotels and motels in a variety of price ranges. Rooms along the River Walk are generally the most expensive in the city.

For a rundown of the properties in San Antonio, contact the **San Antonio Convention and Visitors Bureau**, *Tel. 800/447-3372.* Here's a selection of some of the many family accommodations in San Antonio:

Hyatt Hill Country Resort, 9800 Hyatt Resort Dr., *Tel. 800/233-1234,* is a full-service resort that offers the area's most luxurious getaway with an 18-hole golf course and a four-acre water park with a cascading waterfall and man-made Ramblin' River for inner-tube floaters. This 500-room resort nestles on 200 acres of a former cattle ranch, rolling land sprinkled with prickly pear cacti and live oaks. With its limestone architecture and Western decor, the four-story hotel has captured the atmosphere of the Hill Country, from windmills to gingerbread trim featuring the Lone Star (which often decorated homes of the German pioneers who settled area).

Admiralty Park, 1485 N. Ellison Dr., off Loop 1604, *Tel. 800/999-RVSA,* is an RV park is located only minutes from Sea World and Loop 1604. It includes a heated pool, brick patios at each site, free clubhouse movies, cable TV hookups, and more.

Practical Information

Address: San Antonio Missions National Historic Park, 2202 Roosevelt Ave., San Antonio, TX 78210

Telephone: *210/534-8833 Headquarters; 210/932-1001 Visitors Center*

Operating Season: year round; closed Thanksgiving Day, Christmas, New Year's Day

Hours: 9am-5pm daily

Cost: free

Website: *www.nps.gov/saan/index.htm*

Movies About The Alamo

- *The Alamo*— 1960 film starring American icon John Wayne as Davy Crockett
- *Alamo: Thirteen Days To Glory* — a 1987 made for TV movie starring James Arness as Jim Bowie
- *The Man From The Alamo* — This 1953 film starring Glenn Ford explains events through the eyes of a survivor of the battle
- *Davy Crockett, King of The Wild Frontier* — A Disney classic, this 1954 film stars Fess Parker
- *Davy Crockett and The River Pirates* — After watching this TV series, every child growing up in the 1950's wanted a coon skin cap. Sing along with the famous tune "The Ballad of Davy Crockett"

℞

Learning about the Missions

These books are good for children ages 9-12:

Nartelli, Judith. *Ricardo Walks the River Walk : A Story of Old San Antonio.* Eakin Publications, 1998.

Ragsdale, Crystal Sasse. *The Women and Children of the Alamo.* State House Press, 1994.

Santella, Andrew. *The Battle of the Alamo.* Children's Press, 1997.

Warner, Gertrude. *The Mystery at the Alamo* (Boxcar Children No. 58). Albert Whitman & Co., 1997.

Carlsbad Caverns National Park
New Mexico

Rated as one of the largest in the world, Carlsbad Caverns draws visitors from around the globe to tour this extensive underground labyrinth. Since the early 1900s, when cowboy Jim White first entered the dark cavern, visitors sought out its cool, damp recesses to view spectacular formations.

Are We There Yet?

The park is located 23 miles southwest of Carlsbad, New Mexico on US 62. El Paso lies 150 miles west of the park.

The closest community to the caverns is White's City, located seven miles from the park. Here you'll find camping, souvenir shops (and we mean a lot), gasoline, and picnic supplies.

What's There To Do Here?

Inside the park, you'll be met by 46,775 acres of pristine desert dotted with cacti and small vegetation, little changed from its earliest days. For a quiet look at the Chihuahuan desert, take the 9.5-mile Walnut Canyon scenic drive along the Guadalupe Ridge for an uninterrupted view of the quiet beauty of the desert.

But much of the beauty of Carlsbad Caverns National Park cannot be seen from above ground. To see the spectacular formations that have made this cave famous, you must descend below ground to a world that is perpetually 56 degrees, dark, and damp.

You can enter the cave in one of two ways. The natural entrance tour is a somewhat tough climb. This tour, about three miles in distance, takes about three hours to complete.

Many families opt for the elevator tour instead. A high-speed elevator whisks from ground level to the Big Room 750 feet below. This room is 8.2 acres in size, with a ceiling 255 feet high. This tour takes about half the time of the natural entrance tour, and spans a little over a mile in length.

Enjoy a look at the caverns at your own pace. Instead of keeping up with a group, you can rent CD-ROM audio guide called the Official Cavern Guide for a small charge and listen to information about the cave as you walk. (Got a tired kid and need a break? Your cave entry tickets are good for three days so feel free to break up the tour if you need to.)

Highlights of the tour include beautiful formations such as the Temple of the Sun, the Frozen Waterfall, and the King's Palace. Formed by deposits left by one water drop at a time, the king-sized formations are a testimony to the million years it took to create this cavern.

If your family is especially interested in caves and wants a more in-depth look (so to speak), there are several other tour options:

Kings Palace Guided Tour. This tour takes about an hour and a half and travels through four chambers to the deepest portion of the cave that's open to the public. It's a rugged walk (not as tough as the Natural Entrance tour, though) and children four years and younger cannot participate. Reservations required. Call *800/967-CAVE*.

Slaughter Canyon Cave. This two-hour tour takes you into a wild cave without electricity–the only light comes from your flashlights and headlamps. The cave has some spectacular formations including one of the world's tallest columns. You must make reservations for this tour, *Tel. 800/967-CAVE*. Only children age six and older can participate and everyone needs to bring along good walking shoes (there's a half-mile climb before the cave tour even starts). You'll also need to bring along some good flashlights (check the batteries!) and water.

Wild Cave Tours. These tours are for those with a real interest in caves and range from one hour excursions appropriate for kids six and up to four hour trips that mean wriggling on your belly to view some formations that few visitors ever have the opportunity to see; these longer tours are available only for children 12 and older. Each of these tours has its own requirements. Call *800/967-CAVE* for more information and reservations for these interesting tours.

When Are We Going?

The park is open year around except Christmas Day. Expect big crowds in June, July and August (especially on the weekends) but get there early for the best chance to beat the rush.

Even in the summer months, bring a sweater or jacket for everyone. The cave stays about 56 degrees Fahrenheit year around.

How Long Are We Staying?

Most families take the tour of the Big Room, a one-mile self-guided trail that takes about an hour. There is easily a full day's worth of activities at the cave, though, for those with more interest including longer trails, naturalist programs, films, and more. The evening bat flight programs (see *Bat Fun* sidebar below) are reason enough to extend your stay through dusk.

Bat Fun

If you can possibly extend your stay to the dusk hours, then you're in for a real treat. Every night Every night from Memorial Day through the end of September, hundreds of thousands of Mexican free-tailed bats head out for an evening of insect feeding at sunset.

During the summer months, a Ranger Talk about the bats is given at the cavern entrance. (Call the park for the starting time or check at the visitors center.) The best months for viewing the bat flights are August and September when you'll even have the chance to see baby bats joining in the nightly sojourn.

What Should I Bring?

Bring rubber soled shoes for everyone. A light jacket is also a must. If you'll be taking one of the wild cave tours, you'll need knee pads, gloves, flashlights, and batteries.

What Are We Doing Next?

Don't plan to spend your entire visit to Carlsbad underground. In the splendor of New Mexico's sunshine, the town of Carlsbad has plenty of activities to keep you busy.

Home to 25,000 residents, Carlsbad is nestled on the banks of the Pecos River in the Ocotillo Hills, the beginnings of the Guadalupe Mountains. Carlsbad was founded in 1888 as the community of Eddy, named for Charles Bishop Eddy. Later, city residents voted to call their town Carlsbad after a famous health resort, Karlsbad, in a part of Europe that is now Czechoslovakia. Carlsbad and Karlsbad had identical mineral waters valued for their health properties.

In the early days, Carlsbad was a ranching center, partly because of its abundant water. Today those waters make Carlsbad distinct from many other desert communities. The Pecos River slices right through the center of town, endowing the community with beautiful picnic grounds and top-notch fishing.

One of the best ways to enjoy the Pecos is a stroll along the downtown Riverwalk, just off US 180. This Riverwalk has four and a half miles of paths spanning both sides of the river. Plenty of shady picnic spots will give you a chance to stop and enjoy the scenic beauty of this downtown park.

The waters of the Pecos are filled with swimmers and skiers in the summer months, but year around you'll find children feeding the ducks and fishermen hoping for a lucky catch.

If you're looking for catfish, then you've come to the right place. Channel cat populate the Pecos, especially the stretch just south of the city. Other top fishing spots are Lake Carlsbad and Lake Avalon, stocked with trout, perch, bass, catfish, walleye, and bluegill.

You'll find wildlife of a different sort at the **Living Desert Zoo State Park**, Mills Drive, *Tel. 505/887-5516*. This park offers visitors a look at the plants and animals of the Chihuahuan Desert in their natural surroundings. Set high above the town of Carlsbad, the park is home to 60 species of birds, mammals, and reptiles as well as 1,000 plants from the Chihuahuan Desert and an equal number of exotic cacti from deserts around the world

In the aviary, birds of prey such as the Mexican eagle keep a sharp eye on their visitors. Many of the birds housed in the aviary, as well as animals in other displays, have been injured and cannot survive in the wild.

Bobcats and mountain lions, the largest felines in North America, are housed nearby in exhibit areas strewn with automobile-sized boulders. Here they rest above the visitors, keeping an eye on the activity at the park. Nearby, hoofed animals are contained in large fields to give them room to roam. Many of these creatures stay close to the trail, however, so have your camera ready for a close-up shot of a pronghorn antelope, buffalo, mule deer, or elk.

Wildlife still abounds in the **Lincoln National Forest**, 1101 New York Ave., Alamogordo, NM 88310, *Tel. 505/434-7200*, a sprawling refuge 50 miles northwest of Carlsbad. This forest is located in the Guadalupe Mountains, where some areas are as wild as the days when the first settlers came to this rugged land.

The most popular spot in the park is **Sitting Bull Falls**, *Tel. 505/887-6516*. A day use area, the falls include picnic tables and restrooms. Enjoy a picnic and a swim on warm days, or just sun yourself on the limestone ledges.

Which One Is My Room?

There is no lodging or camping in the park. The closest community to Carlsbad is White's City, located at the turn off for the national park.

The Carlsbad area is home to several campgrounds, including **White's City Campground**, *Tel. 800/CAVERNS*; **Lake Carlsbad Campground**, *Tel. 505/885-4435;* **Windmill RV Park**, *Tel. 888/349-7275 or 505/885-9761;* **Carlsbad Campgrounds**, *Tel. 505/885-6333*; and **Brantley Lake State Park**, *Tel. 505/457-2384*.

For city information, contact the **Carlsbad Chamber of Commerce**, PO Box 910, Carlsbad, NM 88220 or call *505/887-6516*.

Ask for a free copy of the **New Mexico Vacation Guide** by calling *800/545-2040*. The 180-page guide includes a state map and information on attractions, recreation, and camping.

Practical Information
  Address: Carlsbad National Park, 3225 National Parks Highway, Carlsbad, NM 88220
  Telephone: *505/785-2232*
  Operating Season: year round, closed Dec. 25
  Hours: Visitors center open 8am-7pm during summer months, 8am-5pm during non-peak times. Self-guided cave tours are available 8:30am-5pm during summer months and 8:30am-3:30pm during non-peak seasons.
  Cost: $6 individual entrance fee— lasts three days Cave tours range from $7 to $20.
  Restrictions: No pets in the amphitheater or cave (there is a kennel at the park; call *505/785-2281* for information). No flash photography during the bat flights.
  Website: *www.nps.gov/cave/index.htm*

White Sands National Monument
New Mexico
  This is the Sahara in basic white: Miles of blindingly white sand that rolls over the desert, rising and falling, changing with the winds.

Are We There Yet?
  White Sands is located in southeast New Mexico. The Visitors Center is located on US 70/82 15 miles southwest of Alamogordo or 52 miles east of Las Cruces.

What's There To Do Here?
  A visit to White Sands is simple: go out and have fun. Run and jump and play in the miles of undulating white dunes, enjoy a picnic, play explorer, just have a good time. Four trails are available although you can walk anywhere. The marked trails are a great way to get oriented, though. (With a lack of landmarks, it's easy to become lost in the dunes. Your footprints are blown away most days so don't count on following them back.)
  There is a boardwalk that's great for strollers as well as wheelchairs.
  A great program for young visitors is the new **Junior Dunes Ranger Program**. The program has three age levels: pre-school, age 6-8 and age 9 and up. Activities include everything from scavenger hunt bingo to coloring pages and the program is free. To sign up your child, just stop by the visitors center when you arrive and ask for the activity guide for your child's age. Once the activities are completed, return to the visitors center and pick up your child's patch and certificate!

When Are We Going?
The peak visitation months are March through August, mostly in the summer, although the park is open year around. During the summer months, you'll find the dunes hot so bring plenty of sunscreen, light colored clothing, sunglasses, and hats.

How Long Are We Staying?
You can spend anywhere from an hour to a full day exploring the dunes (and longer if you want to camp) but most people will find two to three hours plenty of time for a romp in the sand.

What Should I Bring?
Sunscreen and protective sun equipment (hats, sunglasses, even lightweight long-sleeved shirts for fair-skinned people) are essential. The sun glares off the white sand so you'll be totally exposed. Bring along beach toys for the kids to enjoy in the sand as well.

What Are We Doing Next?
Ruidoso is filled with cultural attractions. A multitude of art galleries attest to the inspiration found in this landscape. The city is also home **to The Hubbard Museum of The American West** (formerly the Museum of The Horse) *Tel. 505/378-4142.* Appropriately housed adjacent to the Ruidoso Downs race track, this establishment displays a collection of over 10,000 horse-related items and pays tribute to the relationship between jockey and horse. Children can try on western duds and have their photo taken in a jockey's saddle wearing a helmet and goggles. Open year round from 9am-5pm. Adults $6, $2 for children 6-16, children under 6 free. Located on 841 Hwy 70 W, 1/4 mile from the race track.
Other attractions include:
International Space Museum and Planetarium, *Tel. 877-333-6589.* From the IMAX movies to the International Space Hall of Fame, this museum is a moving tribute to those who have dared to reach beyond earth's boundaries. Open 7 days a week, 9am- 5pm Adult— $2.50 for museum, $6 for IMAX movie, children 4 -12 $2 museum, $4.50 for IMAX movie, children 3 and under free Turn East on Indian Wells Road At intersection of Indian Wells Road and Scenic Drive turn left on Scenic Drive, travel for 100 yards to Hwy 2001.
Take a ride on one of three passenger trains which travel a two mile stretch of **Alameda Park** and see hundreds of miniature locomotives displayed in a 100 year old depot. Toy Train Depot, 1991 White Sands Blvd. 505/437-2855 Open Wednesday-Sunday from noon to 5pm.
Watch whimsical otters and monkeys at play at the **Alameda Park Zoo,** 1321 N. White Blvd. *Tel. 800/545-4021*, home to over 90 different

species. Open every day but Christmas and New Years from 9am - 5pm. Adults $2.20, children 3 -11 $1.10, children under 2 free.

Mescalero Apache Indian Reservation *Tel. 505/671-4494.* This reservation is home to over 3,000 Native Americans. Don't miss St. Joseph's Apache Mission, with an icon of an Apache Christ. Powwows are performed at various times of the year.

For more information on the region, contact the **Ruidoso Chamber of Commerce**, *Tel. 505/257-7395.*

Which One Is My Room?

You'll find only primitive camping in the park. Permits are required and you'll have to pack in your own water.

Other campgrounds are available outside the park in Alamogordo, 15 miles away, and Oliver Lee Memorial State Park, 22 miles from the park. You'll also find accommodations in Las Cruces, 52 miles away.

You can contact the following for more information on accommodations:
- **New Mexico Department of Tourism**, *Tel. 800/733-6396*
- **Cloudcroft Chamber of Commerce**, *Tel. 505/682-2733*
- **Ruidoso Valley Convention and Visitors Bureau**, *Tel. 505/257-7395*

Special Events at White Sands

Throughout the summer months, full moon programs are planned. Special astronomy programs include telescope viewing, slide programs, meteor shower viewing, and other activities depending on activities. Star talks are planned for many Friday nights throughout the summer; call the park for dates.

Practical Information

Address: White Sands National Monument, PO Box 1086, Holloman A.F.B., NM 88330

Telephone: *505/679-2599 or 505/479-6124*

Operating Season: year round; closed Dec. 25

Hours: Visitors Center 8am-7pm (8.-5 p.m during non-summer months); Dunes Drive 7am-10pm (7am-sunset off peak)

Cost: $3 age 17 and older (admission good for seven days). A White Sands Park Pass, good for one year, is $20

Restrictions: The park occasionally closes if missile testing is going on at the White Sands Missile Range. During these times, the park is closed for up to two hours (as well as the US 70/82 from Alamogordo to Las Cruces.) Also, dogs must remain on a leash.

Website: *www.nps.gov/whsa/index.htm*

Did You Know.....?

• New Mexico is a sparsely populated state, with only twelve people per square mile.

• Each August the city of Gallup hosts the Inter-Tribal Indian Ceremonial.

• Each October the city of Albuquerque hosts the world's largest hot air balloon festival.

• New Mexico is also known as The Land of Enchantment."

• The state song is "O, Fair New Mexico."

• Yellow and red, which represent the colors of Spain, were chosen for the state flag

• The design on the state flag is called a Zia. It is an ancient sun symbol.

• The state motto is "Crescit eundo," which means "It grows as it goes."

• The official state tree is the Pinyon Pine.

• Hatch, New Mexico is considered the Green Chile Capital of the World.

• The state capital is Santa Fe.

• The Rio Grande river runs the entire length of the state.

• The Anasazi, or "Ancient Ones", once lived in New Mexico, and so far archaeologists have unearthed over 25,000 Anasazi sites.

• The leaves of the state flower, the Yucca, can be useful for making baskets and sandals.

Arches National Park
Utah

Like its name suggests, this park has the largest concentration of sandstone arches in the world. Truly a natural wonder, this park is a good place for enjoying beautiful scenery and is also a great destination for any budding photographer, young or old, you might have in the family.

Are We There Yet?

Arches is located in the southern section of Utah near the town of Moab. From Moab, take Utah 191 north for five miles.

What's There To Do Here?

The main activities here are centered around hiking. Before you head off down the trail, make a stop at the visitors center, located near the park entrance. Here you can watch an orientation program about the park's beautiful formations.

Most families choose to see the park on the road trail. This is a 48-mile trip through the park which takes you to the major attractions for a good view. Courthouse Towers might look familiar to you— this majestic site was featured in the movie Thelma and Louise. The trip would not be complete without seeing the beauty of Delicate Arch, and be sure to stop by nearby Wolfe Ranch, where a settler's log cabin dating from the 1800's still stands.

Some other family activities include picnics, biking, photographing the arches, and hikes with rangers into Fiery Furnace. This moderately strenuous tour, lasting anywhere from 2 1/2 to 3 hours, is held from March through October; check with the visitors center for times. There is a charge for this guided tour: $8 for adults, $4 for ages 6-12, with children under the age of 6 admitted free.

When Are We Going?

The peak visiting months are March through October. The summer months are toasty at this latitude: expect the mercury to regularly hit 100 degrees during the summer. Bring the sunscreen!

If you visit the park in the winter, plan on opposite extremes. Winter temperatures are often below freezing and can fluctuate to over 50 degrees throughout the day.

How Long Are We Staying?

If you just want to check out the visitors center and drive the road tour, plan on a stop of at least two to three hours. Schedule longer if you will be hiking or picnicking in the park.

What Should I Bring?

Cool clothing is important in the summer months, along with good walking shoes.

What Are We Doing Next?

Southern Utah is dotted with national parks. In this southern part of the state, vacationers will find a more rugged beauty, a place rich with national parks that offer year around recreation. The city of **St. George**, population 40,000, enjoys the warmest climate in Utah. Here the atmosphere is semi-tropical with summer days averaging in the 90s and winter months usually topping out at 60 degrees (although winter sports can be found nearby at Brianhead Ski Resort.)

"St. George is the gateway to one of the largest concentrations of national monuments in the US," said Penny Shelly, Executive Director of the Washington County Travel & Convention Bureau. **Zion National Park**, carved by nature from Navajo sandstone, and **Bryce Canyon National Park**, with 13 natural amphitheaters, are two nearby scenic attractions. For more information, see the Bryce Canyon National park entry in this book.

The Zion Canyon Cinemax Theatre shows the giant six-story screen production called *Treasure of the Gods* at the 500-seat theater near the park entrance. A popular summer activity is the outdoor musical drama *UTAH!* about the state's early days.

Which One Is My Room?

The park campground, Devils Garden Campground, has 50 tent and trailer sites and these are at a premium during summer months and even as early as mid-March and as late as October. This campground is located 18 miles from the park entrance and the facility includes flush toilets and water, at least until freezing weather. To snag one of these sites in the peak months, you'll need to go by the Visitor's Center EARLY in the morning (between 7:30 and 8am) or be at the entrance station by 8am. These spots fill up very fast. The National Recreation Reservation System offers both telephone and online reservations. See their website, *www.ReserveUSA.com,* or call either *877/444-6777* or *877/833-6777*.

If you don't get one of those sites, you'll find other accommodations in the area: **Moab Chamber of Commerce**, *Tel. 435/259-7814; e-mail info@moabchamber.com.*

and **St. George Chamber of Commerce**, *Tel. 435/628-1658; e-mail hotspot@stgeorgechamber.com.*

It's best to book ahead, especially in Moab, since outdoor sports fans mob the place from spring to autumn.

Arches in the Movies!

During your stay in Arches National Park any movie lover in your family will recognize several familiar landmarks. This 73,000 acre expanse of land has provided a rugged backdrop for a variety of popular Hollywood films, including:
- *Indiana Jones and The Last Crusade*
- *City Slickers II: The Legend of Curly's Gold*
- *Thelma and Louise*
- *Cheyenne Autumn*
- *Warlock*

Practical Information
Address: Arches National Park, PO Box 907, Moab, UT 84532
Telephone: *435/719-2299*

Operating Season: Year round; closed Christmas Day
Hours: Visitor Center open from 8 AM - 4:30 PM daily, with extended hours spring through fall)
Cost: $10 per vehicle; admission is good for seven consecutive days
Restrictions: No food is available in the park. Stock up before you come!
Website: www.nps.gov/arch/index.htm

Learning about Utah

Fradin, Dennis Brindell. *Utah*. Children's Press, 1997. Ages 9-12.

McCarthy, Betty. *Utah* (America the Beautiful). Children's Press, 1989. Ages 9-12.

Salts, Bobbi and Steve Parker (Illustrator). *Utah is for Kids*. Golden Books, 1991. Ages 4-8.

Sirvaitis, Karen. *Utah* (Hello USA). Lerner Publications Co., 1996. Ages 9-12.

Thompson, Kathleen. *Utah* (Portrait of America.) Raintree/Steck Vaughn, 1996. Ages 9-12.

Bryce Canyon National Park
Utah

This southern Utah park has some beautiful formations caused by erosion. A great place for hiking and outdoor photography, this park is also a favorite with those looking for a place to view the night sky far from city lights.

Are We There Yet?

The park is located off US89. From US 89, take Utah 12 east to the junction of Utah 12 and 63. Turn south on Utah 63 and continue to the park.

If you are traveling from the east, take Utah 12 west to the intersection of Utah 63. Turn south.

The park may seem like it's located a long way from civilization, but if you visit on a peak weekend you'll see that civilization has come to Bryce Canyon. To cut back on the number of cars in the park, the park is instituting a shuttle bus service between mid-May and the end of September. Use of the shuttle isn't mandatory, but if you bring your vehicle in the park you'll have to pay $5.

What's There To Do Here?

Hiking is the top activity in the park, with over 50 miles of trails from which to choose. For an easy hike of one mile or less, families might consider the 1/2 mile walk on Rim Trail between Sunset and Sunrise Points, the one mile long Bristlecone Loop, and Mossy Cave, which is only 0.9 miles.

Adventurous families can stay up late and take a ranger-led special nighttime hike under a full moon. Tours are limited to thirty people, and tickets must be bought on the day of the hike at the visitor center.

See the sites like a real cowboy, on horseback, as actual wranglers take your family on a guided two hour tour. These authentic cowboys have twenty years of experience, so there is no need to worry if you have never saddled up. Kids can even pick from the two hundred horses and mules available for their ride. Children must be at least seven years of age to go on this tour, which is offered from spring through fall. For further information call either *435/679-8665* or *435/834-5500*.

Kids ages 12 and under can take part in the **Junior Ranger Program** here. Children attend a ranger-led activity so they'll need about a day's visit to the park to complete their booklets and pick up a Junior Ranger certificate.

When Are We Going?
Summer months are by far the busiest in the park; watch out for busy weekends, especially the Fourth of July.

Early spring and autumn months are beautiful times in the park and offer a more peaceful experience, without the heavy crowds of summer.

How Long Are We Staying?
Because of its distant location, you'll probably want at least one full day to enjoy some hikes and get a feel for the park.

What Should I Bring?
Good walking shoes are a must. In the summer, don't forget hats, sunscreen, and sunglasses for everyone.

What Are We Doing Next?
The Anasazi State Park Museum, eighty miles from Bryce Canyon in Boulder, UT, is an opportunity to learn about an ancient civilization who were the forerunners to the Pueblo people. Now referred to as Coombs Site, there are over one hundred Anasazi (or "cliff dwellers") buildings, as well as a number of artifacts on display including pottery no larger than a quarter. For more information call *435/335-7308* or *email anasazi@utah.gov*.

Get information on other southern Utah attractions and its many national parks by calling the **Garfield County Travel Council**, *Tel. 800/444-6689*.

Which One Is My Room?
The **Bryce Canyon Lodge** offers guest rooms and cabins from April 1 through the end of October. For reservations, write Xanterra Parks and Resorts, 14001 East Iliff Ave., Suite 600, Aurora, CO 80014; *Tel. 303/297-2757*, *www.nps.gov/brca/lodging.html*. For further information visit their website at *www.brycecanyonlodge.com*.

Campers have two options in the park, both on a first-come, first served basis. The campgrounds have no hookups but they're still plenty popular–if you don't get there shortly after lunch you won't get a space.

Practical Information
Address: Bryce Canyon National Park, PO Box 170001, Bryce Canyon, Utah 84717-0001
Telephone: 435/834-5322
Operating Season: year round; visitors center closed Thanksgiving, Dec. 25, Jan. 1
Hours: visitors center hours vary by season
Cost: $20 per vehicle for 7-day pass
Website: *www.nps.gov/brca*

Did You Know.....?
- The man who invented television, Philo T. Farnsworth, was born in Beaver, Utah.
- Utah's nickname is The Beehive State.
- The capital of Utah is Salt Lake City.
- Bryce Canyon National Park was named in honor of Ebenezer Bryce, a pioneer who settled in the area along with his family in 1875.
- The state bird of Utah is the common American Gull.
- The official state fish is the rainbow trout.
- Each year over 1.5 million people from every corner of the globe visit Bryce Canyon National Park.
- Entertainers Donny and Marie Osmond are from Utah, as is football quarterback Steve Young.
- The first department store in America, Zion's Co-operative Mercantile Institution, was built in Utah.
- The official state animal is the Rocky Mountain Elk.
- The long-running television series "Touched By An Angel" was filmed in Utah.
- The limestone, sandstone and mudstone spires in the Bryce Canyon National Park are called "hoodoos."
- The state flower is the sego lily.
- Utah was named in honor of the Ute tribe, who are also known as "people of the mountains."

Zion National Park
Utah

Zion National Park, carved by nature from Navajo sandstone, is known for its spectacular natural formation. The park is home to the world's largest arch as well as numerous wildlife, from mountain lions to majestic golden eagles.

Are We There Yet?

The park is located in southern Utah, 46 miles from St. George. From I-15 take Exit 40 to reach the park and the Kolob Canyons entrance.

What's There To Do Here?

Hikers will find a full vacation's worth of activity right in the park. Keep your eye out for birds during your walks, as Zion is home to over 290 species. Other activities include:

Horseback riding. From March through October you can take guided horseback tours of the park. Check with the visitors centers for times. *Tel. 435/772-3810* for Zion Lodge trail rides desk

Swimming. Cool off during summer visits on the Virgin River.

Bicycling. A family-friendly choice for biking is the Pa-rus Trail, free from cars and with good views.

Ranger Activities. The park has a good program of ranger-led activities with topics that range from natural to cultural history of the area. The programs are free and change frequently; check with the visitors centers for times.

Junior Ranger. Zion has a great Junior Ranger program for ages six to 12. Kids take part in the Junior Ranger program and other interpretive programs such as guided walks, patio talks, and evening programs to earn awards in the program. Children can earn a Junior Ranger Program certificate, an Assistant Junior Ranger button or a Junior Ranger patch for taking part in activities such as a morning in the Zion Nature Center to learn about spiders, a petroglyph party to search out ancient drawings, and rock hunting. The program only takes place during the summer months; for more information write or call Zion National Park, Springdale, Utah 84767, *Tel. 435/772-0169*.

When Are We Going?

Summer is the peak season at Zion. Be prepared for warm temperatures during these months, although nights can get cool. Spring and fall are beautiful times to visit the park, with fewer visitors and displays of native wildflowers.

How Long Are We Staying?

At a very minimum, you'll want a full day to explore this park. Plan for a longer visit if you'll be horseback riding, hiking, or bicycling.

Navajo Language

There are currently over thirty-five different Native American tribes residing in Utah, consisting mainly of the people of the Navajo nation. During the second world war, the complex language of the Din'e (a word which translates as "The People") helped to transmit military information. See if you can learn a few Navajo words:

- bear— shush
- bird— tsidi
- buzzard— jay-sho
- cat— moasi
- deer— be
- dog— lha-cha-eh
- eagle— atsah
- fox— ma-e
- horse— lin
- owl— ne-ahs-jah
- rabbit— gah
- snake— klesh
- turkey— than-zie

What Should I Bring?

Sunscreen, hats, and sunglasses are important accessories during the summer months. Bring along swimsuits and an old t-shirt if you'll be inner tubing.

What Are We Doing Next?

The **Zion Canyon Cinemax Theatre** shows the giant six-story screen production of *Treasure of the Gods* at the 500-seat theater near the park entrance.

A popular summer activity is the outdoor musical drama *UTAH!* about the state's early days. *Tel. 888/256-3456, www.zioncanyontheatre.com.*

Bryce Canyon and Arches National parks are other good options in southern Utah. See those headings for more activities in the area.

Which One Is My Room?

You'll find family accommodations at the **Zion Lodge**, *Tel. 303/297-2757.* Family accommodations are also available outside the park in communities such as Kanab, Springdale, and others; for information on these accommodations call **Travel Services Utah**, *Tel. 800/259-3843*, or check out the website at *www.zionpark.com.*

Camping is available in the park at the south entrance. Campsites are on a first-come, first-served basis; some sites have electrical hookups. During the summer months, you'll want to arrive before noon to get a space.

Practical Information

Address: Superintendent, Zion National Park, SR9, Springdale, UT 84767-1099

Telephone: *435/772-3256*

Operating Season: year around; visitors center closed Dec. 25

Hours: 8-7 during summer months; shorter hours during non-peak season

Cost: $20 per vehicle for seven-day pass

Website: *www.nps.gov/zion/index.htm*

Learning About Zion

Madsen, Susan Arrington (editor). *Growing Up in Zion: True Stories of Young Pioneers Building the Kingdom.* Deseret Books, 1996.

Marsh, Carole. *Utah: Indian Dictionary for Kids!* Gallopade Publishing Group, 1995. Ages 9-12.

Marsh, Carole. *Utah Facts and Factivities.* Gallopade Publishing Group, 1996. Ages 9-12.

Petersen, David L. *Zion National Park* (A New True Book). Children's Press, 1993. Ages 4-8.

Grand Canyon National Park
Arizona

No other destination in the National Park System is as instantly recognizable as Grand Canyon. Definitely one of the "must sees" in the system, this park offers a variety of activities depending on your adventure level.

Are We There Yet?

Grand Canyon National Park is located off Route 180 about 80 miles northwest of Flagstaff or off Route 64 from I-40 from Williams 60 miles north of the park.

Once you're in the park, you can take advantage of free shuttle service from mid-March through mid-October. The shuttle moves vacationers from the Grand Canyon Village along West Rim Drive (which is closed to private auto traffic during peak months). There's also a shuttle between the North Rim and South Rim; for information and prices contact **Trans Canyon Shuttle**, *Tel. 928/638-2820.*

What's There To Do Here?

Start your visit with a stop at the visitors center on the South Rim, located near Grand Canyon Village to learn more about the creation of this spectacular canyon. The Grand Canyon invites long looks out at the canyon from both the North and South Rims. You'll find many scenic overlooks and one of the best activities is just to look out at the canyon. Watch children carefully at these overlooks, however; drops can be sheer. Other activities include:

Ranger programs. Interpretive programs for all ages are led daily during peak season. Programs are free; to learn times and subjects check the park newspaper you'll get at the park entrance.

Mule Rides. A fun (though bumpy!) way to explore the canyon is with a full or half day ride by mule. From the North Rim you can take a full or half day trip (from the South Rim you can book a one day or a two-day trip). These don't go all the way to the bottom of the canyon but give you a sense of exploring the region. For reservations, call **Grand Canyon Trail Rides**, *Tel. 435/679-8665.*(Check on the status of mule rides on the South Rim; due to road conditions, rides had been temporarily

Overnight Mule Trips. From the South Rim you can take a two-day, one-night trip down into the Canyon to see the Colorado River. You'll spend the night at Phantom Ranch below the rim. Reservations are a must for these excursions; you can call **Xanterra Parks and Resorts** , *Tel. 303/297-2757,* up to 11 months in advance. Only families with older children can take one of these trips, however: all rides must be over 4 feet 7 inches tall (and less than 200 pounds). Also, pregnant vacationers, look elsewhere for activities.

Flightseeing. Air tours are conducted for a true bird's eye view of the canyon. For details, contact **Grand Canyon Chamber of Commerce**, PO Box 3007, Grand Canyon, AZ 86023.

Bus Tours. If you'd like to take a guided bus tour to let someone else do the driving for a while, call *303/297-2757* or write **AmFac Parks & Resorts**, 14001 E. Iliff, Aurora, CO 80014.

Did You Know.....?

- Nearly five million tourists flock to Grand Canyon every year.
- Grand Canyon was formed roughly five million years ago, and some of the rocks lining the bottom are two billion years old.
- Grand Canyon offers over 400 miles of trails.
- There are 1,500 plant species growing in Grand Canyon.
- Some of the Hollywood movies to film here include Vacation, Maverick and Fools Rush In.
- Grand Canyon's first trail, Bright Angel Trail, opened in 1891.

When Are We Going?

If you are like millions of other travelers, you'll be visiting this park from April through October. One of the most popular sites in the park system, Grand Canyon sees five million visitors a year so be prepared for crowds during summer months. Even in off peak months, you'll find crowds on some weekends.

The summer months are beautiful at the canyon, with temperate days that can even be downright chilly thanks to the elevation. Bring layers any time of year. If you visit during the winter, expect snow (and don't be surprised to see snow on the North Rim during fall and spring months as well.)

How Long Are We Staying?

We'd really recommend an overnight visit if at all possible and more than one night certainly won't be a waste. You can do the park as a day visitor but because of crowds and limited parking you'll want to get here very early if you don't plan to spend the night.

What Should I Bring?

Your packing list will reflect the activities you choose. At the very least, bring layers of clothing including a jacket even during summer months since evenings can get nippy. A hat, sunglasses and sunscreen are important. Good shoes with non-slip soles are a must-have. If you will be taking a pack trip on a mule, be sure to bring long pants.

What Are We Doing Next?

A popular addition to the Grand Canyon experience is the **Grand Canyon IMAX theater**. The theater is located in the town of Tusayan and features the *Grand Canyon—Hidden Secrets,* 35 minutes in length.

Time has never revealed the mystery behind the Anasazi's disappearance, but the villages of "the ancient ones" are still standing as a testament to their existence at the Navajo National Monument in Tonalea. At the visitors center there are artifacts and two videos which illustrate both the beauty of the land and its people.

Throughout the summer months there are demonstrations of Native American crafts such as silversmithing and basket weaving. \ Learn about the plants once used by the indigenous people of the area as you walk the trail which lead from the visitors center to the Betatakin cliff dwelling. Three to four-hour free guided tours are also available, weather permitting.

Children will enjoy the Junior Ranger program, which educates youngsters on the lives of Native Americans through storytelling, nature walks, and learning how to paint a Navajo design. For more information on this national park, write Navajo National Monument, HC-71, Box 3, Tonalea, AZ 86044-9704 or call *928/672-2700.*

More dwellings left behind by The Ancient Ones can be found at **Canyon de Chelly National Monument** in Chinle, Arizona. To journey past the White House ruins requires either a park ranger or an authorized guide from **Thunderbird Lodge**. Run by members of the Navajo nation, this 73 room lodge offers half day and full day jeep trips to the cliff dwellings, which were erected between AD 350 and 1300. The lodge also offers authentic Navajo cuisine (continental meals are also available) and a gift shop filled with Native American crafts. To receive further information about Canyon de Chelly National Monument write to PO Box 588, Chinle, AZ 86503 or call *928/674-5500*. For more information on Thunderbird Lodge, call *800/679-2473*.

Which One Is My Room?

Before we discuss lodging options, we're going to give you a word of advice: make your reservations early! With five million visitors a year, you can bet that every campsite and lodge room books up. Paris remembers traveling to Grand Canyon with her parents as a child and the family booking a lodge room once they arrived. That was years ago (we won't say how many) and today's travelers don't often have that kind of luck. Make your plans early.

Here are your options for the South Rim. Each of these accommodations are handled by **Grand Canyon National Park Lodges**. For reservations at any of these properties, call *303/297-2757, Fax 303/297-3175,* or write **Xanterra Parks and Resorts**, 14001 E. Iliff, Aurora, CO 80014.

El Tovar. This is one of the most famous lodges in the national park system, perched right on the South Rim. The lodge was built in 1905 by the Santa Fe Railroad and is worth a visit even if you aren't staying here.

Bright Angel Lodge. Built in 1935, this lodge has hotel rooms as well as cabins, all built in a rustic style. Don't miss the fireplace in the lodge, constructed of rocks that represent each of the geologic periods at the park.

Kachina and Thunderbird Lodges. These lodges are modern and located on the South Rim near El Tovar. Both lodges are identical.

Maswik Lodge. This lodge offers modern rooms similar to a motel. You can choose from motel rooms or cabins (which are closed during the winter season). This lodge is a good choice for those with an eye on the budget.

Yavapai Lodge. This lodge is the largest in the park and offers motel-like accommodations. It's not on the rim but you can walk to the South Rim from your room. It's also near the visitors center as well as the general store and other facilities in Grand Canyon Village.

Phantom Ranch. This lodge is below the canyon rim and offers cabins and dormitory accommodations.

The North Rim also offers accommodations during the season, including:

Grand Canyon Lodge. This lodge is right on the rim at Bright Angel Point and offers motel-like accommodations and cabins. The lodge was built in the 1920s features huge windows that overlook the canyon.

You'll also find lodging outside the park in the communities of **Williams** (60 miles away) and **Flagstaff** (80 miles away). For information and reservations at Williams, call *800/863-0546*, and for Flagstaff call *928/774-4505*.

Another option is camping on the South Rim. The campsites take reservations up to three months in advance. Campsites run between $15 and $20 during peak months Write to **Grand Canyon National Park**, Backcountry Information Center, PO Box 129, Grand Canyon, AZ 86023 or fax your request to *928/638-2125*. You'll pay $10 for the permit and $5 per night per person.

Practical Information

Address: Grand Canyon National Park, PO Box 129, Grand Canyon, AZ 86023

Telephone: *928/638-7888*

Operating Season: South Rim open year around; North Rim open mid-May to late October

Hours: 24 hours daily

Cost: $20 per car

Website: www.nps.gov/grca/index.htm

Learning About the Grand Canyon

McAnally, Kathleen. *Letters from the Canyon*. Grand Canyon Association, 1995. Ages 4-8.

Minor, Wendell. *Grand Canyon: Exploring a Natural Wonder*. Scholastic Trade, 1998. Ages 4-8.

Vieira, Linda and Christopher Canyon (Illustrator). *Grand Canyon: A Trail Through Time*. Walker and Company, 1997. Ages 4-8.

Montezuma Castle National Monument
Arizona

Montezuma Castle is one of those sights that has to be seen to be believed. Nestled in a cliff face, this ancient dwelling was constructed about 600 years ago as the home to prehistoric Sinagua Indians. And, no, it wasn't the home of Montezuma the Aztec leader as was first thought.

Are We There Yet?

Montezuma Castle is about 50 miles south of Flagstaff or 90 miles north of Phoenix. The park is located off I-17 at exit 289.

What's There To Do Here?

Have a look at the visitors center to learn more about the ancient residents of this desert "apartment house" then take a walk on the 1/3-mile trail to the foot of the cliff. You cannot go up into the castle but you can view it from the trail.

When Are We Going?
Summer is the peak season at this park but be prepared for high temperatures during this time. Spring and fall months are excellent times to visit.

How Long Are We Staying?
Plan on about a two-hour visit to see the exhibits and take the trail.

What Should I Bring?
Bring along sunscreen, hats, and sunglasses during the summer months. A bottle of water for the trail is nice to have as well.

Which One Is My Room?
There are no accommodations in the park. You will find accommodations in **Camp Verde**, Chamber of Commerce, *Tel. 520/567-9294*, about five miles away.

Practical Information
Address: Montezuma Castle National Monument, Box 219, Camp Verde, AZ 86322
Telephone: *520/567-3322*
Operating Season: year round
Hours: 8am-5pm winter; 8am-7pm summer
Cost: $2 per person (age 16 and under free)
Website: *www.nps.gov/moca/index.htm*

Petrified Forest National Park
Arizona
Fossil lovers will enjoy Petrified Forest, a park that is home to the world's largest concentration of petrified wood as well as many fossils dating back 225 million years.

Are We There Yet?
This park is located one hour west of Gallup, New Mexico or two hours east of Flagstaff and is easy to reach from the interstate highway. From I-40 heading west, exit at mile marker 311; from I-40 east exit at Holbrook then take US 180 east to the park. Entrances to the park are found on the north end at I-40 and the south end at US 180.

What's There To Do Here?

Most visitors make their first stop at the Painted Desert Visitor Center, located at the north entrance. Here you'll learn more about what makes petrified wood and the fascinating natural history of this region. Another recommended stop is the Painted Desert Inn National Historic Landmark, located two miles from the north entrance. Here kids can visit an old trading post that now serves as a museum. Often you'll find Native American demonstrating local crafts as well.

When Are We Going?

Summer months are the most heavily visited, but even then you won't find thundering crowds. During the summer months, be prepared for high temperatures so bring cool clothes, sunscreen, and hats.

In the winter months, visitation is very low and the park cools off to temperatures ranging from 20s to 40s, with occasional snow.

How Long Are We Staying?

Most visitors stay about two hours, enough time to enjoy the visitors centers and a drive through the park.

Practical Information

Address: Petrified Forest National Park, PO Box 2217, Petrified Forest National Park, AZ 86028

Telephone: *520/524-6228*

Operating Season: year round; closed Christmas and New Year's Day

Hours: 7:30am-5pm; extended hours during summer months

Cost: $10 per car

Website: *www.nps.gov/pefo/index.htm*

Learning About the Petrified Forest

Diamond, Lynnell. *Let's Discover Petrified Forest National Park.* Mountaineers Book, 1991. Ages 6-11.

Marsh, Carole. *The Phantastic Painted Desert and the Phenomenal Petrified Forest.* Gallopade Publishing Group, 1996. Ages 9-12.

Petersen, David. *Petrified Forest National Park* (True Book). Children's Press, 1996. Ages 9-12.

Mesa Verde National Park
Colorado

We think that Mesa Verde is a great park for families with school-age children. While its trails may be too much for younger children, older kids will love the almost dollhouse-like quality of the dwellings tucked in the cliffs. The ancient history of the site is a wonderful introduction to the West.

Are We There Yet?

The park is located in southwestern Colorado between Cortez and Mancos off US 160.

Once you reach the park entrance, however, don't think you're there. You've got a drive of over 20 miles ahead to get to the archaeological sites. It's a slow, winding drive so allow about 45 minutes to reach this area.

What's There To Do Here?

We visited Mesa Verde with our daughter on the way to some of Colorado's dude ranches and a look at the archaeological sites brought back memories of our own childhood visits to the area.

You'll want to budget at least half a day here (remember that 45-minute drive in and out). Begin your journey back in time at the **Far View Visitors Center** for orientation to the park and to buy tickets to one of the many tours. Join the one hour, ranger-guided tour of Cliff Palace, built by the Anasazi around 1200 AD and forgotten by the world until 1888, when two cowboys looking for wandering cattle rediscovered this architectural wonder.

There are also ranger-guided tours of Balcony House and Long House, which is open from Memorial Day weekend through Labor Day. It must be noted that these tours are very strenuous, involving climbing ladders, maneuvering steep descents, and crawling through tunnels, and it is advised that anyone with a heart condition or those afraid of heights should avoid the tours.

Spruce Tree House, with a paved, albeit steep, trail, is an easier trip. Tours are self-guided from spring through fall, and ranger-guided in the winter months. This dwelling was erected between 1211 AD and 1278 AD and accommodated roughly 80 people.

Your family can also take a self-guided tour of **Step House**—a ranger is on hand to answer any questions you might have about the dwellings.

Next make a stop at the **Chapin Mesa Archaeological Museum** to view life-like dioramas and artifacts both from the "ancient ones" as well as from the tribes that descended from the Anasazi, including Ute, Pueblo, and Navajo.

When Are We Going?

Summer months are the peak season but don't be too worried about high temperatures during this season. Due to the altitude, days are generally pretty comfortable.

The park is open year around but you will find that tours of the cliff dwellings are limited to spring, summer and fall.

How Long Are We Staying?

We just stopped by Mesa Verde on our last trip to the park for about a half day, but if you want to do all the tours and see the museums, plan on at least one whole day.

What Should I Bring?

Everyone in the family must bring good hiking/tennis shoes. It's a tough walk and uneven. We'd also suggest bringing some water along for the journey.

Mesa Verde Warning – Steep Dropoffs!

Parents with small children must keep an eye on the kids! You'll see that there are steep drop offs that are not protected by railings.

What Are We Doing Next?

The **Durango-Silverton Narrow Gauge Railroad**, which winds through the San Juan National Forest and offers one of the most scenic rail journeys in the country, is a real treat or enjoy the historic Victorian architecture, art galleries, and theaters of Durango.

Explore the lives of the "ancient ones" through film, interpretive exhibits, and actual artifacts at the **Anasazi Heritage Center**, located 17 miles from Mesa Verde in the town of Dolores. Children will enjoy grinding corn and weaving on a loom in the same manner as the early Indians. *27501 Highway 184, Dolores, CO 81323, Tel. 970/882-4811.*

Which One Is My Room?

Years ago, Paris and her family stayed at the **Far View Lodge** in the park; it's still a fun and convenient place to stay, with no modern distractions to take away from the serenity of the area. The lodge, which offers half-day and full-day motor coach tours of the sites, is open from early April through to the end of October; for reservations call *800/449-2288* or make your reservation online at www.visitmesaverde.com/accommodations.

Conveniently located only 4 miles from Mesa Verde's entrance, **Morefield Campground** offers 435 sites on a first-come, first served basis and offers a coin-operated laundry ,hot showers and a RV dumping station. The park has several campgrounds as well. Morefield Campgrounds offers 400 sites on a first-come, first-served basis and offers restrooms, coin operated showers, and more.

You'll also find motel accommodations in Durango, Mancos and other surrounding communities. We can especially recommend Lake Mancos Ranch, a traditional dude ranch with a relaxed atmosphere and lots of Western fun. Since 1956 the ranch has specialized in family fun. Children and teenagers are divided by age into groups called the Cowpokes, Buckaroos and Mavericks to take morning trail rides with their new friends and enjoy other activities as well. Three-to-five year-olds are the yearlings, a group with organized activities and guided pony rides. The adults form the Wild Bunch, and share encouragement when those new-found muscles start to speak out about mid-week!

For more information, write: 42688 County Road N, Mancos, CO 81328 or call *800/325-9462*. You can make reservations for both Skyline and Lake Mancos through **American Wilderness Experience**, *Tel. 800/444-0099*.

Practical Information

Address: Mesa Verde National Park, PO Box 8, Mesa Verde, CO 81330-0008

Telephone: *970/529-4465*

Operating Season: year round; some areas and services closed in winter

Hours: ranger tours from 9am-5pm daily; Far View Visitor Center open from mid-April through mid-October 8am-5p.m.; Chapin Mesa Museum open 8am - 6:30pm from mid-April through mid-October

Cost: $10 per vehicle for 7- day pass. Tickets for tours are $2.50 per person per tour

Website: *www.nps.gov/meve/index.htm*

Learning About Mesa Verde

Arnold, Caroline. *The Ancient Cliff Dwellers of Mesa Verde*. Clarion Books, 1992. Ages 4-8.

Martell, Hazel Mary. *Native Americans and Mesa Verde* (Hidden Worlds). Dillon Press, 1993. Ages 9-12.

Petersen, David. *Mesa Verde National Park* (New True Books). Children's Press, 1992. Ages 4-8.

Dinosaur National Monument
Colorado & Utah

Ready for a visit to a *real* Jurassic Park? Here it is, tucked right on the border of Colorado and Utah. Jurassic dinosaur bones, a veritable graveyard of bones in a fossilized riverbed, were the reason this park was founded. Today your family can visit a fascinating visitors center to have a look at these bones and learn more about dinosaurs, then take a nature walk or enjoy an exciting white water river trip in other areas of the park.

Are We There Yet?

The park is located just off US 40 in northwest Colorado and northeast Utah. The visitors center is located a mile from Dinosaur, Colorado (really!) off US 40. The Dinosaur Quarry Visitors Center, where the dinosaur bones are located, is in Utah, seven miles north of Jensen on Utah State Highway 149.

What's There To Do Here?

River rafting. Your family can take a trip on the Green or Yampa Rivers inside the park with several private operators. Trips range from one day to six. Some commercial operators include (note: Don Hatch and Adrift offer short one-day trips):

- **Adrift Adventures**, *Tel. 800/824-0150*
- **Adventure Bound**, *Tel. 800/423-4668*
- **American River Touring Association**, *Tel. 800/323-2782*
- **Colorado Outward Bound School**, *Tel. 303/837-0880*
- **Dinosaur River Expeditions**, *Tel. 800/247-6197*
- **Don Hatch River Expeditions**, *Tel. 800/342-8243*
- **Holiday River Expeditions**, *Tel. 800/624-6323*
- **National Outdoor Leadership School**, *Tel. 307/332-6973*
- **OARS**, *Tel. 209/736-4677*

Dinosaur Exhibits. The must-do of this park is Dinosaur Quarry Visitor Center in Utah. This is where you'll see the dinosaur bones and learn more about these ancient residents. During the summer months talks on these giants are offered.

Headquarters Visitor's Center. Located on the Colorado side of the park, there are no dinosaur bones here but you'll find plenty of information on park activities here as well as a 10-minute slide show on the park.

Driving Tours. Two self-guided car routes take you through the park. The Tour of the Tilted Rocks is a 22-mile trail starting near the Dinosaur Quarry Visitor Center. Schedule one or two hours for the drive past petroglyphs and nature trails. The second driving tour is located near the headquarters visitor center. This is a 62-mile trip so plan on between two hours and half a day for this excursion to nature trails and picnic areas.

Hiking. Your family can set off on many of the self-guided nature trails. One of the best for families is the **Desert Voices Nature Trail**. This one winds for one and a half miles and, best of all, has trail signs specially for kids and designed by kids. Trail guides are available for all the nature trails and the car trails; call *800/845-DINO* for information.

Fishing. Some excellent fishing sites are found in the park; one of the top is Jones Hole, tucked in a 500-million-year-old fault. Only artificial flies and lures are allowed and a license is required. For the non-anglers in the family, there's plenty of other fun here as well including a fish hatchery, petroglyphs, and a waterfall.

When Are We Going?

The peak visitor months are during the summer. During that time the busiest area is the Quarry Visitors Center region of the park; some of the other areas remain quiet even during the busiest weekends.

During the summer months, expect the temperatures to be hot and the air dry. The air is thinner at this elevation (4500 to 9000 feet) so take it easy, walk slowly, and drink plenty of water. Be sure to carry water with you on your hikes and drink often. Sunscreen, hats, and sunglasses are important for all members of the family.

During the winter months, this park can experience cold weather and the Harpers Corner Road closes because of snow. Also, commercial river trips are not available during the winter months. Whenever you visit, expect the river water to be very cold because it is released from Flaming Gorge.

Dinosaurs, Dinosaurs, Dinosaurs!

Here are a few of the dinosaurs whose remains have been found at Dinosaur National Monument:

- Allosaurus— "Different Lizard" A dangerous predator which grew to thirty-eight feet in length.
- Apatosaurus— "Deceptive Lizard" Commonly referred to as the Brontosaurus, these dinosaurs grew up to ninety feet in length.
- Camarasaurus—"Chambered Lizard" A plant eater which weighed approximately 20 tons.
- Camptosaurus— "Bent Lizard" A herbivore that could weigh up to 2,000 pounds.
- Ceratosaurus— "Horn Lizard" A carnivore that lived during the late Jurassic period. Approximately twenty feet in length and weighing up to one ton, its distinctive feature was a horn on its nose.
- Diplodocus— "Double-Beamed" One of the largest creatures to ever walk the face of the earth, this dinosaur, which weighed up to 20 tons, was a herbivore with a long neck and tail.
- Dryosaurus— "Oak Tree Lizard" A fast-running plant eater which weighed up to 200 pounds
- Ornitholestes— "Bird Robber" A fast-running meat-eater which was six feet in length and weighed 25 pounds.
- Stegosaurus— "Covered Lizard" A herbivore with a spiked tail and large upright plates lining its back.

☙

Parents should watch children near the rivers; because of currents swimming is not recommended.

How Long Are We Staying?

The amount of time you'll want to stay in this fascinating park just depends on how much interest your family has in dinosaurs, if you want to take a river trip, and how many trails you'd like to explore. You'll want at least a half day to see the Quarry Visitor's Center and do the tour of the Tilted Rocks car tour. If you'd like a longer visit, you'll find plenty of activity for several days to a week of camping and exploring.

Which One Is My Room?

There is camping in the park at several campgrounds. No reservations are accepted. The quietest campground are Gates of Lodore and Green River which remain quiet even during the busiest summer weekends.

Green River campground offers 88 sites with water and rest rooms. Echo Park offers 17 sites with water but only vault toilets. Gates of Lodore has 17 sites with water and rest rooms. Each of these campgrounds charges a fee. Free camping is available at Deerlodger Park (eight sites) and Rainbow Park (only two sites), each with vault toilets only.

There are no RV hookups in the park.

What Are We Doing Next?

Colorado National Monument is 150 miles away in Fruita, Colorado. Covering over 20,000 acres, this park is a desert oasis for families looking to get away from it all. Explore the canyons on foot, bike, or horseback and see the abundant wildlife which live in the area, including bighorn sheep, mule deer and golden eagles. Admission is $5 per vehicle. Call *970/858-3617* for more details.

Practical Information

Address: 4545 Highway East 40, Dinosaur, CO 81610-9724

Phone Number: *970/374-3000* headquarters; *435/781-7700* for visitor information

Operating Season: The park is open year around, although the visitors centers close Thanksgiving, Christmas, and New Year's Day (the headquarters visitors center closes on other federal holidays as well.)

Hours: The Headquarters Visitors Center is open all year; 8am-6pm in the summer and 8am-4:30pm during winter (weekdays only during winter months); The Dinosaur Quarry Visitor Center is open all year 8am-4:30pm.

Cost: $10 per vehicle

Restrictions: No rocks can be removed from the park. Swimming is not recommended in the rivers because of currents.

Website: www.nps.gov/dino/index.htm

Learning About Dinosaurs

Daeschler, Ted. *The Dinosaur Hunter's Kit: Discover the Traces of a Lost World.* Running Press, 1990. Recommended for ages 9-12.

Digging into Dinosaurs (Ranger Rick Naturescope Series). National Wildlife Federation, 1991. Recommended for ages 9-12.

Dixon, Dougal. *Dinosaurs: Giants of the Earth.* Boyds Mills Press, 1995. Recommended for ages 9-12.

Glut, Donald F. and Helen I. Driggs (Illustrator). *The Age of Dinosaurs : A Fact-Filled Coloring Book* (Start Exploring). Running Press, 1994. Recommended for ages 9-12.

Long, Robert A., and Samuel P. Wells (Illustrator). *All New Dinosaurs and Their Friends: From the Great Recent Discoveries.* Bellerophon Books, 1985. Recommended for ages 9-12.

Mayes, Sue. *Dinosaurs* (Young Nature Series). EDC Publications, 1993. Recommended for ages 4-8.

Petersen, David. *Dinosaur National Monument* (A New True Book). Children's Press, 1995.

Wilkes, Angela. *The Big Book of Dinosaurs: A First Book for Young Children.* DK Publishing, 1994. Recommended for babies through preschool age.

Rocky Mountain National Park
Colorado

If your family is ready for a Rocky Mountain high, this is the place to be. This beautiful park offers some of the most scenic mountain vistas in Colorado.

Are We There Yet?

From I-25, take the exit for highway 34 or highway 36 to Estes Park. Continue on Highway 34 to the north entrance or Highway 36 to the south entrance (headquarters).

If you are traveling on I-70, exit for Highway 40 to Granby. Travel north on Highway 34 to Grand Lake and continue to the park's west entrance.

What's There to Do Here?

Any time of year you visit you'll find a wide range of activities and attractions in the park:

Visitors Centers. The Headquarters Visitor Center and Kawuneeche Visitor Center will give you a good overview of the park through exhibits and videos.

Moraine Park Museum. Rock lovers in your family will find geological exhibits at this museum which is open daily May through mid-October.

Alpine Visitor Center. Learn about alpine tundra ecosystems here, open daily from Memorial Day through mid-October.

Never Summer Ranch. This stop is great fun for learning about the history of dude ranches; the ranch is open only from mid-June through Labor Day.

Hiking. You'll find 359 miles of trails ranging from walks to mountain climbs. Be sure to stop by one of the visitors centers or information booths for trail guides.

Horseback riding. Contact Hi Country Stables, which is located within the park, regarding horseback rides. *Moraine Park— 970/586-2327, Glacier Creek— 970/586-3244.*

When Are We Going?

July and August are the busiest months at the park but you'll find pleasant conditions in the months before and after that peak time as well.

How Long Are We Staying?

You can see the park as a day trip but book an overnight stay if you'll be doing some hiking.

Did You Know.....?

- The world's first rodeo was held in Deer Trail, Colorado on July 4, 1869.
- "Nil sine Numine", Latin for "Nothing without Providence", is the state motto.
- Colorado's official state song is "Where The Columbines Grow."
- Colfax Avenue, located in Denver, is the longest continuous street in the United States. Colorado's nickname is The Centennial State
- The stegosaurus is the state fossil.
- The Rocky Mountain Bighorn Sheep is the state animal.
- The state tree is the Colorado Blue Spruce.
- Colorado was admitted into statehood on August 1, 1876.
- Colorado means "colored red" in Spanish.
- The Rocky Mountain Columbine is the state flower.
- The Lark Bunting is the state bird.
- Denver is the state capital.
- Some of the famous personalities who were either born or raised in Colorado include: comedian Tim Allen (Denver), astronaut M. Scott Carpenter (Boulder), actor Lon Chaney (Colorado Springs), boxer Jack Dempsey (Manassa), and actor Douglas Fairbanks (Denver).

What Should I Bring?
Good walking shoes are a must, along with a jacket any time of year.

Which One is My Room?
You'll find five campgrounds in the park. **Moraine Park** and **Glacier Basin** each take reservations, *Tel. 800/365-2267*. Three campgrounds are operated on a first-come, first-served basis. Reservations for Moraine Park and Glacier Basin can also be made online at http://reservations.nps.gov.

Lodging facilities are available outside the park in the community of **Estes Park**, Chamber of Commerce, *Tel. 800/443-7837*, and **Grand Lake**, Chamber of Commerce, *Tel. 800/531-1019*.

What Are We Doing Next?
Denver is only 65 miles away, and **Six Flags Elitch Gardens** stands in the heart of the city at 2000 Elitch Circle. The brave at heart will want to try the family flying coaster. Admission. Call *303/595-4386* for more information.

Adjacent to Six Flags Elitch Gardens is **The Children's Museum of Denver**, filled with hands-on exhibits to spark a youngster's imagination. Open seven days a week Monday- Friday 9am - 4pm and Saturday and Sunday from 10am - 5pm Admission $6 per person. *Tel. 303/433-7444*

Hop aboard an original 1904 St. Louis World's Fair steam train **at Lakeside Amusement Park**, open Memorial Day through Labor Day. There are rides for the thrill seeker in the family as well as 15 rides specifically geared toward children age 7 and under. Admission $2 per person. Located at I-70 and Sheridan Boulevard. *Call 303/477-1621* for further details.

Practical Information
Address: Rocky Mountain National Park, 1000 Highway 36, Estes Park, CO 80517
Telephone: *970/586-1206*
Operating Season: year around
Hours: 24 hours daily
Cost: $15 per car for a 7-day permit
Website: *www.nps.gov/romo/index.htm*

Learning About the Rocky Mountains
Luton, Joanne and Brad Luton (Illustrator). *Rocky Mountain Wildlife Coloring Book*. Grand Teton Natural History Association, 1995. Ages 4-8.

Petersen, David. *Rocky Mountain National Park* (A New True Book). Children's Press, 1993. Ages 4-8.

Ruurs, Margriet et al. *A Mountain Alphabet*. Tundra Books, 1996. Ages 9-12.

Staub, Frank J. *Mountain Goats* (Early Bird Nature Books). Lerner Publications Co., 1994. Ages 4-8.

Chapter 8

THE WEST

Great Basin National Park
Nevada

This quiet, expansive park is perched between desert and mountains, covered in sagebrush. One of the top attractions of the park is Lehman Caves, where you can take guided tours year around.

Are We There Yet?

This remote park is located five miles west of the town of Baker, Nevada on Highway 488. The park is located over 230 miles from Salt Lake City on the Nevada-Utah border.

What's There To Do Here?

Along with hikes, the top activity is a tour of Lehman Caves. Cave tours are limited to just 25 people so consider purchasing your tickets in advance; call the park with a major credit card up to 30 days in advance. Walk-in tickets are also offered every day. Kids programs are also available every Friday and Saturday afternoon at the Upper Lehman Campground, and the entire family can circle round the campfire during the summer months at an evening program.

When Are We Going?

Summer months are the peak times for this park. Winter months are quiet here with regular snowfall (and some parts of the park may close due to weather).

THE WEST

Redwood
NP

NEVADA

Great Basin NP

Yosemite
NP

Sequoia NP

Lake
Mead
NRA

CALIFORNIA

How Long Are We Staying?

You'll want to budget half a day at the least for this park to see the visitors center, take a walk, and do a cave tour. A full day will keep the visit from feeling rushed.

What Should I Bring?

Don't forget a jacket for the cave tour: year around the temperature is 50 degrees! Good, nonslip shoes are a must for the cave as well.

If you visit during the winter months (anytime before April) bring along food and drink as well. There's a cafe at the park but it closes during cold weather months.

Which One Is My Room?

For $10 a night, you can camp at one of the five campgrounds at the park. These sites include water during the summer months, restrooms, and picnic tables. Primitive sites are also available at no charge.

Other accommodations are found outside the park. You'll find a few rooms in Baker, but most accommodations are in Ely, Nevada, located 70 miles west of the park or Delta, Utah, 100 miles east of the park.

What Are We Going to Do Next?

Bryce Canyon, which is 188 miles away, and **Zion National Park**, 202 miles away, are both extensively covered in this book.

Did You Know.....?

• Lehman Caves in Great Basin National Park first began to form over five million years ago.

• There are more mountain ranges in Nevada than in any other state.

• Nevada is the largest producer of gold in the US.

• The state flower is sagebrush.

• "All for our country" is the state motto.

• The official state animal is the Desert Bighorn Sheep.

• Tennis star Andre Agassi and former First Lady Patricia Nixon were both born in Nevada.

• The state capital is Carson City.

• The official state song is "Home Means Nevada."

• Nevada has three nicknames: Sagebrush State, Battle-Born State and Silver State.

• The official state bird is the Mountain Bluebird.

• Nevada means "snow-clad" in Spanish.

Salt Lake City, home to the 2002 Olympics, is only a distance of 230 miles. At the **Salt Lake Cauldron Park** your family can relive the excitement of the winter games at the visitor center, where the glory of athletic competition is depicted in photographs and an interactive theater. You can also see **Hoberman Arch** and the actual cauldron used to start the event. While admission to the park and visitor center is free, there is a fee to enter the Salt Lake 2002 Theater ($3 adults, $2 for children). Open Monday through Saturday 10am - 6pm, closed Sunday. The park is located between 1300 East and Guardsman Way on the north side of 500 South

Reach for the stars at **Clark Planetarium**, which houses Utah's only 3D IMAX theater and exhibits on space exploration, including the landscape of Mars. Open 7 days a week. 110 South 400 West. For more information contact Tel. 801/456-STAR (7827).

If you like your attractions more down to earth, head to **Wheeler Historic Farm**, where you can tour an authentic Victorian house and find out about life on the farm during the 19th century. Children will love to feed the many barnyard animals, and you can take a tractor-drawn wagon ride through this 75-acre farm. Admission is free, although there is a small fee for some of the activities and special events. Open from dawn to dusk daily, Wheeler Historic Farm is located at 6351 South 900 East. Call 801/264-2241 for more details.

Practical Information

Address: Great Basin National Park, 100 Great Basin National Park, Baker, NV 89311

Telephone: 775/234-7331 (ext. 242 for cave tickets)

Operating Season: year around; closed Thanksgiving, Dec. 25, Jan. 1

Hours: Summer 8am-4:30pm; shorter hours off season

Cost: admission free; 30-minute cave tour is $2 for ages 12 and older; 11 and younger get in free; 60-minute cave tour is $6 for those 12 and up, $3 for ages; 90-minute cave tour is $8 for ages 12 and up, $4 for 11 and younger (note: children under the age of four are not permitted on the 90-minute tour)

Website: www.nps.gov/grba/index.htm

Lake Mead National Recreation Area
Nevada

Lake Mead National Recreation Area, located 25 miles east of Las Vegas, is a popular destination for boating, water skiing, and fishing. The park is truly colossal in scale: over 1.5 million acres. Here you'll find quiet coves for swimming or fishing and wonderful photo opportunities as well.

Wildlife thrive in this remote park so have your family keep their eyes open for bighorn sheep, coyotes, ringtail cats, and even desert tortoises.

Are We There Yet?
The park is located off I-15.

What's There to Do Here?
Start your visit at the Alan Bible Visitor Center, located on US 93 four miles from Boulder City, the community that sprang up to house workers employed on the massive Hoover Dam. The visitors center can offer information on special park programs and provide maps to help you plan your stay. There's also a botanical garden here with some of the typical desert foliage you might see during your visit.

Hiking is a popular activity but a tough one because there are few maintained trails. If you do head out, carry plenty of water and be advised that temperatures are oven-like during the summer months. During those hot weather months, a far more popular activity is watersports. Fishing for largemouth bass, rainbow trout and other species is common.

When Are We Going?
Summer season is the peak time for use of this park. Like other locations, visitation really skyrockets during the holiday weekends.

How Long Are We Staying?
You can visit Lake Mead as a day trip from Las Vegas, heading out for an afternoon swim if you like.

What Should I Bring?
Drinking water is a must during the summer months, along with sunscreen. Bring swim shoes and an old t-shirt to protect sensitive skin for young swimmers.

What Are We Doing Next?
Your family will find a world of activities in **Las Vegas**. Here is just a sample of the variety of attractions offered by The City That Never Sleeps:

If you are searching for a locale that will educate as well as entertain, look no further than the **Lied Discovery Children's Museum**. In the Discovery Store kids can pretend to shop for groceries while at Desert Discovery, for those five and younger, children can put on hard hats and burrow through a mountain of soft-sculpture "boulders" and learn about the nocturnal creatures that live in the area at Desert In The Dark. For toddlers there is Baby Oasis. Located off the strip at 833 Las Vegas Blvd. Open Tuesday through Sunday 10am-5pm, $6 adults, $5 children 5-17 and free to children under one year of age. For more information call *702/382-3445*.

On the strip you'll find **Madame Tussaud's Wax Museum**. Get up close to superstars such as Jennifer Lopez (her figure is able to blush) and Britney Spears (a "breathing" wax figure. Professional dancers are even on hand to teach you Britney's dance moves). Buffy The Vampire Slayer is on display, as well as legendary performer Elvis. Located between the Venetian Resort Hotel Casino and Las Vegas Boulevard. Open from 10 AM- 10 PM daily, with shorter hours during the winter months. Ages 13- 59, $19.95, ages 6 - 12, $9.95, and those under 5 admitted free.

Is there a budding Indiana Jones in your family? Take a journey back to ancient Egypt at the **Luxor Hotel**, where you will be surrounded by a pharaoh's treasures at the King Tut's Tomb exhibit. This 15 minute self-guided audio tour displays the bounty found in King Tutankhamun's tomb in rooms identical to those in the ancient burial chamber.

The **Star Trek Experience at the Hilton** is custom made for the sci-fi lover in the family. The museum houses over 200 pieces of memorabilia from both the TV cult class and the numerous Star Trek movies. Next, voyage through the galaxy on a simulated ride and try to escape capture from the Borg at Borg Invasion 4D, a blend of live action and 3D special effects.

Other choices include the **Valley of Fire State Park**, with amazing Native American pictographs, and **Lost City Museum**, a fascinating collection of historic structures. Raft trips below Hoover Dam as well as tours of the dam itself are also popular.

Which One is My Room?

The park offers guests five motels, eight campgrounds, and seven RV campgrounds. For information on facilities, contact Lake Mead National Recreation Area, *Tel. 702/293-8907*.

Practical Information

Address: Lake Mead NRA, 601 Nevada Hwy., Boulder City, NV 89005
Telephone: *702/293-8907* and *702/293-8990* (weekends)
Operating Season: year-round
Hours: 24 hours daily. Visitor center open 8:30am -4:30pm
Cost: $5 per vehicle for 5 days
Website: *www.nps.gov/lame/index.htm*

Redwood National Park
California

The majestic California redwoods are the focal point of this beautiful national park. It's one that has special family memories for Paris–one of her first baby pictures was taken beside the old "Tunnel Tree" in the Mariposa Grove. Sadly heavy snows caused that tree to fall in 1969 but you'll still find several "drive through" trees where you can take your own special family photos.

Are We There Yet?

The park is located in northern California. From San Francisco take US 101 for 397 miles to the Redwood Information Center, located two miles west of Orick.

If you are coming from the north, head south on US101 from Brookings, Oregon to Crescent City, California, home of the park headquarters. The park is four miles northeast of the city.

What's There To Do Here?

One of the most popular activities is definitely a drive through the giant trees. As mentioned, the Tunnel Tree is no longer standing but you'll still find drive-through trees in the area on Highway 101 (admission charges for each). The Klamath Tour Thru Tree is off the Terwer Valley Exit in the town of Klamath, the Shrine Drive-Thru Tree is near the town of Myers Flat off the Avenue of the Giants exit, and the Chandelier Tree is off Highway 101 in Leggett.

Be sure to stop by the information centers in the national park for more about these spectacular coastal redwoods.

Another popular activity is a visit to the tidepools on Enderts Beach Road, three miles south of Crescent City off Highway 101. Bring along the beach shoes to explore the tidepools (and even to do some whale watching!)

Your family can also view the scenery on horseback by contacting Redwood Trails, *Tel. 707/488-2061.*

When Are We Going?

Summer is the peak time for this park.

How Long Are We Staying?

Allow at least half a day to look at the highlights of the park.

Special Events

The Tolowa and Yurok tribes are proud of their cultures, and every summer American Indian dance demonstrations are held to honor their heritage and teach the significance of their tribe's dances. This event is free to the public. The renewal dance of the Tolowa is held at the Hiouchi Information Center, while the Yurok dance is held at the Thomas H. Kuchel Visitor Center. For information call *Tel. 707/464-6101 ext. 5064 or 5265.*

∽

What Should I Bring?

Bring a jacket, even during the summer months, as well as walking shoes and beach shoes that can get wet if you'll be exploring the tide pool areas.

Which One Is My Room?

There are campgrounds in the state park areas; for information or reservations write **PARKNET**, PO Box 85705, San Diego, CA 92138-5705 or call them at *Tel. 800/444-7275*. These parks fill up during the peak season so from May through September write or call for reservations.

For more options, call the **Orick Chamber of Commerce**, *Tel. 707/488-2885*, or the **Crescent City Chamber of Commerce**, *Tel. 707/464-3174*.

What Are We Doing Next?

San Francisco is a short trip away, and **Fisherman's Wharf** will lure you with a myriad of attractions including:

• the whimsical sea lions on Pier 39; The Great San Francisco Adventure, a 30-minute movie detailing the city's colorful history (adults $7.50, $4.50 for children 4 - 12, call *415/956-3456*)
• the Italian hand-crafted carousel decorated with San Francisco landmarks ($2 a ride),
• Aquarium of The Bay, where sharks, eels and other sea creatures swim past as visitors watch from the safety of a 300 foot clear tunnel, and children can pet a leopard shark or bat ray at the touch tank (*Tel. 1-888-SEA-DIVE*).

An escape from the hustle and bustle of Fisherman's Wharf can be found at some of San Francisco's cultural attractions, such as **The Exploratorium**, a hand's on museum with over 600 exhibits showcasing the wonders of science and the arts. Housed in The Palace of Fine Arts. Admission.

Enjoy the beauty of San Francisco at the **Japanese Tea Garden** in Golden Gate Park. What began as a World's Fair exhibit in 1894 has evolved into one of San Francisco's most beloved locales.

Practical Information

Address: Redwood National and State Parks, 1111 Second St., Crescent City, CA 95531

Telephone: *707/464-6101*

Operating Season: year round. Visitors centers closed Thanksgiving, Dec. 25, Jan. 1

Hours: visitor center hours generally 9am-5 p.m .daily (10am-4pm during winter months at some locations)

Cost: free

Website: *www.nps.gov/redw/index.htm*

Sequoia & Kings Canyon National Parks
California

Standing beneath the enormous trees of Sequoia National Park is enough to make the tallest of vacationers feel like a small child again. This beautiful park is the second oldest in the national park system, protecting these giant trees since 1890.

Sequoia is not only home to the Big Trees but also the largest mountain in the continental US: Mount Whitney. Sequoia is located near Kings Canyon National Park. The two parks are connected by a loop drive, so visiting both is easy.

Are We There Yet?

Sequoia National Park and Kings Canyon National Park are located in Fresno County, California. You'll have to enter the parks from the west. Travel Highway 180 from Fresno to Kings Canyon National Park and then enter Sequoia or take Highway 198 from Visalia directly to Sequoia. The parks are connected by the Generals Highway (which sometimes closes during the winter months).

What's There To Do Here?

General Sherman Tree. This whopper is a must-see. This 274.9 foot tree holds the record as the world's largest living thing. What makes it largest? Not its height, although when you stand at the base of this mighty trunk and look up it would seem to hold the record. What makes this one Guinness material is its bulk: 52,500 cubic feet of wood.

The Tunnel Log. Ever wanted to drive under a tree? Here's your chance. This sequoia fell in 1937 then the Civilian Conservation Corp cut an eight-foot-high tunnel right through the tree. (Driving a jumbo van? Have no fear–there's a bypass nearby. The park doesn't want anyone stuck in the tree.)

Horseback Riding. During the summer months, equestrians and wanna-be riders can enjoy many trails. Several operators offer horses and equipment. Give these operators a call for more information:

- **Cedar Grove Pack Station**, *Tel. 559/565-3464; 559/564-3231* during winter months
- **Grant Grove Stables**, *Tel. 559/335-9292; 559/337-1273* during winter months
- **Mineral King Pack Station**, *Tel. 559/561-3039; 520/855-5885* during winter months
- **Horse Corral**, *Tel. 559/565-3404* year round

Tour Crystal Cave. The budding spelunkers in your family will enjoy a tour of Crystal Cave, home to many beautiful cave formations. Guided tours are offered but you must purchase tickets at the Foothills or Lodgepole visitors centers; you can't get them at the cave itself. (It's about an hour's drive from the visitors centers to the cave, so plan ahead.) Tours take about 45 minutes and bring a jacket for everyone–year around the cave is a nippy 48 degrees! Strollers aren't permitted in the cave. Cave tours are offered from mid-May through September only. Tours cost $9 for adults and $5 for kids 6-12 (kids under six are free)

Mt. Whitney. This mountain is the largest in the continental US. The mountain is located on the eastern side of the mountain chain, though, so you can't really view it from the most popular park areas. Get a good view of the summit from the **Interagency Visitor Center** on Highway 395, south of Lone Pine, California.

When Are We Going?

Sequoia packs 'em in during the summer months, especially August when numbers really peak. In those summer months the temperatures can be varying, depending on the part of the park you visit. Be prepared for 100 degree temperatures but, tucked in the damp shade beneath the majestic sequoias, you'll find the temperatures much cooler.

Winter visitors are in for a special treat as visitors numbers are especially low during these months. Some parts of the park are blanketed in heavy snow during the winter months and sometimes the Generals Highway, which connects Highway 180 and Highway 198, closes due to heavy snows.

How Long Are We Staying?

You'll want to plan most of a day to see the park's main attractions and to drive through the park itself. Driving distances are long, two hours from end to end plus another two to see the General Sherman giant tree.

What Should I Bring?

A light jacket is useful most of the year.

Which One Is My Room?

Except during the winter months, campers will find three options in Sequoia National Park:

Giant Forest/Lodgepole Area. The Lodgepole camp offers 204 sites, which can be reserved up to 5 months in advance. $20 per day in the summer months, $18 a day in winter. For information call *559/565-3774*. For reservations call *800/365-2267*, for international calls *301/722-1257* or reserve online at *http://reservations.nps.gov*. The same telephone numbers apply for the

Dorst camp, with 201 sites available. Opens in mid-May, weather allowing. $20 per day. These sites offer restrooms, drinking water, picnic tables, and RV disposal stations.

Foothills Area. In the Foothills region of the park, you'll find several campgrounds. The Potwisha camp offers 42 sites year around for $18 per night; facilities include flush toilets, phone, and sanitary disposal station. The Buckeye Flat camp has 28 sites but is only open from mid-April to mid-September. Sites cost $18 per night and facilities are limited to flush toilets. The South Fork camp has 13 sites for $12 a night from mid-May through October (free in the winter); the only facilities are pit toilets. This campsite does not accept reservations.

Mineral King Area. This area also offers several campgrounds (although trailers and RVs aren't recommended for this steep road.) The Atwell Mill camp has 21 sites and is open spring to mid-November; sites are $12 per night from Memorial Day through September. Facilities include water (only through September) and phone. Cold Springs camp has 37 sites for $12 a night with the same facilities. This campsite does not accept reservations.

Kings Canyon National Park is also home to two camping areas:

Grant Grove Area. These campsites are close to those giant trees and are open all year, although don't be surprised to see snow on the ground anytime from November until the early days of May. The Azalea campground has 113 sites for $18 a night; facilities include flush toilets, phones, pay showers and a sanitary disposal station. Sunset camp has 200 sites and is open only Memorial Day through mid-September; sites are $18 a night and include use of flush toilets, pay phones, restaurant, and more. Crystal Springs offers 63 sites from mid-May to late September only; rates are $18 per night and include flush toilets, phone, service station, restaurant, and more. *No reservations accepted.*

Cedar Grove Area. This area includes the Sentinel campground with 83 sites from May to October. Sites are $18 a night a facilities include flush toilets, laundromat, service station, and more. Moraine campground offers 120 sites also open May to October; rates are $18 a night and facilities include market, fast food, laundromat, and more. Sheep Creek has 111 sites from May to October for $18 a night with the same services. No reservations accepted.

Bringing along your own trailer or RV? You'll need to know the following:
- You can't take a trailer to Buckeye Flat, Atwell Mill or Cold Spring Campgrounds.
- None of the park campgrounds have hookups.
- If your rig is over 22 feet long, avoid the Generals Highway between Potwish and Giant Forest and instead use Highway 180.
- Avoid Mineral King Road due to the steep grade.

Bear Warning!

All campers should know that all food supplies, including ice chests, will need to be stored at all times in metal, bear-proof boxes throughout the park. These boxes measure 2 feet by 2 feet, so don't bring anything larger than that.

A Special Note on Marmots & Bears

Expect to see bears in these parks, most anywhere below 8,000' elevation. These four legged giants are joined by another critter: the marmot.

Marmots are found in the Mineral King area of the park during the spring and early summer months. These little guys aren't necessarily looking for your picnic basket, though; they might consider your car nutrition as well. They've been known to eat radiator hoses, wiring, backpacking equipment and more.

How do you avoid the marmots? Knock on your hood before starting up the car to scare out any would-be hitchhikers.

Black bears are another problem, and a serious one at that. It's important to teach children that, for the bears' own good, they cannot be fed. Bears who are fed become acclimatized to human contact and quickly become pests.

How can you help protect the bears? By taking simple precautions with your food and supplies. The National Park Service recommends these steps:

- Metal Storage Boxes. Cut off the source of the smell and the bear won't know there's food around. You'll find that the park provides metal storage boxes so tuck your food (and the ice chests–these smart animals recognize them as a food box!) inside. Put anything with an odor in the boxes, even items you wouldn't consider foodstuff, such as toothpaste.
- Air-tight Containers. Metal storage box not available? Then follow the same rule and cut off the source of the smell. Zippered plastic storage bags can be a great first step; continue the effort by then locking food and supplies in your trunk.
- Keep items out of sight. It's not just enough for the bear not to smell the food–he can't see it either. Cover up everything if your car doesn't have a trunk.
- Never leave your camp unattended until all the food is stored.
- Always store the food–not just at night.
- Be tidy.
- Keep your backpack with you. Like ice chests, bears recognize backpacks. Don't leave yours unattended.

What if you do see a bear? The park service recommends:
- Never approaching a bear, even a small one.
- Act right away. Yell, throw things, make noise.

- Join forces. Have the family stand side by side to make a more intimidating target, but don't, under any circumstance, surround the bear.
- Be extra careful of cubs. Like any family, bears defend their young.
- Let the bear have it. If a bear grabs your backpack, let him have it.

What Are We Doing Next?

The closest attractions are **Yosemite National Park**, which is covered extensively in this book, and **Devils Postpile National Monument**. At only 800 acres, Devils Postpile is an intimate park with grandiose views. The towering basalt lava columns are a breathtaking sight, and when the sun shines upon it the aptly named Rainbow Falls makes a kaleidoscope of colors. Due to inclement weather, this park is open only during the summer months. Admission is $7 for adults and $4 for kids. For further details call *760/934-2289* or *email DEPO_Superintendent@nps.gov*. Devils Postpile, P.O. Box 3999, Mammoth Lakes, CA 93546.

Straight out of the pages of a fairytale, **Hearst Castle** in San Simeon, only 175 miles away, was once home to publishing magnate William Randolph Hearst. Several tours of this opulent establishment are available, with the least taxing being Tour One, lasting one hour and 45 minutes, including the bus ride

Did You Know.....?

- Sacramento is California's capital.
- California has many nicknames including The Land of Milk and Honey, The El Dorado State, The Golden State and The Grape State.
- Inyo National Forest is home to the world's oldest living species, the bristle cone pine.
- The state tree is the redwood.
- The grizzly bear is the state animal.
- Fresno is known as the Raisin Capital of The World.
- California's motto is "Eureka", a Greek word which means "I have found it."
- The world's largest amphitheater is the Hollywood Bowl.
- The hottest place in the United States is Death Valley.
- West Coast swing dancing is the official dance of California.
- The United States National Christmas Tree, found in Kings Canyon National Park, is serenaded with carols every holiday season.
- San Luis Rey is the largest mission in California.
- The state bird is the California Valley Quail.
- In 1510 Spanish writer Montalvo described in one of his works a fantasy haven called Califia. This word is the origin of the name California.

to and from the castle. The tour includes a forty minute movie, *Hearst Castle Building The Dream,* as well as a guided walk through Casa Del Sol, the 18 room guest house which once temporarily housed such prominent celebrities as Charlie Chaplin and Clark Gable, a look at both the Neptune and Roman pools, and a tour of several rooms in the main house, Casa Grande. Open daily, except for Thanksgiving, Christmas and New Years Day. The first tour begins at 8:20 AM and the last at 3:20pm, although these hours are extended during the summer months. Admission is $18 for adult and $9 for children between 6 and 17, those under the age of six are admitted free of charge. For recorded information call *805/927-2020* and for tour reservations call *800/444-4445.*

Practical Information
Address: Sequoia and Kings Canyon National Parks, Three Rivers, CA 93271-9700
Telephone: *209/565-3341 for recorded information*
Operating Season: year round
Hours: 24 hours daily except two areas (Mineral King and Highway 180 to Cedar Grove) close from November until late spring
Cost: $10 family pass for seven consecutive days (good for Sequoia and Kings Canyon)
Restrictions: Restrictions include gathering only dead wood, quiet time from 10pm-6am, putting all food in metal boxes, and not using soap in rivers.
Website*: www.nps.gov/seki/index.htm*

Yosemite National Park
California
One of the grandest parks in the entire system, Yosemite is a true wonder of nature and a great—although very popular—family destination. Plan your visit carefully to miss the peak weekends and to ensure that you'll have accommodations when you arrive.

Are We There Yet?
There are multiple ways to get into the park. From Modesto and Manteca you'll enter on Highway 120 west. From Fresno, enter on Highway 41. From Merced, come in on Highway 140 west. The Tioga Pass entrance (which closes during winter months until early June) is reached on Highway 120 east from Lee Vining and Highway 395.

What's There To Do Here?
A great activity in the park is the Junior and Senior Ranger programs. The Junior Ranger program is for young travelers age 8 to 10 years old while the Senior Ranger activities are for ages 11 and 12.

To sign up your child for the program, stop by the Valley Visitors Center and pick up an activity paper and information sheet. The fee is $3. Obtaining the ranger patch is easy and fun: kids attend one ranger program, pick up one bag of trash, and complete an activity packet.

Ansel Adams Gallery (next to Visitors Center in Yosemite Village). The famous black-and-white photographer is remembered in this gallery filled with his work as well as the photographs of other photographers. You can also rent cameras and buy film here. A children's storytime is offered every Saturday afternoon. *Tel. 209/372-4413.*

Bridalveil Falls. This very recognizable waterfall, the height of a 62-story building, is a true symbol of Yosemite. Be prepared to get spritzed a little on the path – it's part of the fun.

El Capitan. Another symbol of Yosemite, this sheer monolith rises up from Yosemite Valley and presents a challenge to dedicated climbers. Have a look at the face of the rock and see how many climbers you can point out.

Half Dome. Even more distinctive than Bridalveil Falls and El Capitan, this monolith does, indeed, look like it's just half there. It's easy to pick out – just look for the mountain that looks like it has split in half.

Mirror Lake. You'll have to do a little walking to get to this lake and meadow but the one-mile journey is well worth it.

Ribbon Fall. It may not be as famous as Bridalveil Falls, but it is taller. Ribbon Fall is, in fact, taller than most other waterfalls in the world. You might not get to see it in action if you come in late summer, however; the water often dries up during hot weather.

Visitor Center in Yosemite Village. Stop by to talk with rangers and see exhibits on this fascinating park, its wildlife, and its history. The adjacent museum and cultural exhibits next door present an educational stop for children looking to learn more about the first residents of this valley.

When Are We Going?

Summer is definitely the peak season and you can pretty much expect a crowd during those months. At least try to avoid weekends and holidays– Memorial Day, July 4th, and Labor Day. Spring and fall make great times to view the park.

How Long Are We Staying?

You can see the highlights of the park in one day but try to budget at least one night to get a real feel for the park.

What Should I Bring?

Put camping gear, a jacket, good walking or hiking shoes, and hats on the packing list. And don't forget the camera!

What Are We Doing Next?
There are many attractions near to Yosemite. For a complete rundown, contact the following visitors bureaus or check out, a commercial web-site with information on all sorts of activities in the region. Here's a list of local visitors bureaus that can provide you with additional information:

- **Coulterville Visitor Center**, Highway 132/49 , PO Box 333, 5007 Main Street Coulterville, CA 95311, *Tel 209/878-3407*
- **June Lake**, High Sierra Direct, PO Box 467, June Lake, CA 93529, *Tel. 760/937-2177*
- **Lee Vining Chamber of Commerce & Mono Lake Visitor Center,** PO Box 130, Highway 395 & 3rd Street, Lee Vining, CA 93541, *Tel. 760/647-6629*
- **Mammoth Lakes Visitors Bureau,** 437 Old Mammoth Road, Suite Y , PO Box 48 Mammoth Lakes, CA 93546. *Tel:* Toll free in US and Canada *888/GO-MAMMOTH, 888/466-2666* (US and Canada) *760/934-2712* outside of US and Canada
- **Mariposa Visitors Center,** Mariposa Town Center, 5158 Highway 140, PO Box 425, Mariposa, CA 95338, *Tel. 800/208-2434 or 209/966-2456*
- **Merced Conference & Visitors Burea**u, 710 West 16th Street, Merced, CA 95340, *Tel. 800/446-5353 or 209/384-7092*
- **Tuolumne County Visitors Bureau,** West Highway 120, 55 West Stockton St., PO Box 4020, Sonora, CA 95370, *Tel. 800/446-1333*
- **Yosemite Sierra Visitors Bureau**, Highway 41, PO Box 1404, 49074 Civic Circle, Oakhurst, CA 93644, *Tel. 800/208-2434 or 559/683-4636*

Which One Is My Room?
There are several accommodations in the park, all operated by Yosemite Concession Services Corporation, but a word of warning – they fill up quickly! Plan early if you want to get a room in this popular park. The best known accommodation (and the priciest) is in the **Ahwahnee Lodge**, a truly classic park lodge that's worth a visit even if you don't stay here. You can make reservations at the Ahwahnee or at any of the other accommodations in the park, which range from motel-type rooms to tent-cabins (with a floor) up to a year in advance; write **Central Reservations**, 5410 East Home, Fresno, CA 93727 or call *559/252-4848*.
There are many campgrounds in the park as well, and these are equally popular. Campground reservations can be made up to five months before your stay. To make reservations, call *800/436-PARK* between 7am and 7pm pacific standard time (internationally call *301/722-1257*; the TDD number is *888/530-9796*). You may also write **National Park Reservation Service**, P.O. Box 1600, Cumberland, MD, 21502. Personal checks, money orders, MasterCard, Visa and Discover cards are accepted.

Practical Information
  Address: *Yosemite National Park, Superintendent, PO Box 577, Yosemite National Park, CA 953899*
  Telephone: *209/372-0200*
  Operating Season: *year round*
  Hours: *daily, all day*
  Cost: *$20 per car for 7-day pass*
  Website: *www.nps.gov/yose/index.htm*

Learning About Yosemite
  Baron, Kathy. *The Tree of Time: A Story of a Special Sequoia.* Yosemite Association, 1994. Ages 9-12.
  Petersen, David. *Yosemite National Park* (A New True Book). Children's Press, 1993. Ages 4-8.
  San Souci, Robert D. Daniel San Souci (Illustrator). *Two Bear Cubs: A Miwok Legend from California's Yosemite Valley.* Yosemite Association, 1997. Ages 9-12.
  Sargent, Shirley, et al. *Yosemite Tomboy.* Great West Books, 1994. Ages 9-12.

Chapter 9

THE NORTHWEST

Crater Lake National Park
Oregon

Even if it's your first visit to Crater Lake, you'll recognize this park from many photos. The spectacular lake, created by a collapsed volcano, boasts dark blue waters that stand in contrast to often snow-covered lakeshores.

Are We There Yet?

The park, located in southern Oregon, can be reached from the north or south. From the north (summer only), you can take Route 97 south from Bend to Route 138 West and continue to the park entrance. From Roseberg, take Route 138 east to the entrance.

The south entrance can be reached by following Route 97 north from Klamath Falls to Route 62 North. Drive west to the park entrance. From Medford, take Route 62 to the park entrance.

What's There To Do Here?

Enjoyment of this wilderness area is the prime activity at Crater Lake. You can enjoy ranger-led programs and hikes during summer months (remember, around here summer usually means late June.) Several trails are easy to maneuver and take only 30 to 45 minutes to walk, including Sun Notch Viewpoint, a .5-mile round trip excursion with views of Phantom Ship and Crater Lake, Castle Crest Wildflower Garden, a .5-mile loop which leads you through a carpet of wildflowers, and Godfrey Glen, a one-mile hike which overlooks Annie Creek Canyon.

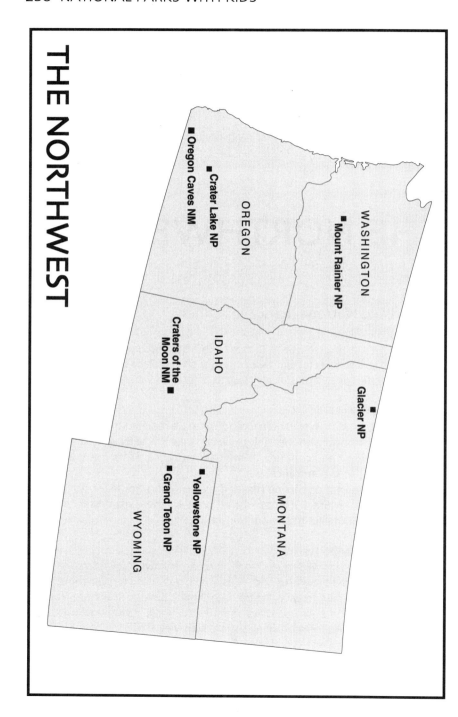

THE NORTHWEST

Several scenic drives are available in the park including a 33-mile Rim Drive that circles the body of water. Another popular option with families are boat tours from Cleetwood Cove. These take place during the summer only.

Kids 6-12 can take part in the Junior Ranger Program. The program takes place at the Mazama Campground Amphitheater from late June to the end of August at 5pm.

When Are We Going?

Summer is definitely the peak time at this park. Paris remembers her first trip to Crater Lake – an early July excursion where there was still snow on the ground and cool temperatures. The north entrance to the park closes from mid-October until mid-June and whenever you come, bring along a jacket.

How Long Are We Staying?

You can visit the park as a day trip but plan on spending most of the day to see the park highlights.

What Should I Bring?

A jacket, good walking shoes, and warm socks.

Did You Know.....?

- There are more ghost towns in Oregon than anywhere else in the United States.
- The deepest lake in the United States is Crater Lake.
- Oregon is the only state flag bearing two separate designs on either side.
- On the front are symbols of trade, farming and mining within a shield encircled by thirty-three stars and adorned on top with an eagle.
- On the back of the flag is a beaver, which is the state animal.
- Oregon's nickname is Beaver State.
- The Western Meadowlark is the state bird.
- The Oregon Grape is the state flower.
- The state tree is the Douglas Fir.
- Salem is the state capital.
- Oregon was admitted into statehood on Valentine's Day in 1859.
- Hells Canyon, which is 8,000 feet deep, is the deepest river gorge in North America.
- "Alis Volat Propiis" is the state motto. It translates as "She flies with her own wings."
- Portland is the home town of Matt Groening, the creator of The Simpsons television show.

What Are We Doing Next?

Oregon Caves National Monument, which is detailed in this chapter, is about a three-hour drive from the park. Only 70 miles away is Lava Beds National Monument, an otherworldly environment of volcanic formations which was once the dwelling place of the Modoc tribe. There are over 435 lava tube caves of varying size in the park, and families can explore on their own or opt for a ranger-guided tour. This park also offers views of cryptic pictures carved into the volcanic rock at Petroglyph point. Admission is $10. For further information call *530/667-2282 ext. 232.*

Which One Is My Room?

Crater Lake Lodge is a classic park lodge. The rooms have great views of the park. Even if you don't stay at the lodge, stop by for a look. For reservations, call *541/830-8700.* The lodge is open from mid-May through mid-October only.

Other options are the Mazama Village Motor Inn, the Mazama Campground (first-come, first served) and the Lost Creek Campground (first-come, first served).

Practical Information

Address: Crater Lake National Park, PO Box 7, Crater Lake, OR 97604
Telephone: *541/594-3100*
Operating Season: Year round, except Christmas and New Years Day; some roads and facilities are closed throughout the winter months
Hours: visitor's center hours vary by season
Cost: $10 per vehicle
Website: *www.nps.gov/crla/index.htm*

Oregon Caves National Monument
Oregon

Spelunkers, grab your flashlights and your good walking shoes. This is a cave park for those with a real interest in caves. It's not an easy trail like Carlsbad Caverns and cave tours are restricted to children above 42 inches tall.

Free tours of five to ten minutes in duration are available for young children unable to attend the standard tour.

Are We There Yet?

The park is located 20 miles east of Cave Junction. Follow Highway 46 from Cave Junction to the park.

What's There To Do Here?

Caving is definitely the number one activity. Cave tours are operated by an independent concessionaire. As we mentioned, kids need to be at least 42 inches tall and able to climb (there will be a test!) for these tours; there's no way to carry little tots. The walk is rugged and the oxygen is thin because of the cave's 4,000 foot elevation so this is not, so to speak, a walk in the park.

Cave tours cost $7.50 for adults or $5 for those under age 16.

Along with the cave, there are also some hiking trails and you can take a naturalist-guided walk once a week.

When Are We Going?

The caves are open year around and the temperature remains constant. In the winter months, the hiking trails are open although they are covered in snow.

The peak season is during July and August. Although the cave itself will be the same any time you visit, expect to see long lines during these peak months. You cannot make reservations for a cave tour so you might have to wait up to an hour if you visit during these months.

How Long Are We Staying?

Most visitors stay half a day, which includes plenty of time to do the cave tour. Budget longer if you'd like to do some hiking.

What Should I Bring?

Be sure to bring good walking shoes; the walking surface can be slippery. You'll also want a jacket and warm clothes because the temperature remains a constant 41 degrees year around.

Flashlights are a good idea and don't forget your camera!

What Are We Doing Next?

You might combine a visit to this park with a stay at the Redwood National Park (see Redwood National Park heading), located about two hours away, or Crater Lake National Park (see Crater Lake National Park heading), three hours away.

A National Historic Landmark town, the streets of Jacksonville are lined with architecture which hearkens back to the days when adventurers in search of gold flocked to this location. Guarded by the Siskiyou Mountains, this picturesque town 65 miles from Oregon Caves is filled with unique shops. For more information call *541/899-8118.*

Exotic animals from around the globe are on display at Wildlife Safari, a 600 acre drive-through park where cheetahs, giraffes, and elephants roam freely. Children will enjoy the animal-themed rides and petting zoo at Safari Village. Wildlife Safari, which is open every day with the exception of

Christmas, is located in Winston, a two-hour drive from Oregon Caves. Admission. Summer hours 9am - 6pm, 10am - 4pm in winter. Call *541/679-6761.*

Which One Is My Room?

The Oregon Caves Company operates the **Oregon Caves Chateau**, Oregon Caves Company, PO Box 128, Cave Junction, OR 97523. This 22-room hotel is open from March through November.

Practical Information

Address: Oregon Caves National Monument, 19000 Caves Hwy., Cave Junction, OR 97523

Telephone: *541/592-2100 ext. 232*

Operating Season: year round

Hours: tour times vary by month

Cost: $7.50 for adult, $5 children 16 and under; admission free with National Park Pass, Golden Eagle Card, or Golden Access Pass.

Restrictions: only children 42 inches and taller allowed in cave

Website: *www.nps.gov/orca/index.htm*

Learning About Oregon

Gregory, Kristiana. *Across the Wide and Lonesome Prairie: The Oregon Trail Diary of Hattie Campbell* (Dear America). Scholastic Trade, 1997. Ages 9-12.

Kudlinski, Kathleen V. and James Watling (Illustrator). *Facing West: A Story of the Oregon Trail* (Once upon America Series). Puffin, 1996. Ages 9-12.

Lawlor, Laurie. *American Sisters: West Along the Wagon Road 1852*. Pocket Books, 1998. Ages 9-12.

Love, D. Anne and Ronald Himler (Illustrator). *Bess's Log Cabin Quilt*. Yearling Books, 1996. Ages 9-12.

Steedman, Scott and Mark Bergin (Illustrator). *A Frontier Fort on the Oregon Trail*. Peter Bedrick Books, 1994. Young adult.

Van Leeuwen, Jean and James Watling (Illustrator). *Bound for Oregon*. Dial Books for Young Readers, 1994. Ages 9-12.

Craters of the Moon National Monument
Idaho

Wonder what's left after a volcano explodes? Then set your sights on Craters of the Moon National Monument. This park showcases the largest lava field of its kind in the U.S., 83 square miles to be exact.

Are We There Yet?

Craters of the Moon is located in the south-central region of Idaho. From Highway 93, travel west from Arco for 18 miles to the park entrance. The park is about 66 miles west of Idaho Falls.

What's There To Do Here?

This 618-square-mile park offers a variety of outdoor pursuits for active families. Take in a landscape filled with lava flows and spatter cones along the various hiking trails, or see the rugged terrain on a seven-mile drive. If your family is looking for adventure, explore one of the many caves in the area. Proceed with caution inside the formations—in Boy Scout Cave ice forms on the cave floor. Sunlight streams in from collapses in the ceiling at Indian Tunnel, making this cave much easier to traverse.

When Are We Going?

The busiest months at this park are July and August. During the summer months, days are warm but pleasant, averaging about 84 degrees.

Winter temperatures are chilly, averaging about 31 degrees so bring warm clothes.

How Long Are We Staying?

You'll want to set aside at least half a day for a visit, more if you'd like to hike.

What Should I Bring?

Good walking shoes are a must. If you'll be exploring the lava tubes, bring along a flashlight. Sunglasses, hats, water, and sunscreen are must-haves during the summer months.

Which One Is My Room?

Craters of the Moon Lava Flow Campground provides 51 campsites. Campers have access to restrooms, picnic tables, and water. Quiet time lasts between 10pm and 6am There are no showers or hookups available. Wood fires are not allowed in the park.

What Are We Doing Next?

A wide expanse of wilderness awaits nature lovers **at The Salmon-Challis National Forest**, which is located only ten miles away. The state's tallest peak provides a backdrop for families wanting to get away from it all. Write to 50 Hwy 93 South, Salmon, ID 83467 or call *208/756-5100.*

Fossils from the Pliocene age are on display **at Hagerman Fossil Beds National Monument**, which is 98 miles away from Craters of The Moon. The fossilized remains of 35 types of plant life and over 140 species of animals have been discovered in this area, including Idaho's official state fossil, The Hagerman Horse, an ancient forerunner of today's horse. PO Box 570, 221 North State Street, Hagerman, ID 83332 *Tel. 208/837-4793.*

Grand Teton (190 miles away) and Yellowstone National Park (200 miles away) are detailed in this book.

Practical Information

Address: Craters of the Moon National Monument, PO Box 29, Arco, ID 83213

Telephone: *208/527-3257*

Operating Season: The park is open year.

Hours: Visitors center open 8am-6pm daily during the summer months; 8am-4:30pm during off peak season.

Cost: $5 per vehicle

Restrictions: No wood fires in the park.

Website: *www.nps.gov/crmo/index.htm*

Learning About Volcanoes

A good introduction to volcanoes for readers age 9-12 is *Volcano, Earthquake and Hurricanes* by Nick Arnold (Raintree/Steck Vaughn, 1997).

Did You Know.....?

- The state horse, the Appaloosa, was first bred in Kamiah Valley.
- Idaho was the 43rd state to enter into the union.
- The state motto is "Esto perpetua," which means "Let it be perpetual."
- Gem State is Idaho's nickname.
- The Idaho Star Garnet is the state gem.
- Gutzon Borglum, Mount Rushmore's sculptor, was born in Idaho, as was poet Ezra Pound, actress Lana Turner, and Olympic skier Picabo Street.
- The Mountain Bluebird is the state bird.
- Boise is the state capital.
- The state song is *Here We Have Idaho.*

Mount Rainier National Park
Washington

Mount Rainier is a magical place filled with wildflowers, ferns, old forests, and even glaciers. The mountain itself is an active volcano.

Are We There Yet?
You'll find several ways to enter the park. If you are traveling from Seattle or Tacoma to Sunrise, head East on SR410 from Enumclaw to the White River entrance. From these cities to Paradise, head South on SR7, then turn east on SR706. Continue through Elbe and Ashford to the Nisqually entrance.

What's There To Do Here?
The park offers over 240 miles of trails but recommends these for family hiking:

Nisqually Vista Trail. This 1.2-mile trail, located at Paradise, has good views of Mt. Rainier and the Nisqually Glacier. The trail starts at the Henry M. Jackson Memorial Visitor Center.

Silver Falls. This Ohanapecosh trail runs for three miles, starting at the Ohanapecosh Campground. The trail follows the river to the 75-foot falls.

Bench Lake and Snow Lake. This Paradise trail, 2-1/2 miles long, is a popular trail during the summer months because of the wildflowers. The trail starts on Stevens Canyon Road one mile east of Reflection Lake.

Naches Peak Loop. This Tipsoo Lake trail, 3-1/2 miles, has good views of Mt. Rainier. You'll see fields of huckleberries during late summer and colorful wildflowers in July and August. The trail starts at Chinook Pass/Tipsoo Lake.

Glacier Basin. This White River trail runs seven miles and follows an old road for a view of the Emmons Glacier, the largest in the contiguous US. You might even see mountain goats (not to mention mountain climbers). The trail starts at White River Campground.

Mt. Fremont. This 5-1/2-mile Sunrise trail traces a path up to the fire lookout for a great view of Mt. Rainier. The trail starts at the Sunrise parking area.

Shadow Lake. Also at Sunrise, this three-mile trail goes to Shadow Lake. The trail starts at Sunrise parking area.

Carbon Glacier. This Carbon River trail runs for seven miles, starting at the Ipsut Creek Campground. The trail gives hikers an up-close and personal view of the glacier but watch for falling rocks.

Tolmie Peak. This Carbon River trail also travels for seven miles, starting at Mowich Lake. Good views of Mt. Rainier make this trail popular.

Mt. Rainier also has plenty of shorter walks for those with young children. From the National Park Inn at Longmire there's a half mile walk called the Trail of Shadows that takes families to a settler's homestead. From the Ohanapecosh Campground, you can take a half-mile walk to see the bubbling Ohanapecosh Hot Springs. Explore a real rain forest on the Carbon River Rain Forest Nature Trail, a short one-third mile walk from the Carbon River park entrance.

Especially for Kids

Check out the Mt. Rainier website for **"Little Tahoma News"** – a special newsletter for children. The Internet address is *www.nps.gov/mora/pphtml/forkids.html.*

When Are We Going?

Mount Rainier is one of the busiest parks in the national parks system so plan your visit accordingly. Top months are May through October so if you will be traveling then, try to visit the park during the week rather than on busy weekends. Parking is very limited during summer weekends.

During the winter months, some facilities and some roads will be closed. The southwest entrance road between Nisqually Entrance and Paradise is closed starting with the first heavy snows until May.

How Long Are We Staying?

If you just want an overview of the park with stops by the visitor's center and the top sites, you can visit the park in a day. However, if you'd like to enjoy the hiking trails, plan for a two to three day visit.

What Should I Bring?

Good hiking shoes are a must, along with layers of clothing. Even during the late spring and early summer months you can expect cool temperatures during the evening hours so come prepared.

Which One Is My Room?

You'll find plenty of camping options at this park. Here's a rundown of your camping options:

Cougar Rock Campground. One of the most popular in the park, this site is 2.3 miles northeast of Longmire and offers 173 individual sites. Facilities include water, flush toilets, trailer dump station, fire grates, tables, hiking trails. There are no showers or RV hookups. From July 1-Labor Day, the site is only available be reservation (see below). At other times, the sites are rented on a first-come, first-served basis and cost $12 per night ($15 for reserved sites). The campground is only open late May to mid-October.

Ohanapecosh Campground. The other top campground at the park, this site is 11 miles north of Packwood and has 188 individual sites. Facilities include water, flush toilets, trailer dump station, fire grates, tables, visitor center, hiking trails. No showers or RV hookups available. From July 1-Labor Day, the site is only available by reservation (see below). At other times, the sites are rented on a first-come, first-served basis and cost $12 per night. The campground is only open late May to mid-October.

White River Campground. This campground, located five miles west of the White River Entrance, is open late June to September and offers 112 individual sites. The cost is $10 per night and sites are available on a first-come, first-served basis only. Facilities include water, flush toilets, trailer dump station, fire grates, tables, hiking trails. No RV hookups available.

Ipsut Creek Campground. Located in the northwest corner of the park, this 28-site campground is currently limited to only high clearance vehicles or walk-in/bicycle-in access because of road damage. Use is currently free.

Mowich Lake Campground. Also in the northwest corner of the park, this campground offers walk-in sites and is open July through mid-October. Use of the campground is free. Facilities include chemical toilets, tables, and hiking trails; there is no potable water and fires are not permitted.

Sunshine Point Campground. Located on the southwest side of the park near the Nisqually Entrance, this park offers 18 sites on a year-around basis. Water, chemical toilets, fire grates, tables available. The fee is $10 per site on a first-come, first-served basis.

Cougar Rock and Ohanapecosh Campgrounds require reservations from July 1 through Labor Day. To make reservations, call the **National Park Reservation ,** *Tel. 800/365-CAMP*, international *Tel. 301/722-1257*or write P.O. Box 1600, Cumberland, MD 21502. Reservations can be made up to four months in advance. Camping fee is $14 per night. cancellation fee—$13.65 Reservations can also be made online at *http://reservations.nps.gov*.

What Are We Doing Next?

Seattle is less than seventy-five miles from Mount Rainier, and no trip to the city would be complete without a view from **The Space Needle**. For a memento of your visit have your photo taken by SpaceShots Photography as you enter the glass elevator which takes you up to the 520 foot observation deck. Open every day from 8am to midnight. Located on 400 Broad Street. For more information call *206/905/2111* or *800/937-9582*.

From your view at the Space Needle you will notice **The Children's Museum** nearby. Located on the first level of Center House at Seattle Center, children will receive a lesson in world cultures in the Global Village, and the budding actor in your family will love Bijou Theatre, complete with costumes and props. Discovery Bay is a play area equipped to entertain even the most restless toddler. Located at 305 Harrison St. For more details call *Tel. 206/441-1768*.

The Rosalie Whyel Museum of Doll Art, voted the best private doll museum in the world, is only a fifteen minute drive from the heart of Seattle in Bellevue. Over 1,200 dolls are on display, ranging from an elegant 1800's French Bru to a familiar face to any child— Barbie. Located at 1116 108th Ave NE. Open Monday-Saturday 10am-5pm, and Sunday 1pm-5pm. For more information, call *425/455-1116*.

Practical Information

Address: Mount Rainier National Park, Tahoma Woods, Star Route, Ashford, WA 98304-9751

Telephone: *360/569-2211*

Operating Season: July through Labor Day marks the full service season with all facilities open.

Hours: all day, daily

Cost: $10 per vehicle for 7-day pass

Website: *www.nps.gov/mora/index.htm*

Did You Know.....?

- Before entering into statehood, Washington was called Columbia.
- Washington's flag is the only state flag to be emblazoned with a picture of a president. It is also the only green state flag.
- Washington is the only state to be named after a president.
- The state motto is Alki, which is a Native American word meaning "bye and bye."
- Washington is sometimes referred to as The Evergreen State.
- Starbucks was founded in Seattle.
- There are over 1,000 dams in Washington.
- Some of the famous people who have called Washington home are legendary crooner Bing Crosby, 1960's musical icon Jimi Hendrix, The Price Is Right host Bob Barker, singer Kenny Loggins, chairman of Microsoft Bill Gates, explorers Meriweather Lewis and William Clark, singer Kurt Cobain, and TV's *Batman*, Adam West.
- More apples are produced in Washington than in any other state.
- The official state bird is the Willow Goldfinch.
- Olympia is the state capital.
- The official state flower is the Pink Rhododendron.
- The state insect is the Green Darner Dragonfly.
- The oldest operating gas station in the United States can be found in the town of Zillah.
- The state song is *Washington, My Home.*
- The official state tree is the Western Hemlock.

Yellowstone National Park
Wyoming/Montana/Idaho

The sprawling Yellowstone Park is one of the gems in the National Park System. Budget as much time as you can for this massive park.

Are We There Yet?

Yellowstone has five entrances. From Jackson, Wyoming, take US 89 to the south entrance. From Cody, Wyoming, take US 16 to the east entrance. The west entrance is accessible from US 191 from Bozeman, Montana; you can also travel US 20 from Idaho Falls, Idaho. The north entrance can be reached from US 89 off I-90 at Livingston, Montana. From Billings, Montana, travel US 212 from I-90 or from Cody, Wyoming take Highway 296 to the northeast entrance.

What's There To Do Here?

Yellowstone is filled with hiking and sightseeing options including miles of trails. You can't come to Yellowstone without watching Old Faithful spew at least once. The park is dotted with other geysers and hot springs as well.

Kids who are ready to learn more about Yellowstone and do some exploration with rangers will find plenty of fun during the summer. The park participates in the Junior Ranger Program for kids from ages 5 to 12. To participate in the program, kids pay a $3 fee for booklet (available in each of the visitors centers) and complete the activities which include joining a ranger-led program, hiking a trail, and answering some questions about the park.

Your family can explore the terrain on horseback (one- and two-hour tours are offered) or on a wagon ride which leads to a cookout site for dinner. Contact Xanterra Parks and Resorts, *Tel. 307/344-7311.*

When Are We Going?

Summer is certainly the number one time to visit Yellowstone. Summer temperatures average in the 70s so days are very pleasant, although nights can cool off into the 30s. During late summer, look for afternoon thunderstorms.

Although by far most guests visit during the summer months, in the winter the park has a magic all its own. Activities include snowshoe tours, cross country skiing, snowshoeing, and snowmobiling. Equipment is available for rent in the park or visitors can bring their own.

How Long Are We Staying?

As long as possible! This mega-park is a vacation destination all its own. At a minimum, budget two days in the park and restrict yourself to just one area, probably the Old Faithful region. Be sure to realize that there will be crowds during the summer season so book your hotel or campground accommodations early if at all possible.

What Should I Bring?

Don't forget good walking shoes as well as socks. Jackets are important any time of year as well as rain gear.

What Are We Doing Next?

Although Yellowstone certainly has enough activities to fill even the busiest vacation, save some time for a look at nearby Jackson Hole, Wyoming. Filled with vacation options ranging from guest ranches to rodeos to float trips, Jackson Hole can make a great base for your vacation if you don't want to stay in Yellowstone. From here, you'll also be able to visit Grand Teton National Park (see separate heading). Glacier National Park is also another nearby destination.

For more information on Jackson Hole, contact the **Chamber of Commerce,** PO Box 550, Jackson, WY 83001 or *Tel. 307/733-3316; www.jacksonholechamber.com.*

Which One Is My Room?

Yellowstone is home to one of the best-known and loved lodges in the national park system: the **Old Faithful Inn.** This classic lodge is a popular choice so book early; for reservations, call *307/344-7311.* The inn is open from early May to mid-October.

Other hotel choices in the park include:

Old Faithful Lodge Cabins (mid-May to mid-September); reservations call *307/344-7311.*

Lake Lodge Cabins (mid-June to mid-September); *Tel. 307/344-7311.*

Grant Village (mid-May to mid-September); *Tel. 307/344-7311.*

Canyon Village Lodge and Cabins (early June to end of August); *Tel. 307/344-7311.*

Roosevelt Lodge Cabins (early June to end of August); *Tel. 307/344-7311.*

Did You Know.....?

• Dunanda Falls in Yellowstone National Park was named after the Shoshone Indian word for "straight down."

• The most common tree you will find in Yellowstone is the Lodgepole Pine.

• The waters of Yellowstone Lake are normally 41 degrees, and the most common fish swimming in those waters is the cutthroat trout.

• There are roughly 600 active and dormant geysers in Yellowstone.

• The stone arch found at the North entrance into Yellowstone is named in honor of President Theodore Roosevelt.

• Yellowstone River was once known as Rive des Roche Jaune, or River of Yellow Rock. This is the origin behind the name of Yellowstone National Park.

∂

During the winter months, only two of the park's hotels are open. **Mammoth Hot Springs Hotel**, *Tel. 301/344-7311* or *travelyellowstone.com.*, on the north side offers 96 guest rooms from late December through early March (as well as mid-May to early October). Built in the 1930s, the hotel has a Map Room which contains a large wooden map of the US made of 165 woods from nine countries.

The newly built **Old Faithful Snow Lodge**, *Tel. 301/344-7311* or *www.amfac.com,* accept winter visitors from mid-December to mid-March (as well as mid-May to early October). This hotel is built in the style of Old Faithful Inn.

Camping is one of the most popular accommodation options in the park. They're so popular, in fact, that many campgrounds fill up by early mornings during the peak summer months. We've listed reservations numbers for those campgrounds which accept reservations; for others plan to be in place early. Camping fees range from $10 to $17 ($31 for RV camping). Remember that you'll need to bear-proof everything at the campgrounds. Here are some of the campgrounds available:

Bridge Bay Campground (mid-May to mid-September); reservations *Tel. 307/344-7311.*

Canyon Campground (early June to early September); reservations *Tel. 307/344-7311.* Includes showers and laundry facilities.

Grant Village Campground (mid-June to early October); reservations *Tel. 307/344-7311.* Includes showers and laundry facilities.

Madison Campground (early May to late October); reservations *Tel. 307/344-7311.*

Fishing Bridge RV park (mid-May to mid-September); reservations *Tel. 307/344-7311.* Includes showers and laundry facilities as well as water, sewer and electrical hookups. This park is only for RV campers; no tent camping or tent trailers allowed.

Mammoth Campground (year round); first-come, first-served.

Norris Campground (mid-May to late September); first-come, first-served.

Indian Creek (early June to mid-September); first-come, first-served.

Lewis Lake (early June to late October); first-come, first-served.

Pebble Creek (early June to end of September); first-come, first-served.

Slough Creek (late May to late October); first-come, first-served.

Tower Fall (mid-May to end of September); first-come, first-served.

Practical Information

Address: Yellowstone National Park, PO Box 168, Yellowstone National Park, WY 82190-0168

Telephone: *307/344-7381*

Operating Season: year round although only the north entrance at Gardiner, Montana is open from mid-December through mid-March

Hours: daily

Cost: $20 for a private vehicle for a seven-day entrance permit; annual passes available for $40

Website: *www.nps.gov/yell/index.htm*

Learning About Yellowstone

Carrier, Jim. *Letters from Yellowstone.* 1987.

Houk, Randy. *Wolves in Yellowstone.* 1997.

Keene, Carolyn M. *An Instinct for Trouble* (The Nancy Drew Files, No. 95). 1994.

Lauber, Patricia. *Summer of Fire: Yellowstone 1988.* 1991.

Peterson, David. *Yellowstone National Park* (New True Books). 1992.

Pringle, Laurence P. et al. *Fire in the Forest: A Cycle of Growth and Renewal.* 1995.

Roberts, Willo Davis and Dan Burr (Illustrator). *The Absolutely True Story: How I Visited Yellowstone Park With the Terrible Rupes.*1997.

Swinburne, Stephen R. et al. *Moon in Bear's Eyes.* 1998.

Skurzynski, Gloria and Alane Ferguson. *Wolf Stalker: National Parks Mystery* (National Parks Mystery). 1997.

Warner, Gertrude Chandler and Charles Tang (Illustrator). *The Growling Bear Mystery* (Boxcar Children No. 61). 1998.

Glacier National Park
Montana

Tucked on the US-Canada border in northwestern Montana, this rugged park is known for its, well, glaciers. There are almost 50 glaciers within the park and many opportunities to view wildlife. The park spans over a million acres and is filled with geologic history, wildlife, and beautiful flora.

Glacier is joined to Waterton Lakes National Park in Alberta, Canada as the Waterton-Glacier International Peace Park, the first park of this type in the world.

Are We There Yet?

The park is located on US 2, accessible from the east or west.

What's There to Do Here?

You'll find several guided activities in the park:

Scenic Drives. The number one drive in this park is Going-to-the-Sun Road, a 50-mile drive that traces the Continental Divide along lake shores and spectacular bluffs.

Hiking. You'll find over 700 miles of trails that invite exploration of the park. To better understand your surroundings while on a self-guided tour, hike The Trail of The Cedars, Huckleberry Mountain, Hidden Lake, Sun Point, or Swiftcurrent Nature Trail, for which signs and brochures are provided.

Horseback Trips. Guided rides are available during peak months. For trips to Lake McDonald, call *406/888-5121,* and for trips to Many Glacier, call *406/732-4203.*

Boating. Glacier Park Boat Company offers guided boat tours as well as boat rentals in the park. Contact the visitors center for details.

Learn the Language of the Blackfeet People

This area is the homeland of the Blackfeet people. Here are a few words in the Blackfoot (or Siksika) language:

Numbers
- one— ni't
- two— ist
- three— niookska
- four— niiso
- five— niisito
- six— naa
- seven— ihkitsik
- eight— naanisoyi
- nine— piihksso
- ten— kiipo

Animals
- bird— pi'kssii
- cat— poos
- dog— omitaa horse— o'ta's
- owl— sipisttoo
- puppy— sisomm

People
- baby— maanipokaa
- boy— saahkomaapi
- brother— niisistowahsin child— oko's
- daughter— itan
- father— inn girl— aakiikoan
- grandparent— aaahs
- mother— na'a
- sister— aakiim
- son— ohko

Guided Hikes. Backpacking trips are available into more remote areas, including guided day hikes. Contact Glacier Wilderness Guides, *Tel. 406/387-5555.*

When Are We Going?

Summer is definitely the peak time for a visit to this park, a time when temperatures are moderate and comfortable.

How Long Are We Staying?

Because of the size of this park, you'll want at least two days to get a feel for the facility.

What Should I Bring?

Bring along a light jacket even during summer months; evenings can be cool.

What Are We Doing Next?

Families will find several area attractions, including the **Blackfeet Indian Reservation**. Here the **Museum of the Plains** explores the history of this region.

South of the park, the **People's Center** and **Native Ed-Venture** showcase the Salish and Kootenai cultures with tours and a museum.

Which One is My Room?

You've got lots of different options at this park with seven lodges and hotels located throughout the park. The premier lodge is **Apgar Village Lodge** with 48 cabins and motel units (each has a private bath). For reservations, contact the lodge at PO Box 410, West Glacier, Montana 59936; *Tel. 406/888-5484.*

Other options include The Village Inn, Rising Sun Motor Inn, Swiftcurrent Motor Inn, Lake McDonald Lodge, and more. For information on these properties, contact **Glacier Park, Inc.**, P.O. Box 2025, Columbia Falls, MT 59912, *Tel. 406/892-2525.* Another option is **Granite Park Chalet**; for information contact **Glacier Wilderness Guides, Inc.**, PO Box 330, West Glacier, MT 59936, *Tel. 406/387-5555; www.glacierguides.com.*

Campers have almost 1000 sites, most on a first-come, first served basis. Two campgrounds, **Fish Creek** and **St. Mary**, accept reservations; call *800/365-CAMP.*

Lodging is also available across the Canadian border at **Waterton Park**, home of Waterton Lakes National Park. Contact the Waterton Park Chamber of Commerce, P.O. Box 55, Waterton Park, Alberta, Canada T0K 2M0; *Tel. 403/859-2203.*

Did You Know.....?

- Montana is also called the Treasure State.
- There are more species of mammals in Montana than in any other state.
- There are more grizzly bears living in Montana than in any other state in the continental US.
- "Oro y plata", which means "gold and silver" is the state motto.
- The Western Meadowlark is the state bird Montana was admitted into statehood on November 8, 1889.
- Many famous personalities were either born or raised in Montana including Battlestar Galactica star Dirk Benedict (Helena), comedian Dana Carvey (Missoula), actor Gary Cooper (Helena), daredevil Evel Knievel (Butte), actress Myrna Loy (Helena), director David Lynch (Missoula), and actress Martha Raye (Butte).
- Bitterroot is the state flower.
- The Ponderosa Pine is the state tree.
- Miles City is referred to as the Cowboy Capital.
- The town of Ekalaka was named in honor of Sitting Bull's daughter.
- Helena is the state capital.

Practical Information

Address: Glacier National Park, Park Headquarters, PO Box 128, West Glacier, MT 59936

Telephone: *406/888-7800*

Operating Season: year-round

Hours: Apgar Visitor Center open all year, (although only on weekends from November through March); Logan Pass Visitor Center open from June through mid-October; St. Mary Visitor Center open May through mid-October

Cost: $20 per vehicle for a 7-day permit

Website: *www.nps.gov/glac/index.htm*

Learning About Montana

Marsh, Carole. *Montana: Indian Dictionary for Kids!* Gallopade Publishing Group, 1996. ages 9-12.

Marsh, Carole. *Montana Facts and Factivities*. Gallopade Publishing Group, 1996. Ages 9-12.

Grand Teton National Park
Wyoming

Just 56 miles from the southern edge of Yellowstone lies Grand Teton National Park, an excellent accompaniment to the one of the nation's top parks. Grand Teton is known for its towering mountains and rugged glaciers, part of the Rocky Mountains.

Are We There Yet?

From Jackson, Wyoming it is a 12 mile drive to the Moose Visitors Center.

What's There To Do Here?

Outdoor activities about in this park, whether your family's idea of fun is a slow stroll or mountain climbing. Seasonal activities include fishing, swimming, canoeing, float trips, bicycling, skiing, snowmobiling, and more.

Start your visit at one of the visitors centers in the park. **Moose Visitors Center** includes videos on the region as well as exhibits on endangered species. **Jenny Lake Visitor Center** offers displays on the unique geology of the park. **Colter Bay Visitor Center** includes a museum of Native American items and an excellent bookstore for learning more about the region. You'll also find museum tours and ranger-led activities here. **Flagg Ranch Information Center** includes information about the region.

Other activities include:

Scenic Drives. The Signal Mountain Summit Road is a favorite for views from Signal Mountain. From here, you'll have a bird's eye view of Jackson Hole and the Tetons. Another beautiful drive is Jenny Lake Scenic Drive, featuring views of Grand Teton.

Menor's Ferry. North of Moose you'll find the Menor's Ferry Trail, under half a mile long. Here pioneer Bill Menor once lived in a cabin and you can ride a replica of a turn of the century ferry.

Snake River Raft Trips. Families with older children will appreciate these exciting excursions including float and fishing trips. Contact the visitors center for information.

Horseback Rides. At Colter Bay and Jackson Lake Lodge you'll find horses for rent, a great way to enjoy the park in a natural way.

When Are We Going?

Summer is the busiest time in the park, so be prepared for crowds. Have your reservations made well in advance, whether you'll be staying in the park or in Jackson Hole.

How Long Are We Staying?

You'll want at least a day to enjoy some of the scenic drives, more if you'll be engaged in activities.

What Should I Bring?
Bring along a jacket even during summer months as well as insect repellent.

What Are We Doing Next?
Yellowstone is the number one activity to combine with a visit to this park.

Which One Is My Room?
Accommodations in the park include:
- **Flagg Ranch Resort**, Box 187, Moran, WY 83013, *Tel. 800/443-2311*
- **Grand Teton Lodge**, Box 250, Moran, WY 83013, *Tel. 307/543-2811*
- **Signal Mountain Lodge**, Box 50, Moran, WY 83013, *Tel. 307/543-2831*
- **Dornan's Spur Ranch Cabins**, Box 39, Moose, WY 83012, *Tel. 307/733-2415*

You'll also find several campgrounds. The largest is **Gros Ventre** with 360 sites; the facility also includes a trailer dump station. Your best chance of finding a campsite is at Gros Ventre; other campgrounds often fill up between 8 and 10am during peak months.

Did You Know.....?
- "Old Steamboat" is the name of the bucking horse that can be seen on the license plates of Wyoming residents.
- Artist Jackson Pollock was born in Cody, Wyoming.
- Patricia Mac Lachlan, author of children's novel Sarah, Plain and Tall was born in the state capital, Cheyenne.
- The Western Meadowlark is the official state bird.
- The state motto is "Equal rights".
- Wyoming was the first state in the US to give women the right to vote.
- Fewer people live in Wyoming than in any other state.
- Devil's Tower was the first National Monument.
- The state nickname is Equality State.
- The horned toad is the state reptile.
- The cottonwood is the state tree.
- The official state flower is the Indian Paintbrush.
- The first JC Penney store opened its doors in Kemmerer, Wyoming.
- Wyoming was named after a Native American word meaning "large prairie place."

Where Are We Going Next?

Yellowstone, which is covered in this book, is the number one activity to combine with a visit to Grand Teton. Another nearby excursion is **Fossil Butte National Monument**, where at the visitor's center dinosaur lovers can view a mural of life eons ago and see 80 fossils on display, including the oldest recorded bat and a 13-foot-long crocodile. Nature enthusiasts will enjoy the Forest Lake Trail, with wayside exhibits of the vegetation found in this area, while future archeologists will want to take the Historic Quarry Trail, which leads you to the site where many fossils were excavated. For more information write Fossil Butte National Monument, P.O. Box 592, Kemmerer, WY 83101 or call *307/877-4455.*

Practical Information

Address: Grand Teton National Park, P.O. Drawer 170, Moose, WY 83012

Telephone: *307/739-3300*

Operating Season: year-round; visitors centers closed Dec. 25

Hours: visitors center hours vary by season

Cost: $20 per car. Admission is good for both Yellowstone and Grand Teton National Parks.

Website: *www.nps.gov/grte/index.htm*

Chapter 10

BEYOND THE CONTINENTAL U.S.

San Juan National Historic Site
Puerto Rico

Known as Fuerte San Felipe del Morro (or El Morro, Old San Juan, *Tel. 787/729-6960*), this fort is one of the most photographed sites in the Caribbean. It contains a museum and is administered by the National Park Service. On its grounds, the Cuartel de Ballaja, once Spanish troop quarters, now houses the Museum of the Americas.

Are We There Yet?

The park is located on the waterfront in Old San Juan. This historic district of this city is hard to maneuver in a car—roads are limited and parking is just about non-existent. You cannot drive into the park; it is a quarter-mile walk from the street, Calle Norzagaray.

What's There To Do Here?

The main activity is a tour of El Morro. This fort, one of the most photographed sites in the Caribbean, contains a museum. On its grounds, the Cuartel de Ballaja, once Spanish troop quarters, now houses the Museum of the Americas.

Start with a video on the site then take a self-guided tour. You'll find a map at the entrances, and exhibits throughout the park are posted in both English and Spanish. Even if you're not a history buff, this site is a family place where you can look out on the sea and enjoy a gentle tradewind. Bring along your camera for this scenic stop.

When Are We Going?
Summer is the most popular (and least expensive) time to visit San Juan. You'll find prices as much as 40% lower than during the winter months. However, summer can be very hot in San Juan so if you visit during this season, start your park visit early and hit the beach or the pool in the afternoon.

Also, realize that summer is hurricane season. Although the Caribbean is a large region and tracking systems give you several days advance warning before an approaching storm, this kind of weather can be a factor in your vacation. Generally June and early July are the safest; September is the worst month for storms.

El Morro Warning!
Remember, El Morro is an old fort, not a playground. This structure was never meant to house small, energetic children and includes a lot of hazards. Keep kids away from the wall's edges and off cannons for their own safety.

How Long Are We Staying?
You'll want two or three hours to have a look at the structures.

What Should I Bring?
Bring along a hat any time of year – it gets warm as you walk. We toured the fort one day in December but it felt like August.

What Are We Doing Next?
Near El Morro you'll find **Casa Blanca**, 1 Sebastian Street, Old San Juan, *Tel. 787/724-4102*, which contains exhibits on 16th and 17th century life and on its most famous residents: Ponce de Leon and his family. (Actually Ponce de Leon died before the home was completed.) Built in the 1520s, the home was the city's first fortress and is now open for tours Wednesday through Sunday.

Puerto Rico is also rich in natural attractions, including what is called one of the finest cave systems in the world. The **Rio Camuy Cave Park**, *Route 102*, *787/898-3100*, located 2-1/2 hours west of San Juan, was formed by large underground rivers. Today the park includes a new visitors center with reception area and cafeteria and a theater with AV presentation. Visitors reach cave level by trolley then follow walkways on a 45-minute guided tour.

Spanish Words and Phrases

You will find that Puerto Rico is bilingual; without a word of Spanish, you'll be able to go anywhere. However, it's fun to learn a few words of Spanish and will be appreciated by people you meet.

Greetings
- Hello! — Hola!
- Good bye — Adios
- See you later — Hasta luego
- Good morning — Buenos dias
- Good afternoon — Buenos tardes
- Good evening — Buenas noches
- Please — Por favor
- Thank you — Gracias
- How are you? Como esta usted?
- What is your name? Como se llama?
- My name is.....— Mi nombre es.....

Days of The Week
- Sunday — Domingo
- Monday — Lunes
- Tuesday — Martes
- Wednesday — Miercoles
- Thursday— Jueves
- Friday — Viernes
- Saturday — Sabado

Numbers One Through Ten
- on — uno
- two— dos
- three— tres
- four— cuatro
- five— cinco
- six— seis
- seven— siete
- eight— ocho
- nine— nueve
- ten— diez

Another natural attraction is **Caribbean National Forest (El Yunque)**, Highway 3 east between San Juan and Fajardo to Route 191 near Luquillo, *Tel. 787/887-2875* or *787/766-5335*, the only tropical rainforest in the U.S. National Forest Service. Forty-five minutes east of San Juan, the rainforest boasts 240 species of trees and flowers, including 20 varieties of orchids and

50 varieties of ferns. Walking trails carve through the dense forest, and guided tours are available.

Kids also enjoy the **Children's Museum** (Museo del Niño), 150 Calle Cristo, San Juan. Young visitors enter the museum through the legs of a large wooden figure then enjoy hands-on displays and activities from a village of playhouses to a "Visit the Dentist" exhibit where children can play dentist. The museum is open Tuesday through Thursday, 9:30am to 3:30pm, Friday 9am to 5pm, and weekends 12:30pm to 5pm

Practical Information
> **Address**: San Juan NHS, Fort San Cristobal, Norzagaray St., San Juan, PR 00901-2094
> **Telephone:** *787/729-6960 for visitor information*
> **Operating Season**: year round
> **Hours**: 9am-5pm
> **Cost**: Adults $3 a day per fort, young adults (13 - 17) $1 a day per fort, children under 12 free
> **Website:** *www.nps.gov/saju/index.htm*

Buck Island National Historic Park
U.S.Virgin islands

Just off the coast of the far northeast side of the island lies St. Croix's natural treasure: Buck Island. Several outfitters take snorkelers on half and full day trips to this island to swim along the Buck Island Reef National Monument. Here, in about 12 feet of water, snorkelers follow a marked trail for a self-guided tour of this undersea world.

This national park is for those members of the family who are good swimmers. While outfitters will give you life jackets, swimming is required in deep water. We'd recommend that all members of the family practice snorkeling in a pool or shallow water before heading out to the historic park. Waters are deep and, if the water is choppy, can be a little difficult for snorkeling. You'll be snorkeling from a boat so everyone needs to be comfortable with a snorkel and mask.

Are We There Yet?
The national park is located around Buck Island, a small island that's 5-1/2 miles from Christiansted. There are no park facilities once you get out there and no admission is charged, but you do need to get there by boat. There are many concessions in Christiansted that offer sails out to the park, complete with all the snorkel gear you need.

What's There To Do Here?

Snorkeling is the top thing to do here and, we must say, the snorkeling is great. With crystal clear waters, you'll see all types of tropical fish and coral formations.

As we mentioned earlier, however, this is a trip for those who are comfortable swimming and snorkeling. Pick a nice day for your excursion (we went once on a choppy day and wore ourselves out swimming against the current).

When Are We Going?

The busiest months for this park are the winter months, from mid-December through mid-April. While it won't make much difference for your park visit (there's plenty of water for all the tour boats and snorkelers), it will make a difference in the rest of your vacation. During this peak season, the price of guest rooms runs up to 40% more than during the summer months.

How Long Are We Staying?

Budget about half a day for the excursion.

What Should I Bring?

You'll want swimsuits, lots of sunscreen, hats and sunglasses for the boat ride, towels, and even an old t-shirt to swim in during the snorkeling. We'd also recommend a disposable underwater camera, a great way to get photos of your family as well as the colorful tropical fish underwater.

What Are We Doing Next?

From 1733 to 1917, Denmark owned St. Croix before selling all of the U.S. Virgin Islands to the United States for $25 million in gold. Concerned for the security of Panama Canal, the U.S. made the islands a territory, giving its residents right of American citizenship, except for a vote in the presidential election.

While the stars and stripes may wave there today, the island still boasts its own unique spirit, however. English is spoken with a Caribbean lilt, and driving is on the left side of the road.

What results is a melange of American and Caribbean, with a peppering of other cultures as well. The island is rich in history and has flown seven flags throughout the years: Spanish, Dutch, British, French, Knights of Malta, Danish, and American.

That combination of cultures, mixed with a rich history and natural beauty, brings visitors to St. Croix, an island that offers a sampling of the other Virgin Islands. "St. Croix is a combination of St. Thomas and St. John," explains Elizabeth Armstrong, president of the island's hotel association. "St. Croix has such a good mixture: the rolling hills, the beaches, and the small towns."

The mixture comes together to create a country atmosphere combining the shopping and history of St. Thomas with the natural beauty of St. John. The result is the largest Virgin Island, an 82 square mile landmass dotted with pastel-tinted brick and mortar architecture in the towns of Frederiksted and Christiansted, named for Danish kings.

To view the structures the Danes designed at a time when Americans were still English citizens, consider an island tour, which can be done in five or six hours. Most start on the north shore in the town of Christiansted, a few minutes from where Columbus landed over 500 years ago and named this island Santa Cruz. (Today residents born on St. Croix are known as Crucians.)

Looking like a building carved from lemon sherbet, the Old Scalehouse once weighed sugar, the product of over 100 stone mills scattered across the island in the late 19th century. The sugar was loaded on ship that later returned to St. Croix with a ballast of brick, used to construct many of the homes and businesses. Near the Old Scalehouse, Fort Christianvaern is now operated by the U.S. Park Department. The yellow fortress, with its dungeons and old cannons, is now open for self-guided tours.

The real beauty of the island lies beyond the city limits. Here, on rolling hills littered with historic sugar mills, the island takes on a country charm. Bucolic cattle dot open fields, small homes cling to the hillsides along winding roads, and the occasional shy mongoose, imported to kill snakes, scamper across the road and under cover.

St. Croix's southern city, Frederiksted, lies just a few miles from the former plantation house. A stop for many cruise ships (a new dock was constructed here in 1994 to replace damage done by Hurricane Hugo), the town is a smaller version of Christiansted. Shopping includes duty-free boutiques featuring china and crystal to a vendor's market for inexpensive t-shirts and jewelry.

St. Croix's best treasures, however, are not the man-made ones but the natural areas found at opposite ends of the island. From Frederiksted, take Rt. 76 or the Mahogany Road north for a trip to the rain forest. The 15-acre rainforest has thick vegetation where the sunlight is filtered through mahogany, yellow cedar, and Tibet trees. This forest is also home of **LEAP**, the Life and Environmental Arts Project, where skilled artisans craft everything from sculptures to spoons from the hardwoods found in the rain forest.

Which One Is My Room?

There are no accommodations in the park but you'll find several family properties not far from the docks.

The Buccaneer, *Tel. 800/255-3881*, is located five minutes east of Christiansted. The resort has a rich history: once owned by Charles Martel, a Knight of Malta, the estate had walls three feet thick, and was tucked just behind a hill to hide it from view of possible pirates. Later, the stately manor was the residence of the young Alexander Hamilton. Today, the original estate is supplemented with modern rooms to complete the 146-room resort.

For comfort and very reasonable prices, check out the **Tamarind Reef Hotel,** *Tel. 800/619-0014.* This 46-room property is located east of Christiansted just off the reef. All of the rooms include a refrigerator, coffee maker, air conditioning, phones, and many also include kitchenettes. The atmosphere here is laid-back and comfortable, perfect for families to enjoy the snorkel trail in the inlet just in front of the hotel.

Practical Information
Address: Buck Island Reef National Monument, Danish Custom House, Kings Wharf, 2100 Church Street #100, Christiansted, St. Croix. VI 00820-4611
Telephone: *340/773-1460*
Operating Season: year round; visitors center open 8am-5pm
Hours: call concessions for tour times
Cost: free; charge for snorkel trip from private concessions
Website: *www.nps.gov/buis/index.htm*

Virgin Islands National Park
U.S. Virgin Islands
Laurance Rockefeller donated land on beautiful St. John to create this park, which covers two-thirds of the island. You'll find historic sites here but the real attraction is along the seashore with beautiful beaches, great campsites, and spectacular water.

The stewardship of the island's natural beauty began with Laurance Rockefeller. Developer of Caneel Bay Resort, the multi-millionaire donated much of the island to the National Park Service in the 1950s. Today, preservation of this island's resources lies in the hands of the park service and a developer named Stanley Selengut, a leader in the world of eco-tourism who operates several eco-friendly properties on the island. St. John leads the world in sustainable tourism resorts where guests make a minimal impact on nature.

Are We There Yet?
St. John has no airport so most visitors arrive from neighboring St. Thomas by boat. Most visitors arrive via ferry service from St. Thomas, *Tel. 340/776-6282* . From Red Hook, it's a 20-minute, $3 one way cruise ($1 for kids under 12); from Charlotte Amalie the journey costs $7 ($3 for kids under 12) and takes 45 minutes. A private water taxi from Red Hook is a wonderful luxury; call **Per Dohm's Water Taxi**, *Tel. 340/775-6501.*

What's There To Do Here?

Your first stop will be the **Cruz Bay Visitor Center**, just a short stroll from the ferry dock. There's a small playground nearby where kids can burn off any energy that built up on the ferry ride then you can have a look at the exhibits in the center and pick up a map of the park.

Trunk Bay is one of the best sites in the park; it is home to a self-guided snorkel trail you can enjoy with a short swim from the beach. Other options are a stroll along the self-guided **Cinnamon Bay Nature Trail**, take a ranger-guided hike along The Reef Bay Trail (advance reservations are a must; for more information contact the visitor's center), or walk along the Petroglyphs Trail, where perhaps you can unlock the mystery behind the carved symbols left behind by either Amerindians or African slaves. Visit the ruins of **Annaberg Sugar Plantation** and some of the island's prettiest views.

When Are We Going?

Unlike most parks in the national park system, the peak months at this destination all during the wintertime – and with good reason. Winter visitors find beautiful, sunny days in the 80s, a good explanation for peak visitation from December through April here. The months of May through November are the quietest times.

How Long Are We Staying?

Because of the ferry ride from St. Thomas, plan to spend the day on St. John to enjoy the snorkel trail, take it easy on the beach, and see a little of the island.

What Should I Bring?

Bring all your beach gear as well as snorkels and masks. Fins are optional but bring beach shoes if you don't wear fins to protect against sea urchins and coral. Load up on the sunscreen!

What Are We Doing Next?

Most of the activity on St. John centers around the park but save some time for a look around Cruz Bay, the small town at the ferry port. Here you'll find some fun shops where the emphasis is on hand-made items: clothing, pottery, jewelry, and artwork.

Which One Is My Room?

At **Cinnamon Bay Campgrounds**, Cruz Bay, *Tel. 340/776-6330, Fax 340/776-6458*; Toll free reservations *800/539-9998*, is located in the national park. Campers keep the bare sites, tents, and screened shelters of this popular campground full year around. This campground is located on the grounds of the national park and features accommodations near beautiful Cinnamon Bay Beach, St. John's longest stretch of sand.

Tents (which measure 10' x 14') are outfitted with four cots with bedding, a solid floor, an ice chest, water container, and cooking and eating utensils. Outdoors, a propane stove and lantern, charcoal grill, and picnic table are available.

Cottages (15 x 15 feet) are actually screened shelters with the same features as well as electricity. All accommodations share bathhouses with cool water showers.

The atmosphere is very relaxed, as campers enjoy the Caribbean at their campsite, on the beach, and on daily ranger-led tours of the national park. Don't be surprised to see a family of wild burros roaming the grounds.

Most family cottages are units 10 A through D, a seashell's throw from the water. Tent-site 21 is the closest to the water, and bare-site 24 is best for beach buffs. We hear that you practically have to inherit a reservation to secure these most-popular sites, but give it a try anyway.

If you don't get a campsite in the national park, you'll still find other options on tiny St. John. Campers can opt for **Maho Bay Camps**, Cruz Bay, *Tel. 340/715-0501, Fax 340/776-6226*; Toll free reservations *800/392-9004*. From the minute you arrive at Maho, you'll know that this is no ordinary campground. There is a help-yourself center where guests leave unused food, toiletries, books, and other items for other guests' use and a network of raised boardwalks that connect the tent cabins and protect hillside vegetation. This resort's focus is on environmental camping.

Every 16' x 16' unit has screened sides with roll down privacy shades, a sleeping area with mattress-covered beds and bedding, a futon sofa that pulls down into a sleeper, a cooking and dining area with cooler, propane stove, and fan, and an outdoor balcony. Barbecue grills and bathhouses are scattered throughout the property.

The founder of Maho Bay Camps has established two other properties, both ecologically sensitive. **Harmony**, Cruz Bay, *Tel. 340/715-0501*; Toll free reservations *800/392-9004,* was designed to be a resort in tune with nature. Solar power, recycled materials, low flush toilets, and a complete awareness of the environment makes this an eco-sensitive resort, but with a higher number of creature comforts than are found at its sister property, Maho. These units include energy-efficient refrigerators, a computer to track energy use, comfortable furnishings (either two twin beds in the bedroom studio units or two queen beds in the living room studios), private baths, a deck with furniture, and kitchen.

Estate Concordia, Cruz Bay, *Tel. 212/472-9453, Fax 212/861-6210*; Toll-free US reservations *800/392-9004,* also takes the eco-tourism-with-style approach. Located on the more remote south shore, these units and the neighboring eco-tents are more widely spaced across the landscape than the units at Harmony and Maho. These canvas tent cottages are specifically designed to be light on the land, to rely on high-tech advancements such as ultra light reflective materials, and to provide facilities such as compost toilets, while at the same time being ecologically friendly.

If you're looking for a traditional hotel rooms, you'll find that on St. John as well. The elegant **Westin St. John**, *Tel. 340/693-8000, Fax 340/779-4500;* Toll-free US phone number *800/WESTIN-1,* has long been one of the Caribbean's nicest, a place where guests feel like they're being swept into paradise. Guests are transported to the resort like visiting royalty aboard a private yacht. You'll arrive on St. John at the hotel dock, and soon be off to your room, one of 282 guest accommodations and 67 villas on a hillside over Great Cruz Bay.

Caneel Baỳ, *Tel. 340/776-6111, Fax 340/693-8280;* Toll free US phone number *800/928-8889,* has the air of old-world Caribbean elegance that tells you, without a word, that this resort was a Laurance Rockefeller development. Tucked within the Virgin Islands National Park, Caneel boasts seven beaches and a natural beauty that is surpassed only by the resort's high quality service. Spread out across the lush property, 166 cottages combine "casual elegance" with "St. John camping" to come up with a property where you can feel like you are camping while enjoying plenty of pampering. Cooled by trade winds and a ceiling fan, each cottage has furnishings from the Philippines, screened walls that are open to a pristine view, and cool terrazzo floors as well as an ice chest for daily ice delivery. Children find plenty of fun at Caneel as well. Turtle Town, the children's center, offers plenty of fun and education.

Practical Information

Address: Virgin Islands National Park, 1300 Cruz Bay Creek, St. John, V.I. 00830

Telephone: *340/776-6201*

Operating Season: Year round; closed Christmas Day

Hours: Visitor Center daily, 8am-4:30pm

Cost: free; same-day use fee at both Annaberg and Trunk Bay $4 for adults, free for children 16 and under

Website: *www.nps.gov/viis/index.htm*

Learn More About the US Virgin islands

Aylesworth, Thomas G. et al. *Territories and Possessions: Puerto Rico, U.S. Virgin Islands, Guam, American Samoa, Wake, Midway and Other Islands,* Micronesia (Discovering America), 1995.

Gershator, Phyllis et al. *Tukama Tootles the Flute: A Tale from the Antilles.*1994.

O'Dell, Scott. *My Name Is Not Angelica.* 1989

Vigor, John. *Danger, Dolphins, and Ginger Beer.* 1993.

Denali National Park
Alaska

Mention Alaska and just about everyone is familiar with Mount McKinley, North America's highest peak. The centerpiece of Denali National Park is just one reason for a visit to this sprawling, six million acre park – moose, grizzlies, and Dall sheep are other good incentives to plan an excursion here.

Are We There Yet?

The park headquarters are located about 125 miles south of Fairbanks or about 240 miles north of Anchorage on Alaska Route 3. You can drive on the Denali Park Road for almost 15 miles to the Savage River Bridge. After that point, you'll have to take shuttles and tours (more on that later.)

What's There To Do Here?

Assuming you and your family aren't going to attempt a climb of Mt. McKinley, you'll still find lots of activity in Denali:

Bus Tours. The bus tours are great for spotting those moose, wolves, Dall sheep and, of course, bears. Shuttle buses can move you from spot to spot in the park, all the while you can try your luck at spotting wildlife. To make advance reservations, call *800/622-PARK* or write Doyon/ARAMARK Joint Venture, 241 West Ship Creek Ave., Anchorage, AK 99501. If you don't make reservations in advance, you'll find that half the tickets are sold on site two days in advance of travel.

Narrated Tour Buses. Get a narrated look at the park and learn more about the wildlife. Tours include lunch and you don't have the distraction of people popping on and off the buses as on the shuttle buses. To make advance reservations, call *800/276-7234* or *907/276-7234*.

When Are We Going?

Summer months are the busiest time in this park but because of its size you won't feel crowded.

How Long Are We Staying?

Because of the size of the park and its distance from other sites, you'll want to budget at least two or three days here.

What Should I Bring?

Insect repellent, a jacket, hiking shoes, a camera, and binoculars for spotting wildlife are must-haves.

Which One Is My Room?

The **Denali Park Hotel** offers overnight accommodations in the park if you aren't interested in camping. You'll also find accommodations in the community of Healy, about 12 miles away. A good source of accommodations information in the Healy area is the **Alaska Internet Travel Guide**, *www.alaskaone.com*.

Campers have several options within the park. Three are accessible by car, three other parks can only be reached by shuttle bus.

Reservations are available for most of the campgrounds, call *800/622-7275* or *907/272-7275* (after late February for the following year) for reservations. Only one campground is open year around. You may also mail a reservation request with a check or credit card number (and expiration date) to Doyon/ARAMARK Joint Venture at 241 West Ship Creek Ave., Anchorage, AK 99501. Fax requests are also accepted; call *907/264-4684* with your credit card company and expiration date.

For further help acquiring accommodations, contact the Denali Chamber of Commerce, *Tel. 907/683-4636* or *www.denalichamber.com*.

What Are We Doing Next?

There are a variety of attractions to choose from in nearby Fairbanks including:

Pioneer Park, a 44-acre theme park that is a smorgasbord of activities, including the Pioneer Air Museum, where aircraft which has hovered over

Did You Know.....?

- Thirteen year old Benny Benson designed the state flag back in 1926.
- Anchorage is Alaska's largest city.
- The name Alaska was derived from an Aleut word, "alaxsxaq", which means "the mainland."
- Singer Jewel and Olympic gold medallist in alpine skiing Tommy Roe are from Alaska.
- Alaska is over twice the size of Texas.
- The state flower is the forget me not.
- The Sitka spruce is the official state tree.
- The state song is "Alaska's Flag."
- The moose is the state mammal.
- The state motto is "North to the Future."
- Jade is the state gemstone.
- Alaska provides the majority of America's salmon, herring, crab and halibut.
- The willow Ptarmigan is the state bird.
- Alaska was admitted into statehood on January 3, 1959.
- Juneau is the state capital.

Alaskan skies over the years are on display; the riverboat Nenana, also referred to as "The Last Lady of the River," which now holds a diorama; see actual structures from the time when Fairbanks was a gold rush town as well as a recreation of a Native village, and even play a round of mini-golf. Located at Airport Way and Peger Road. This is a free attraction. Call *907/459-1095* for more details.

River Boat Discovery Tours takes you on a 3 1/2 hour sternwheeler riverboat cruise past such sites as a Chena Indian Village, where Native guides explain the culture and history of the land's people. Also while on the cruise witness a bush pilot take off and land. Admission. Call *866/479-6673* toll free.

Take a tour of an actual gold mine, then pan for gold yourself at **Gold Dredge No. 8**, which also offers a video on the mining process as well as exhibits. Admission. 1755 Old Steese Hwy N., *Tel. 907/457-6058.*

Practical Information

Address: Denali National Park & Preserve, PO Box 9, Denali Park, AK 99755

Telephone: *907/683-2294*

Operating Season: year round

Hours: Visitors center open 7am-8pm during summer; 8a.m.-4:30p.m. from mid-September to early May

Cost: $10 per vehicle for 7-day pass

Website: *www.nps.gov/dena/index.htm*

Learning About Denali

Miller, Debbie S. et al. *Disappearing Lake: Nature's Magic in Denali National Park.* 1997.

Hawaii Volcanoes National Park
Hawaii

Nothing demonstrates nature's capacity for both violent destruction and miraculous rebirth than a volcano, and your family can view this process first hand at Hawaii Volcanoes National Park. The centerpiece of this park is Kilauea, the world's most active volcano, which along with Mauna Loa, a colossus at 13,677 feet, bring about constant formation to this land. Tour at night and you'll have a chance to see red hot lava in the making.

Ready to watch the formation of the earth? Then plan a trip to Hawaii Volcanoes National Park to see the earth at work.

Are We There Yet?

The park is located on the Big Island of Hawaii.

What's There To Do Here?

The volcano is the number one attraction of this park, but before you head off for a look stop by the **Kilauea Visitor Center**, where you can get the latest information regarding Kilauea's activity and view a 25-minute film, "Born of Fire...Born of The Sea," which captures such sights as ancient petroglyphs and an age old ritual, a mixture of dance and chanting performed to this day at the crater's edge as a sign of respect for Pele, the volcano goddess. The film is shown hourly from 9am to 4pm

Another interesting stop is the **Thomas A. Jaggar Museum**, which offers displays of earth science and murals depicting Hawaiian culture. Located only three miles from the park entrance. Open all year from 8:30am to 5pm For more information call *808/985-6000.*

The park offers lots of hiking trails. A good one is **Halemaumau Overlook** where, in just 10-minutes time, you can peer down into the crater. Other hiking trails take travelers through old lava flows, tree fern forests, and more.

Driving tours are another popular option. You can see the summit of Kilauea Volcano with an 11-mile **Crater Rim Drive**. The **Chain of Craters Road** along the coastline is another popular, but longer, option where you might have a chance to see red hot lava.

When Are We Going?

The Christmas holiday season (as well as Easter) are peak times for visitors so plan for crowds at this time.

Volcanic Fumes Warning!

Young children, pregnant women and anyone with breathing problems should be wary of volcanic fumes. Skip the stop at Sulphur Banks as well as the Halama'uma'u Crater.

How Long Are We Staying?

You'll want at least a whole day to view the major sights in the park.

What Should I Bring?

Good packing is important for this park. Bring sturdy shoes–you don't want to be teetering around near a volcano. Along with dependable shoes, bring a jacket, hat, sunscreen, and sunglasses for everyone. Layers are best because temperatures vary throughout the park depending on elevation.

Did You Know.....?

- The state bird of Hawaii is a breed of Hawaiian Goose called a Nene ("nay-nay").
- The hibiscus is Hawaii's state flower.
- The Hawaiian alphabet consists of only twelve letters, which includes all the vowels plus H,K,L,M,N,P and W.
- The official state motto is "Ua mau ke ea o ka aina I ka pono", which translates as "The life of the land is perpetual in righteousness."
- The Hawaiian Islands were created when under-sea volcanoes erupted.
- Kilauea, the name of the world's most active volcano, means "spreading, much spewing."
- Hawaii is the only state which was once ruled by royalty.
- Pele is the name of the Hawaiian volcano goddess (A painting of Pele by a local artist is on display at the Kilauea Visitor Center).

Which One Is My Room?

Since 1846 **The Volcano House Hotel**, the oldest of Hawaii's continually operated hotels, has witnessed the fiery explosions of the island's most active volcano. Located just across from the Kilauea Visitor Center, this establishment offers 42 rooms as well as 10 cabins. Open all year. For further information, call *808/967-7321 or email volcanohouse@earthlink.net.* On the web, go to: *www.volcanohousehotel.com.*

Two campgrounds are available: the **Namakani Paio** campground offers views of tall eucalyptus and ohi'a trees. Restrooms, barbeque pits and picnic tables are available. There is no fee or reservations required. Open all year. For more information call *808/985-6011.* There are only three sites available at **Kulanaokuaiki** campground. Barbecue grills, picnic tables and an accessible toilet available, however, water is not available. This campground is also free with no reservations necessary. Open all year.

Where Are We Going Next?

Once utilized as a safe haven for those accused of breaking Hawaiian laws, **Pu'uhonua O Honaunau National Historical Park** in Honaunau is home today to several archeological wonders. On a self-guided tour you can discover ancient temple platforms and royal fishponds, and see a reconstruction of The Hale O Keawe temple. Demonstrators are often on hand to explain Hawaiian crafts, and for nature lovers, in the winter you may be able to see green sea turtles and humpback whales. For visitor information, call *808/328-2288, email: PUHO_Interpretation@nps.gov,* or see *www.nps.gov/puho.*

Hawaiian Words and Phrases

- makuakane- father
- makuahine- mother
- kuahine- sister
- kunane- brother
- kupunakane- grandfather
- kupunawahine- grandmother
- hoaloha- friend
- ohana- family
- Mahalo- Thank you
- 'O wai kou inoa? What is your name?
- E komo mai!- Welcome!
- Aloha kakahiaka- Good morning
- Hau 'oli la hanau- Happy Birthday
- Pomaika'i- Good luck
- kipa mai- come visit
- A hui hou kakou- until we meet again
- Aloha- hello, goodbye, love

Practical Information

Address: Hawaii Volcanoes National Park, PO Box 52, Hawaii National Park, HI 96718-0052

Telephone: *808/985-6000*

Operating Season: year round

Hours: park open around the clock; visitors center open 7:45am-5pm

Cost: $10 per vehicle

Email:*havo_interpretation@nps.gov*

Website: *www.nps.gov/havo/index.html*

INDEX

Things Change!

Phone numbers, prices, addresses, quality of food, etc, all change. If you come across any new information, we'd appreciate hearing from you. No item is too small! Drop us an email note at: Jopenroad@aol.com, or write us at:

NATIONAL PARKS WITH KIDS
Open Road Publishing, P.O. Box 284
Cold Spring Harbor, NY 11724

Travel Notes

Travel Notes

Travel Notes

Travel Notes

Travel Notes

Travel Notes

Open Road Publishing

U.S.

America's Best Cheap Sleeps, $14.95
America's Most Charming Towns &
   Villages, $16.95
Arizona Guide, $16.95
Boston Guide, $13.95
California Wine Country Guide, $12.95
Colorado Guide, $16.95
Hawaii Guide, $18.95
Las Vegas Guide, $15.95
Las Vegas With Kids, $14.95
National Parks With Kids, $14.95
New Mexico Guide, $16.95
San Francisco Guide, $16.95
Southern California Guide, $18.95
Spa Guide, $14.95
Texas Guide, $16.95
Utah Guide, $16.95
Vermont Guide, $16.95
Walt Disney World Guide, $14.95

Middle East/Africa

Egypt Guide, $17.95
Kenya Guide, $18.95

Eating & Drinking on the Open Road

Eating & Drinking in Paris, $9.95
Eating & Drinking in Italy, $9.95
Eating & Drinking in Spain, $9.95
Eating & Drinking in Latin America, $9.95

Latin America & Caribbean

Bahamas Guide, $13.95
Belize Guide, $16.95
Bermuda Guide, $14.95
Caribbean Guide, $21.95
Caribbean With Kids, $14.95
Central America Guide, $21.95
Chile Guide, $18.95
Costa Rica Guide, $17.95
Ecuador & Galapagos Islands Guide, $17.95
Guatemala Guide, $18.95
Honduras Guide, $16.95

Europe

Greek Islands Guide, $16.95
Holland Guide, $17.95
Ireland Guide, $17.95
Italy Guide, $21.95
Italy With Kids, $14.95
London Guide, $14.95
London Made Easy, $9.95
Moscow Guide, $16.95
Paris Made Easy, $9.95
Paris with Kids, $14.95
Prague Guide, $14.95
Rome Guide, $14.95
Scotland Guide, $17.95
Spain Guide, $18.95
Turkey Guide, $19.95

Asia

China Guide, $21.95
Japan Guide, $21.95
Philippines Guide, $18.95
Tahiti & French Polynesia Guide, $19.95
Tokyo Guide, $13.95
Thailand Guide, $18.95

For US orders, include $5.00 for postage and handling for the first book ordered; for each additional book, add $1.00. Orders outside US, inquire first about shipping charges (money order payable in US dollars on US banks only for overseas shipments). Send to:
Open Road Publishing, PO Box 284, Cold Spring Harbor, NY 11724